Dispatches from Latin America

Dispatches

from Latin

Edited by

America

Teo Ballvé

On the Frontlines

and

Against

Vijay Prashad

Neoliberalism

South End Press
Cambridge, Massachusetts

Cover design by Design Action Collective
Text design by Sudhanva Deshpande
Printed by union labor on acid-free paper.
Printed in Canada

Library of Congress Cataloging-in-Publication Data

Dispatches from Latin America : on the frontlines against neoliberalism / edited by Vijay Prashad and Teo Ballvé. -- 1st American ed.
  p. cm.
 ISBN-13: 978-0-89608-768-2 (alk. paper)
 ISBN-10: 0-89608-768-9 (alk. paper)
 1. Social movements--Latin America. 2. Anti-globalization movement--Latin America. 3. Latin America--Politics and government. I. Prashad, Vijay. II. Ballvé, Teo.

HN110.5.A8D585 2006
303.48'4098--dc22

2006024812

South End Press, 7 Brookline Street #1, Cambridge, MA 02139-4146

10 09 08 07 06   1 2 3 4 5 6 7

Contents

A NEW LEFT RISING?

INDIGENOUS MOVEMENTS

GRASSING THE ROOTS

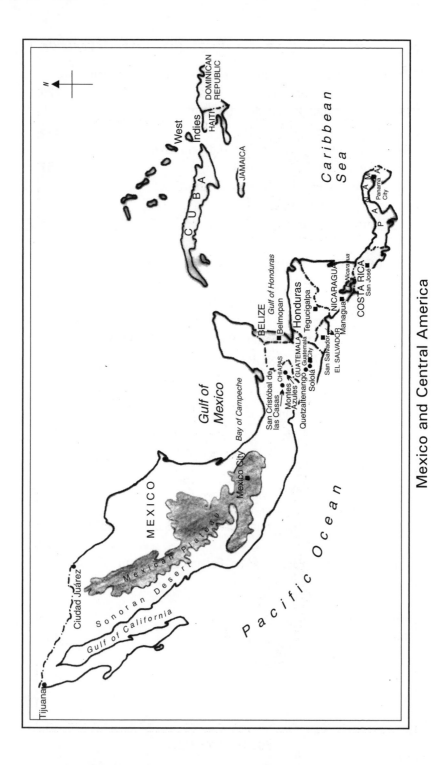

Mexico and Central America

South America

Preface

Vijay Prashad

They Rise From the Earth: The Promise of Latin America

Nadie sabe donde enterraron
los asesinos estos cuerpos,
pero ellos saldrán de la tierra
a cobrar la sangre caída
en la resurrección del pueblo.

Nobody knows where the assassins
buried these bodies,
but they'll rise from the earth
to redeem the fallen blood
in the resurrection of the people.

Pablo Neruda (*Canto General*; tr. Jack Schmitt)

Every generation of North Americans must come to terms with Latin America.

For us, front and center, is the question of neoliberal policy. Latin America suffers and struggles against a bundle of policies promoted by the U.S. government in Washington, DC, by the banks in New York City, London as well as Madrid, and by Latin America's own oligarchies. Poverty and hopelessness, the harvest of neoliberalism for workers and peasants, has led to displacement and migration. Many of those who come north, to El Norte, for work and to rekindle their hopes, are products of the neoliberal policies exported from North America. The battle against the Free Trade Area of the Americas (FTAA) and for a fair U.S. immigration policy is principally a fight for the creation of a just dispensation in the Americas. Resistance against neoliberalism has fueled the rise of left-wing governments and movements across Latin America. They bear within them the answers to many of our common challenges. It is worthwhile to see what they are up to and up against, as well as to see how we, in North America, can get sympathetically involved in the movement for the future of Latin America.

The book you hold in your hands is our attempt to provide a map of Latin America's aspirations and challenges. It is offered to you by Teo Ballvé and myself as a way to get you acquainted with the fast-changing developments in Latin America, from an assessment by Emir Sader of the Lula regime in Brazil to Raúl Zibechi's cartography of worker control over some of Argentina's factories. The large and the small experiments are documented and analyzed. Nothing is seen from a utopian standpoint, because this would doom our appraisal to inevitable failure. These are largely materialist estimations based on the constraints of the histories of each separate Latin American society, of the hierarchies that check the imagination of the population. Oftentimes, we get carried away with this or that current, but in most cases, the writers in this volume are also constrained by the politics of possibility.

LATIN AMERICA IS IN THE HEART

I encountered the United States in the heart of its immigrant population. I spent most of the second Reagan Administration (1985–1989) in the Los Angeles area. Apart from doing all the things that young people do, I involved myself in four sets of struggles. For radicals, it was impossible to avoid the anti-Apartheid campaign, whether in the divestment phase or in our enthusiasm to support one or another of the partisans in the guerrilla wars of southern Africa. It was equally impossible to ignore the wars in Central America (particularly in El Salvador and Guatemala), and hard not to interact with the refugees and exiles who thronged the L.A. basin in the sanctuaries, the barrios, the protests. The third struggle—Jesse Jackson's 1988 campaign for president—enveloped these two and developed in accordance with their rhythms. The legs for this enthusiastic political endeavor came from students involved in the Africa campaigns and from the political exiles and allies of the Central American wars. And the fourth emerged when the dynamics of the 1980s combined with the objective intensification of pressure on workers drove the immigrant workforce to revive a labor movement otherwise given over to the habit of concessionary bargaining. The Watsonville Canning and Shaw strikes of 1985–87, Justice for Janitors within SEIU, 1988 onward, and the 1992–1993 Drywall strike are exemplary of this struggle. Latin America and Africa breathed new life into the exhausted soul of U.S. radicalism.

During those years, the countries of Latin America themselves did not elicit much enthusiasm. Military dictatorships of the worst kind and pro-U.S. puppets who had given over their sovereignty to this or that branch of the U.S. Special Forces seemed to be the regimes on hand. Sections of the U.S. left worked tirelessly, but with little broader public momentum, to expose the dirtiness of the wars, especially the complicity of the U.S. government in many of them (and of its School of the Americas). For most of us, "John Negroponte" and "Otto Reich" were dirty words, associated with assassin's deeds. We watched as the dictatorships slowly fell, the most dramatic developments being in South America (Bolivia, 1982; Argentina, 1983; Brazil, 1985; Uruguay, 1985; Paraguay, 1989; Chile, 1990), but these came after the fleeting victory of the Sandinistas in Nicaragua. Solidarity was the watchword. Many of us worked in groups like the National Network in Solidarity with the Nicaraguan People, the Network in Solidarity with the People of Guatemala or the U. S. Committee in Solidarity with the People of El Salvador (CISPES). Congressman Tom Harkin (Iowa) put it plainly, "Yo soy Sandinista!"

As these military rulers either made negotiated transitions into public life or were ejected into exile, the new regimes encountered a different world. No longer did imperialism require the military to consolidate its dominance, because it now had another, more pointed instrument: the ideology of the free market and of "globalization." The newly democratic regimes, many of them ruled by the parties of Social Democracy, with varying degrees of enthusiasm adopted the mantras of neoliberalism to accommodate their transition from military to civilian rule. The broad agenda of the new regimes, however, continued to suffocate the ability of the mass of population to move forward. Not for nothing, then, did the U.S. left feel despondency toward these developments (not having lived under a military dictatorship also led to a rather cavalier dismissal of the enormity of their removal).

By the assessment of the U.S. left, these new civilian regimes not only acceded to stringent economic policies breathed south from such places as the University of Chicago (*Los Chicago Boys*), but they also took an active role in the suppression of any popular movement. The assault on civil society by Social Democratic regimes came alongside the growth of the NGO sector, a novel move by the dominant classes to canalize the call for systemic transformation into issue-based dissent.

The end of the Cold War further presaged a surface depression in that it meant an end to whatever space had been provided by the Soviet Union's presence and to a renewed aggressive posture by the United States. The U.S. invasion of Panama in 1989 was seen as a dress rehearsal for the new wars of the post-Cold War era. Barbara Trent's *The Panama Deception* (1992) brought home the parallels between the war on Panama and on

Iraq, on how the U.S. demonizes a former ally and then launches a massive invasion (led by aerial bombardment) to pacify the recumbent security forces of the new enemy. The scuffle over the Panama Canal—until 1997, home to the U.S. military's Southern Command—the new discourse of the "drug war" as a cover for counterinsurgency operations and resource extraction, demonstrate the way the United States sought to reconstitute its influence in the region after the era of the military dictatorships. The fall of the Soviet Union and the Third World, the development of the Special Period in Cuba and the isolated degeneration of some guerrilla armies enabled the transformation of a host of Marxist intellectuals into technocrats of such otiose fantasies as neoliberalism.

GLOBALIZATION FROM BELOW

The military went back into the barracks, but this did not itself enthuse us. What many of us active in the anti-war movements in the early 1990s did not see was that the future for Latin America was being incubated in the bad events—the assassinated would rise from the earth, and they did. The economic policies enacted by the civilian heirs to the military regimes had a marked impact on social life in Latin America. The UN Economic Commission on Latin America and the Caribbean (CEPAL, in its Spanish initials) showed that per capita income fell both in the 1980s (the "Lost Decade") and in the 1990s (the so-called "Decade of Recovery"). Reasonable studies indicate that between 1982 and 1993, the number of those living in poverty increased from 78 to 150 million. CEPAL's document on this was aptly titled, *La brecha de la equidad*, or The Breach of Equity. The objective collapse of social indicators in Latin America, and the creation of new economic spaces (automobile industry in Brazil, computer assembly in Mexico), as well as a renewed assault on the raw material resources of the area, produced re-engaged social movements. Indigenous movements, workers' movements, socialist movements, women's movements; some organized on conventional party lines, others as autonomous spaces, some along hierarchies of traditionalism, others in sharp contradistinction to these inherited norms. The force of these social movements has transformed electoral equations and brought the left to power across the continent. Brazil's new unions and the movements of the landless, Argentina's movements of the unemployed, Bolivia and Ecuador's indigenous organizations are some of the faces of this social dynamic. Their gains have been consolidated in left governments that, by and large, understand that their task is to be facilitators of the growth of people's power.

If globalization from above produced the objective conditions of deprivation in Latin America, a globalization from below enhanced the planetary movement for a better world. We in "El Norte" are well aware that the wave of protests against neoliberal globalization that stretched from Seattle (1999) to the shutdown of the Free Trade Agreement of the Americas (FTAA) could not have occurred without the efflorescence of organiz-ation below and around the Rio Grande. The organizations from the South took the lead in providing a framework for understanding globalization. That we now use the word "neoliberalism" (*neoliberalismo*) to describe the phase of capitalism to which we are opposed is a testament to the organizational and ideological preparation of the movements in Latin America. That the World Social Forum (2001 onward) began in Porto Alegre, Brazil is significant, and it is recognized as such around the planet.

But more: those who migrated to the U.S. because of neoliberal policies and joined the labor movement knew full well the social impact of neoliberalism. They had no illusions about its deleterious global effect. These immigrants didn't follow the lazy impulse to blame "foreign workers" for the loss of union strength in the U.S. It is because of this social force that the bureaucrats of the AFL-CIO had to squelch their tendency toward national chauvinism. These immigrants were already familiar with the lexicon of neoliberalism, the working of the International Monetary Fund (IMF) and the World Bank, the machinations of USAID, and on. For them, the IMF was the acronym for "I aM Fired," and the betrayal of Social Democracy would be called (as it was in Venezuela) the "great turn around" (*el gran viraje*). Veterans of various battles against the dictatorships and then of the neoliberal structures, these unionists were far more advanced in their familiarity with the world as it has become (all this despite the hiccups from the AFL-CIO leadership, historically in their support for the Latin American dictatorships and recently in their stubborn nativism regarding China and implication in the coup attempt in Venezuela). It was this crucial section of the U.S. workforce that made the marriage between the "turtles" and the "teamsters" possible at Seattle. It is also this section that has doggedly fought to transform the State's understanding of immigrants: they come to labor in North America only because their ability to labor in their ancestral lands has been demolished by the bulldozers of neoliberalism, so why should they be considered criminals? A scrupulous understanding of contemporary migration's dynamics will allow us to figure out what the immigrants tell us about themselves and their homelands.

The U.S. movement suffers from a historic inadequacy in our relations with radical movements across the planet. Since the suppression of the left in the United States there has been a tendency to either dismiss or to valorize, to hate or to love, movements elsewhere in the world. Balanced strategic assessments that are a necessary prerequisite for genuine solidarity are often missing. What we have instead is a desire to use other social movements for our own line struggles, or else to measure these movements based on a theoretical purity rather than on the historical constraints and possibilities in those societies, as well as on a dialectical theory for the transformation of humanity (whether Marxism or something else). For almost fifty years Cuba provided the U.S. left with just this kind of ideological football. Cuba became the object around which people in North America belabored their disagreements. The objective developments and subjective disagreements within Cuba were rarely at the center of the conversation. C. Wright Mills, the New Left guru, critically presaged this use of Cuba in his 1960 book *Listen Yankee*, where he wrote, "I do not worry about [the Cuban Revolution], I worry for it and with it." To worry "for" and "with" is a useful formula for solidarity. It is worthwhile to consider this as you read the essays in this book on Venezuela's Bolivarian Revolution or Mexico's EZLN. Exuberance is intoxicating, but misleading. Close study, patience and a keen ear should be our requirements. Radicals do not seek messiahs (whether Chávez or Marcos); rather we search for social motion that might move forward a just political agenda that gains widespread support as it draws more and more people into its dynamic. Both Chávez and Marcos represent separate strategies in very different political contexts. To compare them is unhelpful; to study them in their context is imperative. To respectfully study does not mean to defer without any assessment or criticism.

Let us not look for our reflection in events in Latin America, but try to understand its revolutionary dynamics on its own terms (and to the revolutionary theory it develops). We learned that lesson in the 1980s as we tried to come to terms with the movements in Central America and Africa, and as we took refuge in the refugees and exiles, and those who imported their bodies and dreams to places like Los Angeles.

Introduction

Teo Ballvé

From Resistance to Offensive: NACLA and Latin America

Back in 1967, the second issue of a fledgling, seven-page mimeographed newsletter boldly proclaimed: "We have been drawn together by 1) our common sense of dismay as we perceive the obstructionist role of the United States in Latin America; 2) our common commitment to the necessity of a far-reaching social revolution in Latin America." This little newsletter was published by a New York-based group calling itself the North American Congress on Latin America, known by its initials, NACLA. With these words, NACLA's organizers sent the small organization and its publication, Quixote-like, out to battle.[1] This book on Latin America's current social and political upheaval is a result of this ongoing engagement.

The founding of NACLA was spurred by U.S. President Lyndon Johnson's 1965 military invasion and occupation of the Dominican Republic. He sent the Marines to crush a popular uprising that sought to reinstate the constitutional rule of Juan Bosch—the country's former center-left President, who had been deposed by a military coup. Elections were organized a year after the Marines arrived, and two young U.S. activists enlisted as independent election monitors. Bosch lost against the U.S.-backed candidate, but his charges that the election was anything but free and fair went uninvestigated by the higher-ups of the monitoring team. Disillusioned with the experience, Fred Goff and Proctor Lippincott—the two young election monitors—returned to the United States and realized there was no source of independent information on Latin America. They began crisscrossing the country to recruit like-minded individuals and groups in the hope of creating an independent research center that could play a critical role in revealing and challenging U.S. foreign policy in Latin America. By the end of the year NACLA was formed, and soon began putting out its flagship publication, the *NACLA Newsletter*, which eventually became the magazine *NACLA Report on the Americas*.

When it was created, much of the organization's energy was expended revealing the "tools" of U.S. foreign policy—the arrows in the imperialist quiver that had often been overlooked. Early issues of the *NACLA Newsletter* examined the role of the U.S. Agency for International Development (USAID), multilateral funding institutions and U.S. banking giants. NACLA also took aim at philanthropic foundations, educational institutions, multinational corporations, the role of private investment and U.S. military policy. As a group of U.S.-based activists, they understood their role in aiding struggles for liberation in Latin America as one of systematically exposing the interlocking structures of political and economic domination of the region by the U.S. government and allied interests.

The organization continued this work as more and more countries of Latin America bent under the weight of military repression (by the mid-1970s only Costa Rica and Venezuela were holding "free" elections). NACLA's coverage revealed the mechanisms, short of outright military invasion, used to achieve U.S. foreign policy objectives. In its crosshairs were the international policies of U.S. trade unions, the political use of food exports and Washington's advancement of aid and comfort to the hemisphere's heinous regimes.

NACLA soon broadened its coverage beyond U.S. imperialism. It began to trace the contours of popular resistance in Latin America both to U.S. power and to local political elites. Chile provided an early instance of this resistance in 1970, as the left led by Salvador Allende was elected to power, proclaiming "a democratic transition to socialism." Immediately, Washington bore its fangs and NACLA mobilized to document the U.S. government's efforts to destabilize the Allende government, publishing a collection of articles that made their way into a book called *New Chile*. In a historic speech before the United Nations, just months before the brutal 1973 U.S.-backed military coup, President Allende remarked, "If you want to know how the U.S. has affected Chile, just read *New Chile* by NACLA."

The U.S. government responded to NACLA's irksome coverage with surveillance and harassment of the organization. As one staffer remembers, "We courteously traded insults with occasional trench-coat-clad defense intelligence or FBI agents who would stride in, badge in hand." Oddly enough, this harassment garnered the organization a ringing endorsement. In an internal memo from 1973, obtained by NACLA through the Freedom of Information Act, one FBI agent wrote: "NACLA literature is voluminous and is published regularly in a quality format that indicates financial stability. General accuracy is difficult to assess because of the volume factor and the sophisticated topical content, however, random samplings indicate a degree of accuracy approximately 80 percent. Regardless of accuracy, the propaganda value of the information can be scored an unqualified success."

Later in the decade, when the simmering conflicts in Central America burst into flames, NACLA continued to devote increasing attention to the programs and parties of the popular and revolutionary movements in the countries we examined. It also took up the urgent mandate of unmasking the lies and hypocrisy of the U.S. counter-revolutionary wars in Central America, providing much of the fodder that launched the U.S. Central America solidarity movements.

Indeed, the dynamic between U.S. imperialism in Latin America—along with complicit local elites—and the concomitant popular resistance on the ground against this domination has been a defining boomerang-like characteristic of NACLA's work. And such was the case when NACLA began covering the dawn of what has come to be called "neoliberalism." It was something familiar, yet wholly new and different. From the beginning, and certainly more intensely after the fall of the Soviet Union, NACLA clamored to understand and uncloak the workings of this New World Order.

Neoliberalism has become a catchall word that requires some specification. Here, it is used as the shorthand for the process of global capitalist restructuring that began in the 1970s in which the extremist ideology of the "free market" was given pride of place as the basis for the whole organization of society. In Latin America, as elsewhere, this restructuring created new and ever-growing accumulations of wealth along with increasingly massive concentrations of poverty and exclusion. The primary tool of this restructuring was the package of policies demanded by the International Monetary Fund (IMF), the U.S. Treasury, the World Bank and Wall Street that came to be called the "Washington Consensus." The policies included wholesale budget cutbacks, the dismantling of social protections, trade liberalization, financial deregulation, privatization of state-run enterprises and the marketization of just about everything. The Washington Consensus gave foreign corporations unfettered access to the region's natural and human resources and financial markets by rolling back hard-won gains in labor protections, social welfare programs and most regulatory capacities of the state. Economic policymaking was effectively siphoned away from politics and social demands, making the region attractive and "safe" for global capitalism.

The rise and the disastrous results of neoliberalism in Latin America began to be methodically documented in the pages of the *NACLA Report on the Americas* in the 1980s as government after government adopted neoliberal reforms at the insistence of the international financial institutions. Most Latin American governments willingly acquiesced to the new strictures of the international financial institutions in exchange for being "bailed out" of their severe domestic economic crises, which in large part stemmed from the astronomic loans borrowed from these institutions by previous authoritarian regimes. As the military regimes began to buckle, the market-based policies were meant to impart a measure of economic and social discipline to the new governments and the newly freed masses. Latin America quickly became the premier economic and social laboratory of neoliberalism. Arguably, nowhere in the world has this model been so expansively and rigidly implemented, and in no other region has the rejection of the model been so clear and so loud.

Similar to Latin America's nineteenth-century independence movements against colonial rule, the current anti-systemic upheaval was first seen by elites—foreign and domestic—as a case of isolated events, as aberrations from the dominant system to which Margaret Thatcher famously declared, "There is no alternative." Such was the case with the February 1989 popular revolt in Venezuela, known as the *Caracazo* (named after the nation's capital where the uprising was fiercest). The country's streets filled with protestors decrying the government's neoliberal structural adjustment policies. The same dismissive attitude was leveled against the 1994 armed uprising of the

Zapatista Army of National Liberation (EZLN). Designed to coincide with the implementation of the North American Free Trade Agreement (NAFTA), which like other "free trade" agreements solidifies the neoliberal model into a binding international treaty, the Zapatista revolt was ridiculed by its critics as "utopian" and "antiquated." Others, like Chase Manhattan Bank were more forthcoming: a 1995 report issued by Chase called on the Mexican government to "eliminate the Zapatistas."

Proposing how to counter the neoliberal onslaught, a 1993 NACLA article concluded, "The fundamental axis of any program which seeks to overcome neoliberalism with real development, equality and national independence rests on the political and social forces capable of opposing and defeating the economic and political actors who sustain and reproduce the current system of domination. Herein lies the challenge we must take up."

The challenge was indeed taken up, and it was taken up with such force and determination that the history of Latin America has been forever changed. Although many of the grievances by social movements in the region can be traced back centuries, the imposition of neoliberalism emboldened older movements and created new ones. Localized and countrywide popular rebellions have toppled governments, ejected rapacious corporations, and have brought the unpopular policies of governments and international financial institutions to a screeching halt. The social and political effervescence of recent years has also manifested itself in the election of left-leaning governments throughout the region—in fact, now a majority in South America. Undoubtedly, the current alignment of forces on the left in Latin America constitutes a globally unparalleled opportunity for radical change. As Gerardo Rénique notes in his essay, "The region's ongoing social and political upheaval—be it through the ballot box or massive direct action—threatens the hegemony of global capital and neoliberal ideology."

This book seeks to highlight, analyze and celebrate this trend. Drawing almost entirely from recently published and updated articles from the *NACLA Report on the Americas*, it examines the continental challenge to neoliberalism throughout Latin America in recent years. The intent is not to delineate a uniformity of experience, tactic or strategy, but quite the opposite: to shed light on the particulars of each moment and the diversity of experience in the fight against a common enemy. For this reason, the geographic focus is centered on places where this fight has emerged and been consolidated most forcefully; and for space limitations is limited to the mainland, with the reluctant omission of the Caribbean—especially Cuba.

The book is divided into four overlapping sections. The first section contains broad-stroke overviews that serve to contextualize and outline the current moment in Latin America. Next, a series of essays take stock of the emergence and performance of the new left-leaning governments, which continue to spread throughout the region. The election of pro-left political forces is an astonishing achievement: for the most part, the parties now in government emerged from political and social movements that had long suffered the excruciating brunt of military regimes, which sought to wipe out a generation of their *compañeros* and *compañeras* (comrades). That these movements survived, and, moreover, that their members now occupy the halls of power is a testament to their determination and courage. But now faced with the difficult task of governing, some have been more successful than others.

The next section on indigenous movements considers how indigenous-based movements have been at the forefront of social mobilizations in several countries. Before 1980, indigenous organizing was largely confined to local communities, and organizations that united different indigenous groups were rare. But indigenous movements throughout the hemisphere have been asserting their presence in national politics in an unprecedented fashion since the 1990s. As the most historically excluded sector of society, indigenous communities were hit especially hard by neoliberalism, particularly since indigenous forms of organizing collective life are inimical to the individualist-driven ideology of neoliberalism. Indeed, for the region's indigenous movements, economic issues are inextricably linked to their cultural survival. And many have abandoned the sterile debate over whether ethnic- or class-based identities are more important for political action; instead, the emphasis is on the natural linkages between the two.

Overlapping with the preceding section, the final section of the book analyzes other social movement actors combating neoliberalism. From the vast tracts of land occupied by rural squatters in Brazil to the worker-run factories of Argentina, as well as new organizing efforts in Mexico, it seems we are no longer observing mere "resistance to neoliberalism," rather, it may be more fitting to describe the footing of Latin America's social movements as one of an anti-neoliberal *offensive*. Not only because popular rebellions have on more than one occasion uprooted entire governments, and put new ones in their place, but also because these movements have actively constructed autonomous spaces of their own, experimenting with new forms of governance and social and economic organization.

But this propitious moment does not portend a predetermined outcome, both because of internal forces and those from abroad. This brings up the familiar feeling of Latin America being poised at a crossroads: it always seems on the verge of something historic, always teetering between possibility and failure. But this book aims to aid us in imagining different ways of seeing and understanding Latin America and the struggles of its peoples. As NACLA has always maintained, understanding the world, and seeing it through new eyes, will hopefully prompt new efforts to change it.

ABOUT THE AUTHOR

Teo Ballvé is a NACLA editor and a contributing news editor for the Resource Center of the Americas http://www.americas.org.

NOTES

1. Parts of this Introduction draw from anniversary issues of the *NACLA Report on the Americas*, special thanks to Fred Rosen and Steve Volk.

Openings

Gerardo Rénique

Strategic Challenges for Latin America's Anti-Neoliberal Insurgency

Today the specter haunting capitalism journeys through Latin America. The region's ongoing social and political upheaval—be it through the ballot box or massive direct action—threatens the hegemony of global capital and neoliberal ideology. In an unprecedented cycle of strikes, mass mobilizations and popular insurrections extending from the early 1990s to the present, the marginalized, exploited and despised subaltern classes have drawn on deeply rooted traditions of struggle to bring down corrupt and authoritarian regimes closely identified with the International Monetary Fund (IMF), the World Bank and Washington D.C.

Besides important electoral victories of left-leaning parties, mass direct action has toppled discredited governments in Peru, Bolivia, Ecuador and Argentina. Recent government proposals to privatize public services and natural resources have been soundly defeated across the region by grassroots movements and organizations acting independently from established political parties—including those of the left. In Mexico, the peasants in the town of Salvador Atenco blocked plans sponsored by an alliance of multinational corporations, local entrepreneurs and the government to build a multi-billion-dollar airport on agricultural lands and protected wetlands. In Cochabamba, Bolivia, the militant mobilizations of neighborhood associations, unions and popular organizations reversed the privatization of the local water system in the famed "Water War." In Peru, broad alliances of peasant communities, farmers, citizen organizations and ecologists in the towns of Cajamarca and Tambogrande halted the Canadian Manhattan Mining Corporation's attempted expansion into agricultural and public lands and water resources.

Confronted by the withdrawal of the state from its most basic social duties, many popular movements and organizations have mobilized to address such aspects of everyday life as housing, nutrition, childcare, education and productive work. One thinks here of the communal kitchens in Peru, squatter organizations in Uruguay, cooperatives of unemployed workers in Argentina, landless peasants in Brazil, the collective self-managed water service enterprise in Bolivia and the autonomous municipalities and *Juntas de Buen Gobierno* (Good Government Councils) in the territories of Chiapas, Mexico, controlled by the Zapatista National Liberation Army (EZLN). Driven by principles of solidarity, self-respect, collective participation and communal interest, these popular institutions constitute a powerful challenge to the individualism, self-interest, and exclusion at the core of neoliberalism. They also constitute a frontal assault on post-Cold War triumphalism and the neoliberal celebration of unrestricted markets, free trade and electoral regimes as the only possible path to a modern, democratic and civilized existence.

In opposition to this agenda, the new wave of subaltern movements offer a politics of hope. Analysis of Latin America's anti-systemic rebellions and social movements becomes all the more imperative as the United States and allied local elites hastily regroup forces to restore the neoliberal order that has been under consistent attack since the early 1990s. The White House's aggressive campaign to force the approval of the Central American Free Trade Agreement (CAFTA); Bush's threat to interfere with the transmissions of TeleSur (the news and TV network established between Venezuela, Argentina, Uruguay and Cuba); and more ominous, the expansion of Washington's geo-strategic reach with the Paraguayan government's recent authorization of a U.S. military base in its territory are but a few of the many telling expressions of U.S. intentions to reassert an imperial presence and to restore the confidence of chastised local elites.

The neoliberal offensive had its foundational moment in that other September 11, the one in 1973, when General Augusto Pinochet, with the support of the U.S. government, led a bloody coup d'état against the first elected Marxist president in Latin America. For the most reactionary sectors of the global ruling elites, the establishment of the Pinochet regime offered an unsurpassed opportunity to voice openly and aggressively an ultra-liberalism that had previously been restrained by both the Keynesian strictures of the welfare state and by political compromise with social-democratic forces and organized labor.

The Chilean junta's free market policies, uncompromising anti-communism and its hostility towards any state welfare functions galvanized an ideological and political offensive, guided by economist Milton Friedman and his disciples known as the "Chicago Boys," against the regulatory and social policies they viewed as fetters to the "invisible hand" of the market. Today, their multinational cadre of followers educated mainly in U.S. universities hold executive posts in multilateral institutions, such as the World Bank and the IMF, and in Latin American central banks and ministries of economy and finance. Not only did Pinochet enjoy the personal admiration of Henry Kissinger, Margaret Thatcher, and others of their ilk, many of his measures, such as the privatization of Social Security, were swiftly incorporated into the emerging global neoliberal orthodoxy.

Neoliberalism, dubbed *capitalismo salvaje* (savage capitalism) reached its peak during the so-called "lost decade" of the 1980s, when privatization of public services and national resources devastated the already highly polarized societies and economies of Latin America. The post-World War II Latin American developmentalist state had broadly acknowledged— though not always honored—demands for labor rights, basic social services, free education, land reform and national control of strategic resources.

On the heels of the Chilean coup, however, Latin America's developmentalist states were swiftly and thoroughly dismantled through the combined efforts of the World Bank and the IMF. The result was an extraordinary deterioration of the material conditions of existence. In response to this onslaught, however, new social actors emerged, who, together with older activists, have created new social movements and revitalized older class-based organizations to defend popular and national interests.

These movements have managed not only to erode the legitimacy of neoliberalism, but also to realign social and political forces in the region. Strikes and mass mobilizations in Peru (2000), a popular insurrection in Argentina (2001) and, most notably, rebellions with prominent indigenous participation in Ecuador (1997, 2000, 2005) and Bolivia (2003, 2005) have overthrown corrupt, repressive and pro-U.S. regimes. It is this popular mobilization of what can be described as a "social left" that has made possible the election of progressive or left-wing governments in Argentina, Brazil, Venezuela and Uruguay.

Tellingly, discontent with neoliberalism has even reached Colombia—Washington's most loyal ally in the region—where Luis Eduardo Garzón, a former Communist union leader, won the 2004 mayoral elections in the capital city of Bogotá. Recently, Uruguay not only elected its first ever left-wing president (the socialist Tabaré Vásquez), but in the ensuing regional elections his coalition, the *Frente Amplio-Encuentreo Progresista* (Broad Front-Progressive Encounter, or FA-EP), managed to win in seven of the counties 19 states including the capital city of Montevideo. Despite their ideological differences and different degrees of commitment to improve the well-being of the masses, these new progressive regimes are all characterized by an independent foreign policy that represents a serious challenge to U.S. unilateralism.

Led by the recently elected progressive governments, the strengthening (or re-establishment) of diplomatic and economic relations between Latin American nations and Cuba constitutes a dramatic reversal of Washington's decades-old attempt to isolate and strangle the Cuban Revolution. Other signs of such newly found independence include: the defeat of U.S. efforts at the Organization of American States (OAS) to isolate Venezuela's elected revolutionary government; rejection by the region's defense ministries of U.S. Defense Secretary Donald Rumsfeld's proposal—supported by Colombia—to form a Latin American multinational force; defeat (for the first time) of a U.S.-backed candidate for Secretary General of the OAS; and the explicit rejection of unilateralism in the foundational charter of the newly created South American Community of Nations. The inconclusive results of the recent Summit of the Americas in Mar del Plata, Argentina—a practical rejection of the Free Trade Agreement of the Americas (FTAA) which had been slated to go into effect in January 2005—represents a severe setback to future U.S.-led trade agreements, which are apprehensively regarded in the region as no less than a renewed strategy of neocolonization.

Brazil not only has played a prominent role in the region's opposition to the FTAA but has also acted as an important deterrent to U.S. interventionism in both Cuba and Venezuela, while prioritizing the expansion of relations with India, China, the Middle East and Southern African nations. Venezuela likewise has privileged economic ties with nations of the Southern

Hemisphere as well as with Russia, India and China. Venezuela's close cooperation with Cuba and president's Hugo Chávez's efforts to use oil—his country's most important resource—as a tool for the economic and political integration of the Caribbean Basin also represents a challenge to U.S. domination. Even the IMF, the most powerful instrument of the neoliberal offensive, has suffered defeats in the ongoing Latin American upheaval. Argentine president Néstor Kirchner, who was elected in the aftermath of the tumultuous rebellions that brought down President Fernando de la Rúa, stood up to the IMF by declaring a moratorium on private debt. His call for a boycott of the transnational oil corporations Esso and Shell for increasing fuel prices was enthusiastically embraced by thousands of demonstrators who occupied gas stations.

In contrast to their independent foreign policies, on the domestic front, these left-wing and progressive regimes have in most cases fallen short on their commitments to the marginalized—mostly non-white—masses. Perhaps the most tragic example of such disappointment is the case of Brazilian President Luiz Inácio Lula da Silva, whose concessions to the Brazilian right as well as to global financial elites have come at the cost of postponing urgently needed land reform and other basic social and democratic measures. Through such reversals, Lula has managed to bolster the confidence and demands of the propertied classes, while spreading a debilitating apathy and uncertainty among the same social movements whose organization, mobilization and electoral participation were central to the ascendancy of his Workers' Party (PT). Although recent disclosures of the PT's bribes to representatives of its political ally the Brazilian Labor Party (PTB) and of its legally dubious bank loans (obtained through a publicist with the largest government contracts) have forced the resignation of the head of the party, the crisis plaguing the PT is not recent. It goes back to the party's decision during its 2002 electoral campaign to leave untouched the interests of financial capital.

The centrist conversion of Latin America's institutionalized left—described by Subcomandante Marcos of the EZLN as "left-handed neoliberal administrations"—resembles the "molecular transformation" that Gramsci saw effecting leftist political formations in times of crisis, blurring whatever distinguished them from those of the right.

The institutional left's increasingly manipulative and disrespectful relationship to the masses stands in marked contrast to the relation of mutual dependence that link Venezuela's Hugo Chávez with his country's popular classes. Massive mobilizations defeated both the U.S.-sponsored coup against Chávez in 2002 and the subsequent oil strike aimed at his overthrow. In turn, Chávez's organizational efforts and social and economic policies are mainly geared to the benefit and empowerment of the most marginalized sectors of Venezuelan society. Despite its limits and shortcomings Chávez's Bolivarian Revolution, grounded in a mixed economy, welfare programs, popular participation, independent foreign policy and popular nationalism, constitutes Latin America's most radical break from the neoliberal blueprint of the so-called "Washington Consensus." His March 2005 declaration on the ineptitude of capitalism and on the need to build "a socialism for the twenty-first century" represents a hopeful departure from the embarrassing opportunism of the more established left parties in the region.

Another important case illustrating the centrality of popular organizations and mass mobilization in overcoming neoliberalism are the 2003 and 2005 popular uprisings that overthrew the last two Bolivian presidents. Unlike Venezuela, where popular mobilization was promoted by the state, the Bolivian mobilizations emerged from below and were led by autonomous indigenous organizations. The 2003 uprising against the ultra-liberal President Gonzalo "Goni" Sánchez de Lozada blocked the exportation of the nation's vast natural gas reserves to the United States via Chile. Goni was forced to scrap the plan and was forced to resign, leaving more that 80 dead and hundreds wounded.

Acknowledging popular anti-imperialist feelings and pressure from the indigenous-based Movement Toward Socialism (MAS)—the country's second-ranking party, led by former coca grower Evo Morales—Goni's successor, Carlos Mesa, organized a referendum in which the majority voted for the Bolivian government to take greater control of the privatized oil and gas industry. Despite widespread popular support for a full nationalization, the questions of the referendum were deliberately structured to preclude any clear roadmap for achieving greater state control of the resources.

After 10 months of intense debates in Congress and demonstrations in the street, in May 2005 the Bolivian Congress unilaterally passed a watered down law that only levied a marginally higher tax on corporations exploiting the reserves. Led by indigenous people organized by the MAS, the Pachakutik Indigenous Movement (MIP), the Federation of Neighborhood Associations of El Alto (FEJUVE) and the Confederation of Bolivian Campesino Workers (CSUTCB), regional, popular and ethnic organizations mobilized around two central demands: a constituent assembly to rewrite the Constitution and the nationalization of the country's energy sector. Demonstrations, marches, roadblocks and occupations of oil and gas fields paralyzed the country for several days. Unable to govern, Mesa finally resigned in June 2005. Polarized among regional, class and ethnic lines, a separatist movement of right-wing non-indigenous elites in Bolivia's richest province of Santa Cruz began maneuvering for territorial autonomy, an unveiled attempt at secession, and backed one of their ranks to replace the outgoing Mesa. Popular mobilization managed to defeat the separatist movement and secured an acceptable interim president.

As in Bolivia, indigenous peoples in Ecuador led by the Pachakutik Movement (the political arm of the Confederation of Indigenous Nationalities of Ecuador, or CONAIE) have also played a crucial role in popular mobilizations that have forced the resignation of two of the last three presidents. Chile during the last decade has likewise witnessed the emergence of a strong and militant movement among the marginalized indigenous Mapuche in defense of natural resources threatened by multinational mining and lumber corporations. Having displaced the more established parties, these new movements act as a pole of attraction for anti-systemic forces including parties and organizations of the "old left" and the "old labor movement."

Unlike the old left, these new movements tend to privilege unity of action over political homogeneity and diversity over uniformity. As such they do not constitute—nor do they aspire to be—a unified centralized movement, and they are frequently subjected to tensions and contradictions bred by ideological and tactical differences, *caudillismo* and opportunism. Such problems, for instance, undermined the role of the indigenous movement in the April 2005 uprising in Ecuador, when a group of parliamentary and cabinet members of the Pachakutik movement sided with President Lucio Gutiérrez in opposition to the majority of members of CONAIE who favored his ouster. The ensuing crisis in the indigenous movement was solved with the expulsion of the dissidents and a renewed commitment to strengthen grassroots oversight and control of leaders and elected officials. By contrast, during the Bolivian rebellion that ousted president Mesa, despite serious political differences (including tensions between movements represented in parliament and those in the extra-parliamentary opposition), the different popular social and political forces managed to create unity of action against both the state and the right-wing opposition.

But it is the EZLN that expresses most fully the potentialities of indigenous organization and mobilization both for the formulation of a new socialist vision and for the establishment of democratic and participatory mechanisms that assure close oversight of political leaders and elected officials. Since its emergence, symbolically staged on January 1, 1994, the day that marked the launch of the North American Free Trade Agreement (NAFTA) between the United States, Mexico and Canada, the EZLN became, in the words of Immanuel Wallerstein, the "barometer and trigger" for anti-systemic movements worldwide. Born at the peak of the neoliberal ideological offensive, when uncertainty and disillusionment with both socialism and collective action were radically transforming the oppositional stance of the left, the EZLN uprising represented a turning point in the articulation and configuration of a new anti-systemic cycle. Voicing the demands of the most oppressed and marginalized sectors of Mexican society, the EZLN's claims for indigenous peoples' autonomy and right to well-being generated an unprecedented movement of both local and international support.

The EZLN's anti-neoliberal, anti-colonial and anti-racist stance, and its strategy of building local democratic power without taking over the state, galvanized actions and political debate within the emerging "anti-globalization" movement. The political encounters organized by the EZLN attracted social and political organizations, indigenous leaders and representatives, social movements and intellectuals from all over the world. An important outcome of these activities was the formation of the National Indigenous Council (CNI), which is the first independent national indigenous organization in Mexican history. The "intergalactic encounters against neoliberalism and for humanity" staged in the Chiapas jungle were forerunners of the World Social Forum. And the recent EZLN Sixth Declaration of the Lacandón Jungle calling for a global left-wing extra-parliamentary alliance of social and political forces coincides with widespread disillusionment with the failure of social-democratic, progressive and left-wing regimes to act decisively against neoliberalism.

The EZLN uprising and indigenous insurgencies elsewhere in the region have also brought to the surface the legacy of colonial oppression and racism that lay at the heart of Latin America's nation-states. The dead weight of this cultural and ideological legacy had rendered subaltern (in particular, indigenous) agency to invisibility in the historical and political formations of modern Latin America, despite the fact that political independence from Spain led by elites of European descent was achieved in the aftermath of widespread popular insurrections both in Mexico and the Andes. The apprehension generated by the violent and sweeping radicalism of indigenous action hardened the law-and-order mindset of the "enlightened" founders of the Latin American republics.

Their racialized fear of the masses together with liberal emphasis on individual rights have stood as the most important obstacles to the creation of truly democratic nation-states, particularly in countries with non-white (indigenous or black) majorities. This legacy has even had debilitating effects within the left, often impeding collaboration between its institutional and its social sectors. Therein lies the current importance of contemporary subaltern and indigenous mobilizations, their articulation with new and old political traditions, their amalgamation of democracy and collective interests, and their simultaneous deployment of reform, insurgency and rebellion.

This dynamic lies at the core of the creation of the revolutionary strategy prophetically envisioned in the 1920s by Peruvian Marxist José Carlos Mariátegui as the fruit of the confluence between socialist strategies and indigenous communitarian traditions and struggles.

Peasant and indigenous intervention in politics has long been manifested through everyday acts of resistance, acts of insubordination and open rebellion. But these remained fragmented and localized until the second half of the twentieth century. Landlord and state responses to subaltern defiance rested on the systemic use of violence and the deepening of colonial forms of domination, humiliation and exploitation. The achievement of autonomy and of a pluri-ethnic state—as currently demanded by indigenous movements—will not only mark the end of the Eurocentric nation-state, but will also force the redefinition of both the national question and the problem of political democracy. The Zapatistas' forms of autonomous self-government (*caracoles,* or conches) express this particular subaltern political culture forged in 500 years of resistance to colonialism and to the Eurocentric logic of state power. In place of the latter, Zapatista forms of people's power offer an idiosyncratic form of direct rule aimed on the one hand at strengthening democracy, dignity and autonomy, and, on the other, at building an alternative way of life, thereby helping to revitalize the universal struggle for democracy and liberation.

ABOUT THE AUTHOR

Gerardo Rénique is Associate Professor of History at the City University of New York and is on the board of directors of the Brecht Forum. He is co-author (with Deborah Poole) of *Peru: Time of Fear.*

Maruja Barrig

Latin American Feminism: Gains, Losses and Hard Times

Peruvian women appear to have made genuine strides during Alberto Fujimori's ten years in power (1990–2000). A Ministry of Women and a Public Defender for Women (an adjunct to the Public Defender for the People) were created. The Peruvian Congress passed a law against domestic violence and a quota law that obliged political parties to present women candidates in at least 30% of the races for local and Congressional office. Female followers of Fujimori were given important positions in his government and were visible in the national parliament. In fact, in his third, brief administration, the Governing Council of Congress was composed entirely of women loyal to the President.

Those achievements were disconcerting. How was it possible that an authoritarian regime, which steadily chipped away at democratic rights, could seem to have such extraordinary "sensitivity to gender?" Confusing things further, the women politicians in Fujimori's administration were distinct from the men recruited by the regime: They were more hawkish, less tolerant and, above all, more loyal to the president and to his shadowy advisor Vladimiro Montesinos. Dismissing former intelligence service agent Leonor La Rosa's accusation that she had been tortured under Montesinos' orders, one prominent congresswoman allied with Fujimori, Martha Chávez, asserted that the woman "had tortured herself."

These policy innovations and the contradictions they

revealed stoked a debate in Peru—which was more impassioned than elsewhere in Latin America—between feminists who responded to the invitation to enter government and those who rejected it. Virginia Vargas of the Flora Tristan Center, one of those who kept their distance, asserted: "For feminism, the boundary between ethics and negotiations is marked by respect for democratic values."[1] Women for Democracy (MUDE), a small group of feminists allied with human rights activists, leaders of grassroots organizations, housewives, political party militants and students, denounced these government measures that seemed to fulfill feminist objectives. To underscore that these policies were not acceptable if they came from an authoritarian and anti-democratic regime, they coined the slogan: "What is not good for democracy is not good for women."

Other organizations followed in MUDE's footsteps. Another group of feminists, the Broad Movement of Women, protested every Thursday in front of the Palace of Justice, while Women for Dignity washed soldiers' uniforms in front of the Joint Command of the Armed Forces. Dozens of other women's groups both in the capital and in the provinces washed the Peruvian flag to symbolize the urgent need for moral cleansing. What has occurred in Peru in the 1990s is unique in some respects, but it may also serve as a small laboratory in which many of the debates that have shaken Latin American feminism—and their resolutions—can be put under the microscope.

Beginning in 1993, feminists in Latin America and the Caribbean worked tirelessly to bring together scattered groups of women across the region and to create spaces where women could debate and articulate their dreams prior to the 1995 Beijing Global Conference on Women. Those efforts produced the national documents of the nongovernmental organizations (NGOs) and led to the parallel sessions that took place alongside the official gathering of the United Nations in Beijing. That process was not always light-hearted and harmonious, as some Latin American feminists remember it. The unofficial story behind the mobilization of women's groups in each country unmasked struggles over leadership and revealed inexperience and mistrust in dealing with public institutions that only yesterday had been part of a repressive state that refused to dialogue.

In the years since the burst of jubilation that was Beijing, the feminist movement in Latin America has splintered into fragments, and other hands appear to have picked up the pieces. As several studies of regional feminism in the post-Beijing era suggest, not only has feminist militancy redefined itself in ways that opened the floodgates for diverse and sometimes irreconcilable strategies, but also the linguistic codes—those countersigns that we activists used to identify ourselves—have been picked up by officialdom and endowed with new meanings, almost with the consent of feminists. As the French academic Françoise Collin commented in an article: "Don't grow old in the barricades or you'll grow old badly."[2] Latin American feminists and feminist discourse thus carved out a place in the processes of democratization and state modernization, with feminists seeking to become part of a state that they had earlier wanted to transform.

Latin American feminism of the 1970s and 1980s put forward two sets of demands: equal rights for women and economic redistribution. On the one hand, Latin American feminists threw themselves into the struggle for new institutional and legal frameworks that would put women's rights on the same footing as universal human rights, which until recently were seen as implicitly male prerogatives. But at the same time, acutely aware of the wide gulf between the rich and poor, these feminists demanded urgent action to improve the miserable living conditions of millions of women in their countries. Those conditions, they knew, swelled the number of maternal deaths, illiterate women, women eking out a living in the informal sector and single mothers.

More recently, the fabric that originally united all feminists has at times been ripped as feminists developed the specialized skills and strategies needed to pursue one or the other set of demands. The connection between the struggles for legal and economic rights grew more tenuous, just as the gap widened between both of those battles and the rapid transformations of Latin American states. These political changes produced a pernicious acceptance of the limits of government, its restricted regulatory role and the sovereignty of the market. Thus in the Andean region, celebrated victories such as the creation of government institutions to serve women and quota laws to increase their political participation have become frayed at the edges by the persistent reality of inequality among women. Continuing poverty among indigenous, shantytown and peasant women presents a daunting challenge. While the new millennium has excited some women with its promises, it has passed over thousands of others, relegating them to daily-life conditions typical of the end of the nineteenth century.

In the years since Beijing, tension has emerged between the advances of women in achieving legal equality and the persistent social and economic inequality in our countries. The convulsive political situations in Bolivia, Ecuador, Peru and Colombia, coupled with the continuing lack of stable legal systems in Nicaragua, El Salvador and Guatemala, make the institutional foundations of the Latin American state shaky, civil rights precarious and social participation largely a myth. How do we, given these conditions, first put in place and then maintain the principles of legal equality for women? And how do we, in an economic model characterized by a growing concentration of wealth and little sharing of benefits, find that minimum threshold required for the exercise of women's rights?

For some researchers, the gains in legal rights for Latin American women in the 1990s have come hand-in-hand with the modernization of the state, and in some countries, have fit together with the struggle for democracy. The gains for women inscribed in Ecuador's 1998 Constitution, for example, cannot be separated from the active participation of the women's movement in the protests against the short-lived government of President Abdalá Bucarám (1996–97), which made that movement a force to be reckoned with for an array of political parties in the Congress. As a result, the country's new Constitution prohibits violence against women (whether physical, psychological and/or sexual), bars discrimination on the basis of sexual orientation, and asserts "the right to make free and responsible decisions about one's sexual life." By contrast, Peru is an example of a country where modernization has been divorced from democratization. As Peruvian feminist Vargas asserts: "The actors of modernization have not been the same as the actors of democratization. The Fujimori government's policy towards women was developed in an authoritarian and anti-democratic framework, and for that reason, women have gone out into the streets to protest."[3]

The advances of women in the legal field may have resulted in a shift in the arena of struggle, from demonstrations and other pressure in the streets in the 1980s to negotiations in parliament and government ministries in the 1990s. But in either battleground, feminists are adamant that what they obtained "was not a gift of benevolent presidents," as one put it.

A landmark achievement in the struggle for legal equality was the Convention on the Elimination of All Forms of Discrimination (CEDAW), and the creation of its committee, which successfully urged country after country in the region to sign on. This United Nations accord was the central inspiration behind the designing of national measures to prevent and punish violence against women. You can find feminists in every Latin American country who point to the passage of legislation punishing violence against women as their most prized achievement. A law of this sort is the product of multiple forces rallying together—from the Catholic Church to international agencies, legislators, public functionaries, First Ladies and even the National Police (as in Nicaragua)—and the surrounding paraphernalia of slogans, publicity spots, research and government commissions.

A second important advance has been the creation throughout the region of national offices of women. These have taken different forms within each government: as an extension of the Ministry of Work and Social Welfare linked to the wide field of "culture" (in Guatemala, Guyana and Jamaica); with the Ministry of Education and Culture (in Trinidad and Tobago and Uruguay); or integrated with other population groups or sectors (such as the Ministry of Youth, Women, Children and the Family in Panama).

There are, however, numerous problems with these government institutions for women. One of them is the way they have treated the female population as "a vulnerable group" in their programs. Another drawback has been their limited access to the real centers of power where policies are formulated, even when they have ministerial rank. Lastly, their budgets are usually small, meaning that these offices rely on international aid. To cite one example, the budget of the former Sub-Secretary of Women's Affairs in Bolivia depended on international funds for 92% of its budget in 1995, 98% in 1996, 97% in 1997, and 90% in 1998.[4] This scarcity of economic resources at their disposal sharply contrasts with the broad mandates that these offices have. Several national offices of women appear to duplicate the work of feminist collectives and NGOs. It is important, however, to add that the feminist movement does not appear to have clear proposals, much less defined strategies, for dealing with these state apparatuses.

The third visible sign of the progress of women has been the growing participation of women in legislatures and local governments, traditionally male bastions, thanks to the passage of affirmative action measures. The majority of Latin American countries gave women the right to vote in the 1950s, but that did not translate into a presence in public policy. Women are underrepresented in local government and in national parliaments, representing until recently in the latter about 10% of the office holders. Feminists fought for the establishment of quotas for women in each party's list of candidates, winning such a law in 1991 in Argentina (30% of the candidates had to be women), and in 1996 and 1997 in the following countries: Bolivia (30%), Brazil (20%, and increasing to 30% in 2000), Costa Rica (40%), Ecuador (20%), Guyana (30%), Mexico (30%), Panama (30%), Paraguay (20%), Peru (30%), the Dominican Republic (25%), and Venezuela (30%).[5]

For feminists, affirmative action corrected an injustice against women. Asked at the start of Fujimori's aborted third term in office about the authoritarianism of the four women from the president's party who headed the Governing Council of Congress, feminist Ana María Yañez of the Peruvian NGO Manuela Ramos declared, "I prefer four authoritarian women to four authoritarian men."[6] That remark ignited a heated debate, including among women. As the Italian activist Alessandra Bocchetti once reminded us, "A body of a woman does not guarantee the thinking of a woman, and nor can many women together guarantee it."[7]

The presence of these arrogant and powerful Congress-women who were loyal to Fujimori prompted the opposition journalist César Hildebrant to demand an explanation from Peruvian feminists. "Why was the worst of the Fujimori Congress and the most glaring moral wretchedness female?" he asked in a November column in *Liberación*. "Didn't these quotas and gender obligations allow the infiltration of the contraband of believing themselves above the law and the owners of a special statute?" To which Yañez replied: "The mechanism of quotas is only a means to promote the entry of women into power. It is not responsible for the quality of the women who attain power."[8]

"What has happened," Vargas asserted, "is that the Fujimori policy towards women has produced what I would call a civic schizophrenia. In the Peruvian model of modernization without democracy, the Fujimori regime has done more than any of its predecessors to create women's institutions, to pass laws recognizing their rights as citizens, and to put women in prominent positions of power, even if they were authoritarian women who were unconditionally loyal to the president. Alongside this, the regime adopted manipulative and clientelistic policies towards poor women. That presented us with an ambivalent panorama: On the one hand, with respect to rights granted from above, female citizenship formally expanded, especially in political terms. But this expansion had no relation to the widening of women's economic rights, much less the widening of democratic processes, but rather coincided with their further reduction."[9]

All of the aforementioned gains for women can obscure the pile of small victories in eliminating or correcting certain laws in the quest for equality as well as in the multitude of helpful government programs mainly in the area of women's health. All of these represent steps forward, the fruit of pressure from women's groups, encouragement from international aid agencies, and the hard work of the policymakers who were exposed for so many years to the resounding voices of feminists.

But as the Bolivian feminist Sonia Montano asserted, women's policies in Latin America have been "low intensity."

They generate tensions at the heart of neoliberal policies and they do not appear to improve the conditions of women in the structures of production and politics. In the 1990s, for example, 70% of the Bolivian population was considered poor, climbing to 95% in rural areas. In Peru, close to 50% of the population is classified as poor. The literacy rate among the female indigenous population, as a group, is the lowest in Latin America. The 1992 national census in Bolivia found that 50% of rural women could not read. In Peru, according to the 1993 National Census, the figure was 43%.[10]

The health statistics are no less alarming. In Bolivia, there are 390 maternal deaths for every 100,000 births. In Peru, there are 265 such deaths per 100,000 births. The situation in rural areas is even more troubling. In Potosí, Bolivia, the number of maternal deaths per 100,000 can reach 600. In the largely rural Andean provinces of Peru, the incidence of maternal deaths is similar to Potosí's. After Haiti, Bolivia and Peru have the highest rates of maternal deaths in Latin America, reflecting the general living conditions, the quality and coverage of health services and public investment in preventive health care. This is one of the most dramatic representations of social injustice and the inequality among women, as a report of the United Nations Population Fund asserts. [11]

Restrictions on reproductive rights also persist and indeed grow more stringent in some countries. The total percentage of maternal deaths caused by unsafe abortions is higher in Latin America and the Caribbean than any other region of the world. Some four million women in the region confront this risk each year. Botched abortions are the primary cause of maternal death in Chile and the second most common cause of maternal death in Paraguay and Peru. In countries such as Chile and more recently El Salvador, abortion is not permitted even to save the life of the mother.

Between the sporadic victories, the boiling oil of conservative reaction is bubbling up. For instance, in 1997, Salvadoran lawmakers eliminated the four legal options for abortion from the country's penal code after intensive mobilizations by pro-life groups. In many countries, the phrase "and of the family" has been added to the title of the national offices of women. And in Chile, conservative forces stymied passage of a divorce law and kept in the civil code the statutory definition of the husband as the "head" of the family.

There were internal cracks in the institutional structures created for women, but were also external shocks. Instability is a constant in our countries where not only policies, but also the structures of the state can change from one government to the next. In Bolivia, the Sub-Secretary of Women's Affairs disappeared in 1997 with the Banzer Administration and became an Office of Women's Affairs. This descent in the hierarchy transformed the agency from a policymaking body into a technical entity. When Andrés Pastrana became president of Colombia in 1999, the Office for the Equality of Women in Colombia was turned into a Presidential Advisory Board for Youth, Women and the Family, losing its former potential.

These small institutional tremors in the national offices of women suggest the vulnerability to seismic catastrophes gutting the rule of law and a calcifying of authoritarianism in many countries. The unstable political situation in parts of South America is coupled with precarious social conditions across the region that call into question the legitimacy of states that have been unable to respond to the basic needs of their people and have postponed the promise of democracy for decades. That state of affairs does not encourage faith in dialogue with government, much less in the sustainability of the advances for women.

The situation that I have described in this article is not new, nor does it come blown in by the winds from the North. It is part of the old and unresolved problem of exclusion, but nowadays these problems run freely in the face of silent or nonexistent public action to address them. Latin American feminism evolved with an acute social awareness, and two decades ago, it illuminated private life as a redoubt of multiple injustices for women. And as some critics complain, there have been changes in some sectors of the women's movement in the region that have stressed technical issues and have changed its behavior.

In the search for the possible, a subtle pragmatism appears to have become lodged in the strategies of feminists playing by the rules proposed by others. Thus, in their report for Beijing+5 presented in a forum of NGOs in Lima in February 2000, the Ecuadorans called attention to how their country's women's movement today gives priority to lobbying and negotiation over mobilization and denunciation. Chilean feminists have arrived at a similar conclusion, maintaining relations with the state's ministry for women's affairs, SERNAM, that are more technical than political. In the post-Beijing era, one outside observer characterized the implementation of the Beijing conference's "Platform of Action" in Colombia as an undynamic process that reflected the differences between the groups and conflicts among the leadership within the women's movement.

An optimistic assessment would suggest the years after the slight earthquake of Beijing to be only steps toward a reconfiguration of forces that will recover the enthusiasm and utopias of the past while creating perspectives and strategies that are in keeping with the difficult challenges of today: the need to deepen democracy and attain economic justice in our countries.

ABOUT THE AUTHOR

Maruja Barrig is a feminist journalist and researcher from Peru. She is a founder of the Women for Democracy collective. This article collects and updates some of the ideas from her essay, "De Como Llegar a un Puerto con el Mapa Equivocado," the introduction to the book, *Las Apuestas Inconclusas: El Movimiento de Mujeres y a IV Conferencia Mundial* (Flora Tristan Center and UNIFEM, 2000). The author thanks both institutions for granting permission to reprint excerpts. Translated from the Spanish by Deidre McFadyen.

NOTES

1. Author's interview with Virginia Vargas, November 2000.
2. Françoise Collin, "Una Herencia sin Testamento," in *Feminismos Fin de Siglo*, special edition of Fempress (Santiago), December 1999.
3. Author's interview with Virginia Vargas, November 2000.
4. "Avances de las mujeres en Bolivia a partir de los compromisos asumidos en la IV Conferencia Mundial de la Mujer," document published by the Committee of NGOs' Following Beijing, La Paz, January 2000.
5. "Participación, liderazgo y equidad de género en América Latina y el Caribe," CEPAL Working Document, Santiago, 1999.
6. Teresina Muñoz-Najar, "Las mujeres del Fujimorismo," CARETAS, August 17, 2000, http://www.caretas.com.pe/2000/1632/articulos/mujeres.phtml.
7. Alesssandra Bocchetti, "Per se/per me," *Sottosopra* (Milan), June 1987.
8. Letters to the editor, *Liberación* (Lima), November 22, 2000.
9. Author's interview, November 2000.
10. "Avances de las mujeres en Bolivia a partir de los compromisos asumidos en la IV Conferencia Mundial de la Mujer," document published by the Committee of NGOs Following Beijing (La Paz), January 2000; Sonia Montaño, "El dicho y el hecho. Cumplimiento de los acuerdos en Bolivia" in *Las Apuestas Inconclusas: El movimiento de mujeres y la IV Conferencia Mundial de la Mujer* (Lima: UNIFEM and Flora Tristán Publications, 2000).
11. Fondo de población de las Naciones Unidas (FNUAP), 1999; "Compromisos legislativos sobre salud y derechos sexuales y reproductivos: Una revisión de los cinco años de las conferencias de Cairo y Beijing en América Latina y el Caribe," document prepared for the Eighth Regional Conference on Latin American and Caribbean Women (Lima), February 2000.

Guillermo Delgado-P.

The Making of a Transnational Movement

"*Allpamanda! Kawsaymanda! Jatarisun!*" ("For our land and our life, we shall arise!") These Quichua words echoed in the streets as a multitude seized the church of Santo Domingo in Quito on May 28, 1990, turning it into a national arena of political dispute. By June 4, a nationwide uprising of indigenous peoples had paralyzed Ecuador. The "Revolution of the Ponchos," as the uprising became known, demanded the inclusion of indigenous peoples in the country's political process and galvanized indigenous social movements throughout the Americas. In other countries, indigenous peoples received the news and throughout that year and later, invited the rebels to their own meetings, to re/present the story. Based on the historical event, cassettes with messages in Quichua were taped; video-makers circulated documentaries, and early Internet availability helped to spread the news in the Americas and the world.

Up until then, the Quichua and their language had been carefully excluded from Ecuador's public life. But from then on, as their voices filled the airwaves and official TV channels, they could no longer be denied. Ecuador would now respect them, and in recognition of its ethnic heterogeneity, would define itself "pluricultural." The Quichua, along with 17 other ethnic nationalities, had begun to rectify 500 years of oppression by calling for the redefinition of their relation with the Ecuadoran nation-state. The lesson was well taken. All over the Americas, a younger generation of indigenous leaders, both women and men, learned from the dignified stand of the Quichua of Ecuador. The Ecuadoran event marked the official presence of an indigenous social subject that had been "invisible" up to that point. This event was crucial in solidifying the bases for a transnational movement of indigenous peoples in resistance against the appropriation of their natural economy, and their biological and cultural wealth.

These social movements of indigenous peoples force us to reconsider the meaning of struggles beyond the general limitations posed by class-only defined organizations. The surfacing of ethnic and gender/sexual consciousness over the past few decades has helped to strengthen the relationship of indigenous peoples to social movements and civil society. Indigenous peoples in rural as well as urban areas have worked to reconstitute proposals specific to their needs. Such demands can no longer be grafted to the whims of top-down politics monopolized by traditional party elites. Indigenous peoples have nurtured horizontal coalition building and have devised ethnically and culturally inspired social movements that have successfully pressured the state into responding to the needs of its people. Indigenous peoples are, indeed, defiant and rightly so.

In Mexico, twelve years after the Zapatista rebellion of 1994, concrete proposals to work out notions of autonomous territories, and their implementation, have stirred up both the right and the left. Critics have interpreted "autonomy" as secession, or a balkanization of the nation-state. "Autonomy" seen from an indigenous perspective, however, talks to the possibility of an indigenous community being able to manage its resources in close agreement and assistance, but not with uncritical interference by the nation-state. "Autonomy" means prioritizing the fulfillment of basic community needs, assuring well-being as a human right. This debate that emerged in Ecuador and Mexico, has now extended all over Latin America. The notion of "autonomy" is closely linked to the demands for "indigenous sovereignty" and "self-determination." Such proposals reject a mistaken assumption about indigenous peoples as stranded in the past. Instead, they focus on communities that struggle to maintain, or to reinvent themselves using their ethnic and social memory, guaranteeing its survival.

Every indigenous community then, negotiates a different form of autonomy with its respective nation-state. Disillusioned by "developmentalist" policies and neoliberalism, indigenous movements have articulated an international network of mutual assistance, though in terms of implementing their own proposals, some examples are better than others. As the Ecuadoran uprising and the decade-old Zapatista movement both show, "autonomous" models will arise from local and concrete practices. In other heavily indigenous countries such as Guatemala, Bolivia and Peru, for example, while indigenous peoples continue to struggle to defend their rights—and the rights of the population more generally—the struggle for autonomy will continue to evolve in tune with the legacies, histories and cultures of each respective peoples.

We must contextualize the circumstances in which these indigenous social movements emerged. Long traditions of twentieth-century nation-state tutelage and "*caciquismo*" are finally being challenged. Most indigenous movements, in fact, continue to explore legal mechanisms to validate their demands. Anthropologist Stefano Varese believes "indigenous peoples have striven to maintain critical distance from the colonizer's worldview and values in an effort to safeguard moral autonomy, cultural independence, and political sovereignty." As such, he adds, they have become "integral part of a growing world's civil society that articulates answers to top-down globalization from the bottom-up."[1]

Probably the most disastrous examples of indigenous peoples' travails within the nation-state have been the linguistic barriers within Western-inspired legal systems that have always ended up castigating them. This is especially the case given Latin America's lax juridical systems, which have persistently failed to protect indigenous human rights. In general, says Franco Mendoza, "the State fails to fulfill its obligations through acts of omission; despite its duty to guarantee justice for all. It is for this reason that as an act of justice, the model of the State must be changed; from the [homogeneous] nation-state to a plural State."[2] Indeed, at least nominally, Latin American countries have reformed their constitutions to include specific language about indigenous peoples throughout this last decade. However, fundamentalist religious missions, nongovernmental organizations (NGOs) of all kinds and colors, traditional party politics and the impact of international economic competition all continue to disrupt and hinder the possibilities of stronger autonomous movements of indigenous peoples.

In the Americas, the indigenous movement has experienced a radical change of leadership. The younger generations have felt that the international leaderships of the 1960s and 1970s had become stale and comfortable. Not much was known then at the grassroots about mobilizations and international decentralized coordination, let alone the circulation of pertinent information about international instruments to advance the rights of indigenous peoples such as International Labor Organization Convention 169. The self-criticism has prompted a more militant, informed and better coordinated internationalized movement since the 1990s.

Indigenous movements, clearly aware of the diminishing power of the nation-state and the overwhelming presence of globalizing forces, have contested "Indigenism," which is a colonialist nation-state policy that assumes the need to "protect" indigenous peoples. At its worst, Indigenism often served to patronize Indians and manipulate their fate. Its hope was to realize their "full assimilation" into dominant society. In a sense, "Indigenism" substituted itself for the Indian, taking the voice away, obliterating indigenous autonomous resurgence and agency. "Indigenism" became a state policy throughout the Americas since the 1940s. The indigenous movements of the Americas have persistently attacked this ideology; Mexico's Zapatistas have strongly spoken to the need to dismiss it and further rethink indigenous agency in a global context.

Recent meetings of indigenous peoples have proposed changing the terms of relationship with "outside" groups and individuals. They have requested, for example, that "researchers" rather than simply presenting indigenous voices in ineffectual studies, actively accompany the struggles of indigenous peoples. This new proposal—or political stand—indicts scholars and sympathizers, often inspired in the Western ethic of "objectivity," requesting, in a very direct way, that they be accountable to the immediate indigenous community, its needs and its expectations.

Naturally, indigenous movements are reacting to the exploitative ethics so embedded among researchers of indigenous matters. They reject the use of themselves as "informants," a term that they feel is disparaging. In a sense, indigenous movements are redefining the terms of collaboration, promoting horizontality and co-working rather than accepting hierarchy. Within the confines of the research relationship itself, they are attempting to do away with the prejudicial dichotomy of "civilization" versus "barbarism." Notions of "horizontal democracy" and "shared proposal making," often claimed by indigenous peoples, call for the creation of grassroots' political spaces as an answer to racism.[3]

The current process of decolonization proposes to restore the use of indigenous languages, to restore linguistic agency as a means to retrieve their own ways of thinking. Parallel to this repositioning is the redefinition of specific terms such as "land." As we enter the twenty-first century, indigenous peoples are also facing the experience of "landlessness" and displacement. According to an indigenous way of thinking, by talking about "land"—a concept that assumes further subdivision—we disregard the complexity of "territory" which, for indigenous peoples, calls for a deeper meaning of relationship between nature, place, social justice and survival. "Land" in a sense is infinitely divisible, a capitalistic imperative, and because of this, destructive of the ecological balance. "Territory," on the other hand, would press the user to reevaluate ecological/ cultural sustainability, concrete alternatives for the forthcoming generations. Naturally, "lands" that contain subsoil natural resources (like oil), or high levels of biodiversity, have the potential to be earmarked by the global market and faceless transnational interests. Consequently, recent struggles of indigenous peoples are focusing on biopiracy, food security and property rights over natural resources.

Women have gained in this renewed momentum of indigenous movements. Indigenous women are re-evaluating gender relationships in the family, the community, their political organizations and the society at large. Indigenous women propose to re-narrate the historical epics of women that directly shaped their own social history and agency. Several indigenous women of indigenous organizations throughout the Americas have retrieved stories about the power women leaders and elders have had in their communities, and are promoting the active participation of women in the communities' social struggles.

Horizontal communications, prompted by progressive international support and recent forms of continental coordination of indigenous women, are helping to redesign NGOs throughout the Americas, and are circulating new strategies to promote gender balance. Of course, the obstacles are weighty: militarization of indigenous territories, the presence of paramilitary forces, femicide, institutionalized violence, structural impunity, population displacements, etc.

Cross-ethnic work has been noticeable as part of the hemispheric forging of indigenous activism. The extensive dialogues between indigenous peoples of the North and the South, inspired by the 1991 meeting in Quito of representatives of 120 indigenous organizations and nations, belonging to the Peoples of the Eagle (North America), the Condor (South American Andes), the Jaguar (Amazon Basin) and the Quetzal (Guatemala), continue to nurture the exchange of information based on common goals.

After that 1991 seminal meeting, the degree of international coordination and political participation has reached new levels of agency and sophistication, particularly since the start of the twenty-first century, reflecting a clear discontent with the effects of neoliberalism and globalization. Indigenous assertiveness in Latin American countries, however, has provoked a veritable criminalization of indigenous demands by dominant powers. This demonizing of social protest dangerously aligns indigenous movements to the global repercussions of the so-called "War on Terror" and the issue of security.

The hemispheric organizing trends of indigenous social movements has also helped to observe and re-evaluate long-lasting consequences of the so-called "development recommendations" of international financial institutions— economic measures that have indirectly affected territories, deforesting them and intensifying economic poverty on indigenous territories. One of the everlasting effects of "development" is that about 100,000 indigenous peoples of Mexico alone can be found working in California's agribusiness in the United States.[4] After the Central American civil wars of the 1980s that expelled indigenous Mayas from their *milpas* (farm plots) and territories, another large percentage of Mayas from Guatemala have settled in Texas, Florida, Washington D.C. and Mexico. Similar experiences of displacement are found in urban Argentina where Aymara, Quechua and Guaraní peoples migrated in the last part of the twentieth century. A busy community of Quichuas engages in trade today as far as Amsterdam.

Seen within a global context, articulating an indigenous identity has not been a problem. The processes of inter-communication and sustained dialogue solidified mutual exchange of intellectual and life projects between the North and the South. The tremendous scholarship produced by First Peoples and Native Americans in the North is beginning to reach the activists and indigenous intellectuals of the South. Globalization also means the circulation of intellectual production and cross-border, cross-ethnic mutual assistance and dialogue. An excellent example of this has been the organizing of the Society of Writers in Indigenous Languages, based in Mexico City with various chapters throughout the Americas.

This transnational indigenous movement constitutes an intellectual space that allows for the ample circulation of proposals, including the need to press for dialogue on policies— especially those sponsored by the international financial institutions—that directly affect the environments and liveli-hood of indigenous peoples. In addition, the social movement continues re/remembering indigenous peoples while rethinking the collective variant of human rights, the struggles to sustain ecologies and the interactions of ethnicity, gender/sex and social class as elements that help to understand and problematize social reality. All of it has redefined the nation-state, seeking a better future—the realization of a *"pachakuti,"* a great transformation.[5] The multiple dialogues between governments, international financial institutions and indigenous peoples maintain open spaces for maneuvering. Such dialogues are tangible examples of achievements of cross-border and cross-ethnic indigenous movements. Lastly, the United Nations has declared 2005–2015 a *Second Decade for Indigenous Peoples*. Presumably, this international gesture will continue to carve spaces for sharper dialogues with indigenous peoples. After all, there is need to consider them as assertive political actors with clear agencies and proposals to construct a livable future.

ABOUT THE AUTHOR

Guillermo Delgado-P. is a human rights activist and anthropologist who teaches in the Latin American studies department at the University of California at Santa Cruz.

NOTES

1. Stefano Varese, "The New Environmentalist Movement of Latin American Indigenous People," in Stephen B. Brush and Doreen Stabinsky (eds.), *Valuing Local Knowledge: Indigenous People and Indigenous Property Rights* (Washington: Island Press, 1996), pp. 122–42. Stefano Varese "Diálogo Intercultural: La afirmación de las identidades más allá de las fronteras," in Ethel Wara Alderete, et al., *Conocimiento Indígena y Globalización* (Quito: Abya-Yala, 2005), pp. 15–34.
2. Moisés Franco-Mendoza, "The Debate Concerning Indigenous Rights in Mexico," in W. Assies, G. van der Haar and A.J. Hoekma (eds.), *The Challenge of Diversity* (Amsterdam: Thela, Thesis, 2000) pp. 57–76.
3. Jonathan Warren, "Socialist Saudades: Lula's Victory, Indigenous Movements, and the Latin American Left," in Nancy Grey Postero and Leon Zamosc (eds.), *The Struggles for Indigenous Rights* (Brighton: Sussex Academic Press, 2004), pp. 217–31.
4. Jonathan Fox and Gaspar Rivera Salgado eds., *Indigenous Mexican Migrants in the United States* (La Jolla: Center for U.S. Mexican Studies, 2004).
5. Guillermo Delgado-P., "Bolivian Social Movements in the First Lustrum of the 21st Century," http://isla.igc.org/Features/Globalization/BSM2k.html, retrieved November 2005.

Laura Carlsen

Timely Demise for Free Trade Area of the Americas

The stage was set for a showdown. When the Bush cabinet announced intentions to revive the moribund Free Trade Area of the Americas (FTAA) at the Fourth Summit of the Americas in Mar del Plata, Argentina, the countries of the Southern Common Market (Mercosur) closed ranks to prevent it. What followed was a diplomatic melee that reflects not so much divisions within Latin America, as a growing resistance to the current free trade model throughout the developing world.

The November 2005 summit was officially billed as a forum to discuss employment, and the FTAA issue was not even on the agenda. However, well before landing in the Argentine beach town, the Bush Administration made clear its intentions to leave with a specific commitment to restart negotiations.

The U.S. government was determined to come out of the meeting with a revitalized FTAA because the Administration feared that if the negotiations were left to languish, momentum could be lost for the initiative at a crucial time. The FTAA negotiations were first launched in 1994, but after 10 years of inconclusive talks and significant differences between the countries, the goal of a hemisphere-wide trade deal remains elusive. Since the FTAA meeting in November of 2003, when the two co-chairs, United States and Brazil, failed to agree on a basic model, substantive talks have been suspended completely.

Against this backdrop, and pending uncertainty over agreements at the World Trade Organization, the United States wanted a formal statement of common purpose from its own hemisphere. The Administration has presented its pro-business trade strategy as an essential pillar of its foreign policy in the region, while Latin America continues continue to move to the center-left. Venezuela's Hugo Chávez has become a lightning rod in the region for criticism of the Bush government, which flared after the invasion of Iraq. In this context, Washington hoped for a clear affirmation of loyalties among nations of the Americas.

These hopes were dashed in Mar del Plata. Despite the efforts of Mexico's President Vicente Fox to push through a commitment to FTAA talks, the 34 nations present, failed to reach a consensus on renewed negotiations due to the firm resistance of the four nations of the Mercosur (Argentina, Brazil, Paraguay and Uruguay) along with Venezuela. Given the impasse, in a last-ditch diplomatic move worked out after several presidents including Bush had already left the Summit, paragraph 19 of the final declaration was split into two positions.

Twenty-nine countries stood behind the resolution that they would "remain committed to the achievement of a balanced and comprehensive FTAA Agreement that aims at expanding trade flows." These nations resolved to "instruct our officials responsible for trade negotiations to resume their meetings, during 2006, to examine the difficulties in the FTAA process, in order to overcome them and advance the negotiations within the framework adopted in Miami in November 2003."

The second position, put forth by the four nations of Mercosur plus Venezuela, states: "Other member states maintain that the necessary conditions are not yet in place for achieving a balanced and equitable free trade agreement with effective access to markets free from subsidies and trade-distorting practices, and that takes into account the needs and sensitivities of all partners, as well as the differences in the levels of development and size of the economies."

The nations of the Mercosur took a stand against renewing FTAA talks to declare their opposition to free trade agreements, along the model of the existing North American Free Trade Agreement (NAFTA), which do not take into account the needs of developing countries while locking in competitive advantages for developed nations. Since the WTO meeting in Cancún in 2003, the focal point for Brazil has been the question of agricultural subsidies. Brazil has called for elimination of all agricultural export subsidies in the United States and the European Union and a schedule for review and elimination of trade-distorting domestic subsidies. The United States has made it clear that it will not enter into a discussion of its agricultural subsidies in the FTAA, so Mercosur refused to agree to further negotiations.

Agricultural subsidies are not the only bone of contention. Other issues have also impeded progress and caused Mercosur members to question the long-term value of the FTAA. While the United States demands almost unhampered access to Latin American countries' markets, it maintains protectionist barriers in many of the same products exported by their countries, including sugar and textiles. Unrestricted U.S. imports could destroy poor country sectors currently serving the domestic market. Intellectual property and the resulting barriers to access to life-saving medicines, government purchases, and investor guarantees are other areas that have been sticking points in negotiations and that are extremely sensitive to developing nations.

Both Brazil and Argentina announced before the Summit that they did not want to discuss the FTAA prior to resolution of long-standing disputes within the WTO. Brazil, in particular, prefers the WTO for trade negotiations because there it can leverage the power of the still-strong Group of 20 of developing countries it helped form at the WTO ministerial in Cancún in 2003. Alliances with emerging economies of India, China, Africa and Latin America gives Brazilian trade negotiators a far broader base to confront the United States and the European Union on subsidies.

In the post-mortem of the Summit, many analysts on both the right and the left have insisted that the FTAA is not dead. At a time when the Bush Administration is encountering serious problems both domestically and globally, the last thing it needed was a defeat in Mar del Plata. Although Secretary of State Condoleezza Rice was visibly upset at the refusal to commit to the FTAA, official U.S. press statements on the Summit stressed agreement on a number of specific U.S. proposals and did not even mention the FTAA setback.

Despite Summit events, proponents of free trade cite the advance of bilateral trade deals as evidence that the U.S. free trade strategy is still alive and kicking in Latin America. Central American nations and the Dominican Republic have entered into a U.S. free trade agreement (CAFTA-DR) and the Andean nations are now in the fourteenth round of difficult negotiations for an Andean Free Trade Agreement (AFTA). Chile signed a bilateral deal with the United States in 2003. They also point out that in Mar del Plata 29 countries called for FTAA talks in 2006, and only five cited a lack of adequate conditions for negotiations. But the numbers argument is fallacious and masks hard realities.

Calling for renewed talks is a far cry from agreeing with the FTAA model promoted by the United States and its allies. In fact, many of the countries that called for the resumption of talks have had serious problems within their own bilateral negotiations due to differing views and a perceived U.S. intransigency. Even Panama, whose government presented the text to continue negotiating the FTAA, has been at an impasse in its own bilateral talks with the United States since January of 2005. Again, the sticking point is agriculture—the demand of small Panamanian farmers to protect their internal markets from import surges in basic staple crops. Although this point is extremely important to the many smaller, largely rural-based economies of the continent, the United States has shown little flexibility.

Caribbean countries have also expressed major differences with the free trade model as expressed in the FTAA in other forums. The Caribbean Community (Caricom) has been concentrating its efforts on negotiations at the WTO, where it has received severe blows lately in banana and sugar rulings. In response, many of its leaders have formulated demands to take into account developing countries' needs through exemptions and compensations that would go against the terms of a NAFTA-style FTAA.

The defeat of prospects for a hemisphere-wide agreement deals a heavy blow to Washington's commercial strategy in the region. Since its inception in 1994, the FTAA has constituted the most ambitious forum for imposing a very specific model of free trade, one dictated by U.S. interests and those of its transnational companies. Meanwhile, Latin American countries have expanded integration with Europe, and China has made major inroads into the region. What appeared a consensus among nations ten years ago has now become a focal point for deep-seated differences in perspectives on development and integration.

The death of the FTAA opens up room for the nations of the region to explore alternatives to a model that has lost support both among governments and civil society. Diversified trade, increased regional agreements, democratization and policies oriented toward national development should be the guides along the new route.

ABOUT THE AUTHOR

Laura Carlsen is based in Mexico City where she directs the Americas Program of the International Relations Center (IRC), online at www.americas.irc-online.org.

A New Left Rising?

Andrés Gaudin

The Kirchner Factor

When Néstor Kirchner assumed the presidency of Argentina in May 2003 with only 22% of votes cast, few imagined his approval rating would reach 90% only weeks later, much less that such support would last. After nearly 20 months in office, he has managed to maintain record popular support. Throughout his term, Kirchner has channeled a broad spectrum of popular protest to his benefit; he has retained the banner of a progressive politician and he has succeeded in neutralizing the stubborn opposition of the old guard in his party, the Justicialista Party (PJ) of the Peronists. He also counts on his party's majority in both houses of Congress. As a testament to Kirchner's popularity, the majority of his party's leadership believes in the inevitability of his re-election and consequently supports it, despite the contest being almost two years away.

Kirchner assumed the presidency after three consecutive terms as governor of the southern province of Santa Cruz, the second-smallest electoral district in the country with less than 1% of the national electorate. Although he was scarcely known at the national level, his candidacy benefited from internal divisions within the party—for the first time in its history the PJ presented more than one candidate. The backing of then-interim President Eduardo Duhalde also helped Kirchner. Duhalde wanted the Peronists to put forth a new politician, one without leverage inside the party and without an electoral base, and someone who would respond to his directives, allowing him to be the real power behind the throne. Also motivating the interim President was his adamant desire to prevent two-term former ultra-neoliberal President Carlos Menem (1989–99) from taking back the presidency. Duhalde and Menem were, and continue to be, irreconcilable antagonists who fiercely vie for the leadership of the party. So Duhalde's support for Kirchner was basically a marriage of convenience. Indeed, they have never had a trusting political relationship, and have locked horns within the PJ over key issues—the privatization of state enterprises, for example.

To gain maneuverability for independent action in such a partisan context, Kirchner set out to create his own base of support. Divided into its factions, the PJ had no room for another *caudillo*. The options outside the PJ included groups and parties running the political gamut from right to left. With his narrow electoral win and the conditional support of Duhalde, Kirchner approached the different sectors of society that felt unrepresented by all parties.

According to his press secretary, Kirchner and his wife, Senator Cristina Fernández—also one of the President's main political advisors—privately admit that only by winning the sympathy of social sectors uncontaminated by the vices of the large parties will they be able to confront the right. By "the right," they mean Menem and the equally neoliberal Ricardo López Murphy of the Recreate Party. In the April 2003 elections in which Kirchner garnered only 22% of the vote, Menem received 24.4% and López Murphy 16.3%. As the runoff election between Menem and Kirchner neared, Menem's defeat was practically certain. He dropped out of the race amid his growing isolation within the PJ and a series of corruption investigations into his previous administrations.

Kirchner wasted no time. Before his verbal confrontations with the International Monetary Fund and private creditors over payments on a debt of more than $165 billion, he set out to gain support by conquering neglected social sectors. He met with human rights groups, making him the first president in two decades of democracy to do so. He declared the non-applicability of statutory limitations on crimes against humanity committed during the last military dictatorship (1976–83) and converted a building symbolic of the dictatorship into the Museum of Memory.

Within the labor movement he focused on the independent Argentine Workers' Central (CTA). The CTA was an especially attractive group because it was at odds with the General Labor Confederation (CGT), which historically acts as Peronism's union arm. Kirchner promised the CTA that he would implement the International Labor Organization's Convention 87, which ensures freedom of association and the right to organize. In essence, this would officially permit the independent CTA to negotiate for higher salaries and better working conditions on a level equal to the CGT.

He attracted progressives and intellectuals by capping rate hikes for public services privatized in the 1990s, and by discontinuing the privileges enjoyed by water and rail companies since the Menem years. Other measures catering to this sector included terminating the concession of the Argentine Postal System, effectively returning it to state control, and the creation of a state-run airline and energy holding company. Kirchner's most popular early effort was the profound renovation of the judicial system and, specifically, the Supreme Court, which was a constant source of corruption during Menem's administrations.

As for the popular assemblies born out of the 2001 crisis and the more combative and militant *piquetero* (movement of unemployed workers), Kirchner took the tack of protecting them while awaiting their natural disintegration; he was steadfast in opposing any heavy-handed responses to *piquetero* direct actions.

The popular assemblies that had occupied street corners and other public spaces, mainly in Buenos Aires, after the December 2001 crisis were already fading away when Kirchner took office. They were "victims" of their middle class origins and co-opted by Trotskyist groups—especially the Laborers' Party—whose militancy, despite their small numbers, isolated the assemblies from the rest of society. Philosopher Ricardo Forster believes the assemblies and the 2001 upheaval "have to be interpreted like May 1968 in France. It looks like they lost, that they were defeated, but underneath they created something irreversible." Forster adds, "If the 2001 protests did not break the political parties—a stated aim in their discourse—they did succeed in creating a different cultural-political programmatic environment. . . . They created a different sensibility."[1]

This social activism that flowed from the December 2001 upheaval caused middle class groups, who sought access to their frozen bank accounts, to temporarily sympathize with the *piquetero* movement. At the beginning of 2002, for example, members of popular assemblies expressed their solidarity with the *piqueteros* and received them as heroes when they would enter the city of Buenos Aires. It was an especially hot summer, and the assemblies greeted the *piqueteros* with sandwiches and refreshments. They even waved flags and threw confetti from their balconies as they marched by. But as *piqueteros* carried on with their blockades of roads and highways, they fell from the good graces of the middle classes, which historically lean to the right. In fact, the middle classes began calling for the repression of *piqueteros* for altering the rhythm of their daily lives with blockades.

Piquetero groups also began to fragment because of left-wing groups' attempts to capitalize on the movement, causing internal divisions. And their platform of demands changed constantly: one day they asked for subsidies, the next day they wanted seeds for a community garden or school supplies for their children. As traditional middle class intolerance of lower-class activism resurged, Kirchner refused the demands for an aggressive response. He believed the *piqueteros* had legitimate grievances and he protected their right to protest until they tired and weakened. He rightly gambled on their eventual fragmentation, and today some of these splintered groups are important allies of his government.

The *piqueteros* were born in the 1990s deep inside the country's interior, a product of the mass unemployment created by the labor flexibilization of newly privatized state companies— above all, the petroleum industry. Gradually *piqueteros* became an urban phenomenon. Today, *piqueteros* are for the most part no longer found in the country's interior; they almost exclusively reside in Buenos Aires and its surroundings. Like the assemblies, they have fallen victim to miniscule parties with Trotskyist roots, causing their atomization. Since there are now nearly 30 *piquetero* groups directing protest actions, mobilizations are more numerous, yet their force has diminished and they have become increasingly unpopular, particularly in the minds of inconvenienced *porteños*—Buenos Aires residents.

The most active and discredited of these groups is the Independent Movement of Retired and Unemployed Workers led by Raúl Castells, who is now on parole after recently spending two months in jail. He had been convicted on charges of extortion involving the owner of a casino in the northern province of Chaco. When detained, he first thanked López Murphy and Menem for the solidarity they had expressed upon his detention, and then, as if justice were still an appendage of political power, blurted: "The military dictatorship was more honest than Kirchner. When they didn't kill detainees, they at least told you that you were apprehended because they didn't like what you thought. But Kirchner won't admit that he arrested me because he does not like how I think." Human rights groups roundly condemned his comments, as did several nationally respected figures including Adolfo Pérez Esquivel, Argentine winner of the 1980 Nobel Peace Prize. Diverse civil society groups issued a joint declaration. "No government that usurps power is better than one chosen by the people. . . . Castells has finally revealed his true political convictions and society now knows what to expect from him," concluded the document.

Kirchner had no need to respond to Castells' accusations. *Piquetero* groups were the first to defend the President, calling Castells "a traitor." Jorge Cevallos, who leads the *piquetero* group Neighborhoods on Our Feet, even asked, "Who is behind Castells? Who is paying him to try and destabilize the government?"

Kirchner's broad appeal has led some analysts to wonder if he intends to distance himself from the PJ, or perhaps build his own party. But he has never said he plans to abandon Peronism. Although he is of basic Peronist stripe, he is not tied to the party establishment or its folklore. But neither has he indicated that he is pursuing the ambitious project of constructing his own political base. Nonetheless, media outlets have coined a term to describe his rapprochement with the most dynamic social sectors. They contend the President aspires to consolidate a movement that "transverses" across all sectors of society; abbreviating the concept, media have begun referring to "Kichnerist transversality."

Echoing this idea in September 2004, leaders with Peronist roots but distanced from its party structures launched the creation of the Coordinating Board for a New National Project. Renowned leftist journalist Miguel Bonasso announced its creation. Bonasso created the Party of the Democratic Revolution (PRD) in Argentina and won a legislative seat in 2003. He borrowed the name from the political party of the same name in Mexico, where he was exiled during Argentina's last dictatorship.

Joining Bonasso is fellow congressional deputy Francisco Gutiérrez, a respected metallurgical union leader, and Eduardo Luis Duhalde (of no relation to the former interim President), who is Kirchner's Secretary of Human Rights and the founder of the Memory and Mobilization Party. The Board is supposed to act as a nexus between society at large and Kirchner, in step with his transversality strategy, but in reality it is not much more than a public relations maneuver. Even some of its creators concede the project is destined for a slow death. They believe it will become irrelevant once stalwart Peronists line up behind Kirchner. Even former interim President Eduardo Duhalde admitted, "If Kirchner keeps on like this, Peronism will support his re-election in 2007."

Faster than anyone could have imagined, the President has shed his narrow mandate and now enjoys tremendous popular support. Importantly, he has become a respected leader with his own political weight and has managed to capitalize on the complex social reality that has existed since he came to office in May 2003.

"Stated simply, the opportunity for change is always accompanied by the risk of chaos," says sociologist Nicolás Casullo in analyzing the Kirchner phenomenon. "Whoever assumed the government in Argentina [at the time of the election] faced the difficult task of transforming protest into politics, of somehow institutionalizing social mobilization that was anti-institutional." Many political scientists and other scholars would agree with Casullo when he says of Kirchner: "He has managed to keep a foot both inside and outside of Peronism while trying to arrive at something else, because without a doubt we are presented with a political project that recovers and legitimizes protest."[2]

In October 2005, Argentina held legislative elections in which 128 of the 257 seats in the lower house and 24 of the 72 senatorial seats were contested. Two and a half years after having won the presidency with only 22% of votes—mostly from supporters of his mentor (Duhalde)—Kirchner struck a resounding victory. He won 49% of votes, gaining an absolute majority in the lower house of Congress and a simple majority in the Senate. What made this electoral victory so significant is that it was won without the support of the Peronist electoral machinery: Kirchner had definitively split from Duhalde and confronted the old guard Peronist caudillos by creating his own political party—the Front for Victory. Indeed, he has succeeded in solidifying his political base, broke the political dependence he was forced to maintain with Duhalde and defeated Menem and López Murphy, his staunchest opponents of the right-wing.

A few days after this victory, the President reshuffled his cabinet. Many of the changes he made were expected, but few analysts had anticipated the replacement of the Minister of the Economy, Roberto Lavagna. The Minister had presided over sustained economic growth and the most dramatic reduction of poverty and unemployment in years. The cabinet changes were seen as an effort to satisfy his new electoral base—social and political sectors dissatisfied with the old-guard partisan structures. Kirchner hopes his new team will help fulfill the ambitious platform he laid out at the beginning of his term. His foreign affairs minister is a self-declared enemy of the U.S.-sponsored Free Trade Area of the Americas (FTAA) and an ally of Venezuela's President Hugo Chávez; his defense minister is a long-time leftist militant and an outspoken supporter of human rights. And Felisa Miceli, who replaced Lavagna, has publicly rejected IMF prescriptions, criticized the private corporations managing public services and said she portends to address the country's vast economic inequality. It seems the President hopes that the new life breathed into his cabinet will extend to the country as well.

ABOUT THE AUTHOR

Andrés Gaudin is a Uruguayan journalist who went into exile in Argentina in 1972. He lives in Buenos Aires and writes for *Latinamerica Press* among others. Translated from Spanish by Teo Ballvé.

NOTES

1. Ricardo Forster, *Confines* (Buenos Aires, September 2003).
2. Nicolás Casullo, *Plan V* (Buenos Aires, June 2004).

Jonah Gindin

Chavistas in the Halls of Power, Chavistas in the Streets

With members of Venezuela's political opposition trying to get rid of President Hugo Chávez by just about any means they can think of, Chávez's supporters have been in a near-constant state of anti-opposition mobilization. The implementation of projects aimed at improving the lives of poor Venezuelans has frequently taken a back seat to this defensive mobilization. But the mobilization itself has created a social momentum that may be carrying *Chavismo*—the loose grouping of Chávez's supporters—toward a deepening of his proclaimed "Bolivarian Revolution."

The gradual development of *Chavismo* as a possible coherent, autonomous political force in the country fills the gaping void left by the disillusionment of the 1980s and 1990s. During the two decades preceding Chávez's election, the Venezuelan left was represented primarily by fragmented neighborhood associations, a radical student movement and a radical syndicalist movement—all three of which were violently repressed.

What distinguishes *Chavismo* from other political movements is the space Chávez's leadership has opened for mobilization from below. With his charisma and masterful ability to engage in political dialogue with the estimated 80% of Venezuelans who live below the poverty line, Chávez has united most of the country's anti-neoliberal forces under his leadership.

The pro-Chávez mobilization has taken two principal forms. The first follows from the government's active creation of participatory community organizations, neighborhood associations and public-works projects.[1] Health committees, for example, work with Cuban doctors and provide a link between the community and the state in *Barrio Adentro*, a program offering free primary health care in poor neighborhoods across the country; land committees oversee and participate in the application of urban and rural land reform; education committees facilitate three adult-educational programs providing free and accessible literacy, high-school, and university-level education to poor Venezuelans in their own communities.

In this political context, the first steps toward the development of participatory budgeting has meant the creation of "community living organizations," each made up of roughly 15 to 30 people, one member of each family in a given neighborhood. The unique character of these organizations is that they act not only as organizing conduits, but also as informal centers of evaluation and criticism. When land reform is not proceeding according to schedule, for example, or community health clinics are not receiving their funding, it is the committee members of the communities in question who bring the issue to the attention of the state—by direct protest when necessary.

"Local leadership exists, regional leadership exists; there exists a new emerging leadership within *el proceso*," notes Pedro Infante, director of the National Coordinator of Popular Organizations. "We are organized, but we are dispersed."[2] Government mobilizing is in part responding to this reality. It is a form of mobilization that is both intentional and unselfish in that it is usually separate from political campaigns or the direct promotion of Chávez. Its clear goal has been to lay the foundation upon which to build participatory power structures in poor communities where organized political capacities have atrophied after decades of exclusion.

The second form of mobilization is a natural byproduct of representative democracy, but also a direct reaction to the legal and illegal campaign to overthrow Chávez. The 2001 coup and four ultimately unsuccessful—though destructive—general strikes and employer lockouts have inevitably put the government, and its supporters, on the defensive. The resulting siege mentality, particularly as a result of the coup, has meant that the organization of a huge swath of Venezuelan society has been specifically predicated on the basis of supporting the President.

The powerful cult of personality surrounding Chávez gave him a resounding victory in last August's presidential recall referendum, and was largely responsible for the government's landslide victory in the October regional elections. But this type of support inevitably discourages the development of an autonomous, popular movement capable of making independent decisions when the need arises.

The student movement still exists, as do recently revitalized progressive trade union movements. Recently created community organizations are complimented by a slightly older variety of small, disparate community-based social movements. Yet, as veteran social activist and writer Roland Denis notes, "These are groups that move within a large wave of rebellion, but without an organic base, without a party, without history, without tradition; groups that must practically invent a movement from scratch. They are movements that are basically sustained by grassroots leaders, community leaders, student leaders, trade union leaders, peasant leaders—fundamentally popular leaders."[3]

The fragmented social movements that predate Chávez have not abandoned their existing structures. But now, community-based activism inevitably involves close coordination with government-formed community organizations, blurring the boundaries between the two. *Chavismo's* linkage to a representative national political body makes it a stunningly large and complex mobilizing force.

In the two months between the announcement of the August 15, 2004, recall referendum and the referendum vote itself, the government organized its supporters into a nationwide social movement-cum-political party of a kind never before seen in the country, or the region, in either structure or scale. In the first speech of the campaign on June 5, Chávez announced the creation of "electoral battle units" (UBEs) and electoral "patrols" to be coordinated by a national committee. The Comando Maisanta, as the committee was called, oversaw UBEs in every state, municipality and neighborhood, and reported directly to the President. Every Venezuelan who did not want to see Chávez removed from office was encouraged to organize him or herself into a "patrol" of ten committed activists. Groups of patrols made up district UBEs, which together made up municipal UBEs and so on.

At the upper-most levels, time constraints made a democratic structure impossible. Chávez appointed the members of the Commando Maisanta and the state-level UBEs, but from the level of the municipality to the community, positions were largely submitted to improvised elections. Almost overnight, an estimated 1.2 million militants had joined the campaign, creating patrols and UBEs in every neighborhood in the country. Nearly 4% of Venezuela's population became active members of UBEs. Certainly, many who joined the UBEs were from land- and health-reform committees, and some were activists in community-living organizations and militants of the community-based social movements. But for a large majority of UBE members, this was their first experience in political activism.

In a recent interview in Caracas, Pakistani social activist and writer Tariq Ali noted that Venezuela presents an important example of how political and social movements can work together. "The Bolivarian movement," he commented, "is both a social movement that mobilizes the poor as nothing else has been able to do in this country, and a political movement, because it finds its reflection in the government, which it continues to re-elect."[4]

The development of a new kind of social movement in Venezuela is one of the Bolivarian Revolution's most important legacies. Through conscious, planned community mobilization and concrete advances in key areas of education, health and housing, *Chavismo* is currently acting in many capacities as a traditional social movement. But its organic link to the state gives it a character and a revolutionary potential lacking in other movements of the region such as Brazil's Landless Rural Workers' Movement (MST) or the Argentine *piqueteros*. *Chavismo's* lack of autonomy from government is certainly problematic, and it is a contradiction that will eventually be unsustainable. But the manner in which this contradiction forces its own resolution need not be negative.

As the backbone of the Bolivarian project, *Chavismo* already has the space necessary to exert intense pressure on the government to deepen the embryonic development of participatory power structures such as Local Planning Councils and the UBEs. As this capacity develops, it may well reach a point where it can do this to such an extent that autonomy becomes irrelevant, or even undesirable: *Chavismo* as a social movement and as a government may eventually more solidly converge.

One crucial test of *Chavismo's* willingness to articulate an autonomous position from the Chávez government came in the aftermath of the 2004 referendum. Community groups and grassroots Chávez-supporters demanded that regional elections scheduled for October 31, just two months after the referendum, be postponed in order to allow time for all parties to hold primaries. Chávez, along with leaders of the pro-Chávez political parties, argued that the elections could not be postponed because pro-Chávez candidates needed to take advantage of the momentum from the referendum victory. In response, community organizations all over the country protested this decision by holding Popular Assemblies to draw up neighborhood manifestos. The manifestos listed the needs and demands of the community, and were then presented to the corresponding Chavista candidate. The community promised its electoral support providing that the candidate agreed to the terms of the manifesto. Should s/he renege, the community promised to recall that candidate, according to their right to do so under the new Bolivarian Constitution. Thus, Chavistas used their Constitutional rights and grassroots organizational capacities to force reticent representative political structures to bend to their will. It was a powerful example of Venezuelan democracy at work, and of the independence of Chávez's own most dedicated followers.

Another fundamentally important product of *Chavismo's* bridge between the grassroots and the government is its incorporation of rank and file elements of the armed forces. As Denis notes, "The popular movement does not consist of only social movements, there are also military movements . . . soldiers and young military officers who go to workshops and participate in the dynamic of the popular movements."[5]

Whatever the post-referendum strategy for the UBEs was at the time of their formation, their continued existence has since become an integral part of the as-yet largely unplanned future of the Bolivarian experiment. Chávez has declared the arrival of a new stage of *el proceso*, what he calls the "revolution within the revolution." But post-referendum Venezuela was going to be a new stage, with or without Chávez's blessings.

The need to defend Chávez has—for the moment—receded, providing an opportunity for proactive *Chavismo* to fill the vacuum. The UBEs are in the process of redefining themselves as social battle units (UBSs), shifting their focus from electoral processes to community needs. Duly reinforced after the referendum and the regional elections, we may now see a nationally coherent *Chavismo* emerge, supportive of the process but capable of the difficult introspection necessary to identify its weaknesses, and ultimately, of the structural transformation that may eventually see the convergence of social movement and state.

ABOUT THE AUTHOR

Jonah Gindin is a Canadian journalist living and working in Venezuela. He writes regularly for Venezuelanalysis.com.

NOTES

1. As sociologist and political analyst James Petras noted in a recent interview (Caracas, December 2, 2004), the Chávez government has not done enough to foster employment through public works. However, an employment mission, "Vuelvan Caras," represents a significant first step, providing scholarships to hundreds of thousands of Venezuelans while training them in specific trades and in forming cooperatives.
2. Interview with author, Caracas, September 15, 2004.
3. Interview with author, Caracas, November 19, 2004.
4. Interview with author, Caracas, December 6, 2004.
5. Interview with author, Caracas, November 9, 2004.

Steve Ellner

Venezuela:
Defying Globalization's Logic

The continued ability of president Hugo Chávez to carry out significant reforms in the face of U.S. hostility and an aggressive U.S.-supported domestic opposition has important implications for progressive Latin American struggles. Chávez's success places in doubt the view that in today's world of global capitalism it is no longer possible for Latin American and Caribbean countries to effectively resist the "free-market" neoliberal order.

The ongoing market-based conditionality of all economic assistance (including debt forgiveness) from the United States and U.S.-dominated international financial institutions may reinforce the view that "there is no alternative" to free-market policies, as Margaret Thatcher famously quipped. But the Chávez experience goes against Thatcher's dictum, and it raises the interesting question of whether the Venezuelan road is applicable to other countries in Latin America and the Caribbean. The rise to power in recent years of center-left governments in Argentina, Brazil and Uruguay puts this question into sharp relief.

From the outset, Chávez's key aim has been to achieve—and hold on to—state power in order to propel radical change. To that end, he has built the nation's largest political party, the Fifth Republic Movement (MVR), which has governed since 1998 in alliance with smaller leftist parties. Before coming to power, he criticized Francisco Arias Cárdenas, his second-in-command in the abortive military coup he led in 1992, for running for a state governor's office in 1995 rather than concentrating on achieving national power. In response to the local path chosen by Arias, Chávez stated, "The conquest of power through a mayoralty or a governorship to have a platform to make further advances is a lie that will always drown you in a swamp."[1]

The radical thrust of Chávez's actions since his initial electoral triumph in 1998 goes beyond style and discourse. Indeed, many of his reforms and actions have undermined the economic interests of powerful Venezuelan and transnational groups. The MVR government, for example, has put a halt to schemes that were set in motion by Chávez's neoliberal predecessors in favor of the privatization of social security, the aluminum industry and the all-important oil industry. Government allocations favor the poor, significantly increasing the percentages of the national budget assigned to education, health, employment and credit for small-scale businesses. Furthermore, Venezuela's activist role in OPEC during Chávez's first years in office, more than any other member nation, helped restore oil prices to their 1970s levels. Finally, since early 2005, a Chávez-appointed "Intervention Commission" has been reviewing the legality of agricultural land deeds, thus threatening large landowners with loss of property.

The U.S. response to Chávez following his election in 1998 was guided by the then-conventional wisdom regarding the inevitability of his eventual coming around to neoliberal policies. U.S. Ambassador John Maisto supported a soft-line approach and successfully argued within the State Department that Chávez should be judged by his actions, implying that nothing would come of his radical rhetoric.[2] At the time, Maisto's thesis seemed plausible. Indeed, during the presidential campaign, Chávez had toned down his position in favor of a moratorium on foreign debt payments and instead concentrated on the proposal for a constituent assembly that would bring about internal political changes by rewriting the Constitution. During his first two years in office, Chávez stressed political reforms. In 2001, however, the MVR government passed legislation with significant socioeconomic content, including an agrarian reform and a law ensuring the state's majority ownership of all oil industry operations. The radicalization of the government coincided with the beginning of the Bush Administration, and the hardening of Washington's global stance following 9/11. These developments in the United States emboldened Venezuela's opposition, which now claimed that Chávez's days as president were numbered.[3] The opposition's adherence to Thatcher's thesis regarding neoliberalism's inevitability may well have influenced its leaders to underestimate Chávez with disastrous results. This miscalculation translated itself into various abortive schemes to oust Chávez without any fallback plans.

By 2002, U.S. attitudes toward Chávez began to coincide with those of the traditional parties of the opposition, which had all along maintained an intransigent stand. The Bush Administration's support for the short-lived coup against Chávez in April 2002, its approval of the equally futile 10-week general strike later that year and its more recent efforts to isolate Venezuela from its neighbors are not merely reactions to specific reforms threatening economic interests. Washington fears the "demonstration effect," that is, the influence the Venezuelan example can have on the rest of the continent.

A quite different demonstration effect had worked in Washington's favor 10 years earlier with the collapse of the Soviet Union. Champions of neoliberalism and globalization had pointed to the fate of Soviet socialism as hard proof that all forms of state intervention in the economy were doomed to failure. By placing in doubt the possibility of any effective challenge to the dominant system of global capitalism, this demonstration effect hurt leftists worldwide, no matter how they felt about the Soviet Union. Washington's fear is that Chávez's Venezuela may have the opposite effect by demonstrating the feasibility of defying the neoliberal model and establishing viable alternatives.

Chávez's hemispheric influence can be felt at both the popular and diplomatic levels. He has become a hero to millions of non-privileged Latin Americans who admire his courage and take careful note of his political successes. Some activists and leaders have reacted in a similar way. Unlike the mixed reaction to Lula's speech at the 2005 World Social Forum in Porto Alegre, Brazil, Chávez received thunderous applause. Chávez emphasized his commitment to grassroots struggle when he told the crowd: "I am not here as the President of Venezuela.... I am only President because of particular circumstances. I am Hugo Chávez and am an activist as well as a revolutionary."

On the diplomatic level, Chávez has been careful to avoid Cuba's error of the 1960s, when Fidel Castro appealed to the left and the general populace throughout Latin America, but in doing so forfeited a strategy of alliances with existing governments. As a result, Washington was able to isolate Cuba from the Latin American community of nations. By contrast, despite his fiery rhetoric, Chávez has maintained cordial relations with neoliberal-oriented presidents such as Mexico's Vicente Fox, Chile's Ricardo Lagos and Peru's Alejandro Toledo, all three of whom quickly repudiated the 2002 anti-Chávez coup. Chávez even lent a hand to embattled Bolivian President Carlos Mesa before Mesa was forced to step down last June, calling on Bolivia's combative social movements to allow him to complete his term.

Chávez's leadership and diplomatic initiatives may

potentially lead to dramatic changes in Latin America—undoubtedly the source of much concern for Washington. The left has made electoral inroads over the last few years, and the triumph of center-left candidates in the presidential elections in Bolivia, Ecuador, Mexico and Nicaragua over the next year and a half would further alter the correlation of forces in the continent.

Such a political shift may lead to collective action on a variety of fronts along the lines Chávez has already outlined. He calls for the creation of a Latin American hemispheric union—the "Bolivarian Alternative for the Americas" (ALBA)—as an alternative to the Washington-promoted Free Trade Area of the Americas (FTAA). Chávez was influential in thwarting Bush's long-cherished plans to set up the FTAA by 2005.

Chávez's advocacy for the collective negotiation of the Latin American foreign debt is even more detrimental to U.S. interests. In this vein, he has insisted at numerous international conferences that 10% of the payment of the foreign debt go to an International Humanitarian Fund that would provide assistance to social programs without attaching the customary neoliberal strings. Chávez gained official support for the Fund plan at the Iberian-American Presidential Summit held in November 2003.

On an even more sensitive subject, Washington has been particularly concerned about the de-dollarization of international oil sales. The U.S. economy is bolstered by the preeminent use of the dollar for international exchange and as the world's principal reserve currency. Under Chávez, Venezuela has bypassed the dollar by establishing non-monetary barter deals for its oil with over a dozen Latin American and Caribbean countries. He has called on the other OPEC nations to reach similar accords. One such swap agreement involves Venezuelan oil in exchange for the presence of some 12,000 Cuban doctors, who have set up shop and work free of charge in impoverished areas throughout the nation. Within OPEC, Chávez has stressed the dollar's declining purchasing power as an argument for increasing dollar-denominated oil prices. And several representatives of the Venezuelan government have raised the possibility of selling a certain percentage of oil in euros. The country's ambassador to Russia and prominent oil expert Francisco Mieres discussed this proposition at a 2001 conference in Moscow called "The Hidden Threats of Currency Crises." More recently, the possibility has been mentioned by Alvaro Silva Calderón, a former Minister of Mines and OPEC's outgoing Secretary-General. Were Venezuela to decide to switch partially to the euro—a move that would make economic sense should the dollar continue to depreciate and the European Union get its house back in order—other OPEC and Latin American nations would likely follow suit.

For Chávez, power and self-determination go hand-in-hand. The defense of national sovereignty and the right of the Venezuelan government to formulate its own policies without foreign interference are at the heart of the Chavista movement. The military officers who rose up in 1992, and followed Chávez in subsequent years, view the defense of national sovereignty as the military's sacred mission. Some of them, such as Adm. Hernán Gruber Odremán, believe that since the end of the Cold War the United States has worked to convert Latin American militaries into veritable colonial police forces, an effort he deems "an offense to national honor."[4]

Chávez sees national sovereignty as well-served by the goal of creating a "multi-polar world." As with much of his rhetoric, this term has been translated into concrete policies. He has taken steps to diversify commercial and military relations in order to lessen dependency on the United States, efforts that have intensified over the last year. In January, he traveled to Beijing in an attempt to gain Chinese support for a plan to build an oil pipeline from Venezuela to Colombia's Pacific coast in order to facilitate exports to China. Indeed, Chinese-Venezuelan trade is expected to more than double this year. Furthermore, Chávez has recently bought military goods from Russia, Spain and Brazil, acquisitions that Washington has attempted to block. Venezuela is currently considering the purchase of Russian MIG-29 fighter jets to replace the F-16s acquired from the United States in the early 1980s.

When Chávez lashed out at "U.S. imperialism" for the first time last year, he directed his fire at the Bush Administration without making reference to U.S. economic domination. Obviously, he had no desire to alienate the U.S. oil companies that continue to do business in Venezuela. Despite the tense political atmosphere, the oil multinationals have shown no signs of wanting to pull out. At the height of the ten-week general strike designed to topple the government, Chevron-Texaco signed a well-publicized contract to exploit gas in the Orinoco Delta region, an agreement that Chávez used to his political advantage.[5]

More recently, however, tensions within the oil industry have manifested themselves. Early in 2005 Exxon-Mobile announced that it was considering arbitration to challenge the government's royalty increase from 1% to 16.66% on sales of non-conventional oil from the eastern part of the country. Exxon-Mobile claims that the hike violates legally binding contracts, but the government points out that earlier agreements were reached when oil prices—and profits—were just a fraction of their current levels. Concurrently, red flags have been raised by the foreign private sector. Deutsche Bank recently downgraded its outlook for U.S.-based Conoco-Phillips, a major investor in Venezuela, due to its concern that the now-profitable relationship between transnational oil companies and the Venezuelan state may soon change.

The Venezuelan experience points in the opposite direction of current writing on globalization that minimizes the role of the nation-state, particularly in underdeveloped countries. Analysts with this perspective have argued that in today's global economy, the assertion of national sovereignty by strong third-world governments has no potential for transformation and, moreover, it may not even be feasible. Writers who support this thesis extend from right to left on the political spectrum. Those on the right, who defend U.S. foreign policy and free-market formulas, associate strong third-world states with local oligarchies and "crony capitalism," which they blame for the abysmal failure of neoliberalism to live up to expectations.

Some leftist writers who analyze globalization also consider the strengthening of third-world states to be a lost cause. As we have seen, Chávez's goal from the beginning was to achieve power at the national level. This goal is highly suspect to some of those who write off the importance of the nation-state and instead laud struggles for local autonomy and express solidarity with groups like Mexico's Zapatistas.

Michael Hardt, for example, co-author of the much-acclaimed book *Empire*, points to two distinct positions concerning "the role of national sovereignty" that have emerged at the World Social Forums. On the one hand, he says, the leaders of most internationally recognized organizations that participate in the Forums defend third-world national sovereignty "as a defensive barrier against the control of foreign and global capital." The second position is supported by a majority of those who attend the Forums and belong to social movements organized around diverse causes that complement one another.

This second group "opposes any national solutions and seeks instead a democratic globalization." While the second position is inherently democratic and confronts capital, argues Hardt, the first one is top-down and potentially authoritarian. Hardt concludes that "the centralized structure of state sovereignty itself runs counter to the horizontal network-form that the movements [identified with the second position] have developed."[6]

But contrary to what Hardt asserts, Chávez's six and a half years in power demonstrate that third-world governments can forcefully uphold national sovereignty and at the same time promote a nationalist, progressive agenda in opposition to powerful economic interests. Hardt's characterization of the dubious democratic credentials of third-world governments of "national liberation" belies the complexity of the transformations currently occurring in Venezuela. Although the Chavista movement began as highly "vertical," two sets of internal elections within the MVR (one for the national party leadership and the other occurring last April for the selection of candidates in local elections) are steps in the direction of internal democratization, in spite of procedural problems that arose.

It is also frequently argued that Chávez's Venezuela is too distinct from the rest of Latin America to have any lasting influence. High oil prices finance popular programs and thus place Venezuela in a separate league. Furthermore, Chávez derives crucial support from a military structure whose officers have historically come from the middle and lower-middle class, in sharp contrast to the caste-like nature of the armed forces found throughout most of the continent.

These are well-taken points, but the Venezuelan "revolutionary process" nonetheless holds important lessons for those in Latin America who champion social justice and the transformations necessary to achieve it. A first lesson is that the cultivation of a substantial electoral majority is essential for the implementation of far-reaching social change by democratic means. Chávez has received about 60% of the vote in the nine elections held since 1998. These results seem to substantiate the observation that a slim majority or plurality of votes, such as the 36% that elected Salvador Allende in Chile in 1970, does not represent a mandate for radical change.

Second, active participation and mobilization are key components of the process. Chávez has relied on more than just electoral or passive support. He has followed a strategy of ongoing popular mobilization to face his insurgent adversaries, actions that have proven essential for his political survival including his comeback after the April 2002 coup. The massive street actions in favor of the Chavista process have been made possible by the conviction among rank-and-file Chavistas that Chávez's rhetoric is based on substance and commitment to thorough change, not manipulation.

A third lesson of the Chávez experience is the importance of timing and the constant deepening of the process of transformation via the introduction of new goals following each political triumph. Victories that were followed by new slogans and proposals include the holding of the national constituent assembly in 1999, the defeat of the coup in April 2002, the defeat of the general strike in February 2003, the defeat of the recall election in August 2004 and the gubernatorial elections two months later in which the Chavistas won in all but two states.

Nonetheless, Venezuela is far from having developed a new economic system that would allow Chávez to package and export a model to the rest of Latin America. At the 2005 World Social Forum he declared himself a "socialist" and added: "We must reclaim socialism as a thesis, a project and a path, but a new type of socialism, a humanist one that puts humans, not machines or the state, ahead of everything. That is the debate we need to promote around the world." Venezuela, however, is hardly establishing socialism, at least in the traditional sense of the word, since no sector of the economy has been slated for nationalization. If a new model is emerging, it is based on prioritization of social needs, the emergence of worker cooperatives and small producers both in the countryside and urban areas, and the state's rejection of alliances with large capitalist groups while not discarding a modus vivendi with them.

Venezuela's ability to influence the Americas is contingent on the successful implementation of Chavista policies and strategies. At this stage, the most important aspects of Chávez's demonstration effect are his nationalism, which leads him to spurn U.S. impositions; his anti-neoliberalism, which puts a halt to privatization; and his social priorities that have translated into special programs in the fields of health and education. The emulation of Chávez's policies by neighboring countries would show, if nothing else, that third-world governments are very much at the center of political struggle and that national alternatives do exist, despite the dire warnings of many outstanding writers on globalization.

ABOUT THE AUTHOR

Steve Ellner has published extensively on Latin American politics and history. Since 1994, he has been teaching graduate courses at the School of Law and Political Science of the Universidad Central de Venezuela (UCV).

NOTES

1. Hugo Chávez Frías, *Habla el comandante* [interviews by Agustín Blanco Muñoz] (Caracas: UCV, 1998), p. 311.
2. Steve Ellner, "Venezuela's Foreign Policy: Defiance South of the Border," *Z Magazine*, November 2000.
3. This attitude went beyond the Venezuelan opposition. An article in *Foreign*

Affairs, for example, ended ominously with the statement: "the political clock in Venezuela is running out." Kurt Weyland, "Will Chávez Lose his Luster?" *Foreign Affairs*, Nov–Dec, 2001.

4. Hernán Gruber Odremán, *Mi voz en la prensa* (Caracas: Fondo Nacional 1999), pp. 14, 47.

5. Some anti-Chavista political commentators accuse Chevron-Texaco of propping up the Chávez regime. See, Tom Fenton, *Bad News: The Decline of Reporting, the Business of News and the Danger to Us All* (New York: Regan Books, 2005), pp. 208–09.

6. Michael Hardt, "Porto Alegre: Today's Bandung," *New Left Review*, No. 14, March–April 2002, pp. 114–15. This article refers specifically to the World Social Forum held that year. See also Michael Hardt and Antonio Negri, *Empire* (Cambridge, MA: Harvard University Press, 2000).

Teo Ballvé

Is Venezuela the New Cuba?

In many ways, the answer is yes. Venezuela has become a regional spokesperson for opposition to Washington. It has attempted to unite progressive forces throughout the hemisphere in the construction of a regional alliance that would challenge the prevailing vision of U.S.-dominated inter-American "cooperation." Within the Americas, the Venezuelan government also stands out in its attempts to aggressively dismantle the historic social injustices still rampant throughout the region. Venezuela is now watched closely by policymakers, intellectuals, academics, journalists and activists of all political persuasions, inspiring heated debate on everything from anti-imperialism and human rights, to democracy and socialism. Venezuela has supplanted Cuba as Washington's preponderant variable in its Latin America foreign policy calculus.

On a governmental level for Latin America and the Caribbean, Cuba was to the Cold War as Venezuela now is to the current pattern of global confrontation over the ideologies and practices of neoliberalism. Like Cuba, Venezuela has elicited a strongly antagonistic response from Washington for playing this honorary role.

Secretary of State Condoleezza Rice recently stated: what U.S.-Venezuelan relations comes down to, is "what kind of hemisphere is this going to be? Is it going to be a hemisphere that is democratic and that is prosperous and where neighbors get along, where neighbors don't interfere in each other's affairs, where people fight drug trade and fight terrorism together actively?"

Immediately, we can dismiss Washington's "concern" for democracy as the basis for its hostility. The history of U.S.-Latin American relations makes this much abundantly clear. And the Bush Administration's behavior regarding the fight against terrorism, the drug trade and other people's prosperity is so riddled with contradictions that those "concerns" can also be dismissed. What remains is the accusation that Venezuela meddles in the affairs of other nations.

U.S. officials have repeatedly accused the Venezuelan government of supporting Colombian rebels and of funding the Bolivian coca-growers movement, but these allegations have been resoundingly rejected for lack of evidence. What Rice really means by Venezuela's "interference" in regional affairs—a charge the State Department tags onto all its public comments on Venezuela—is more honestly stated as "influence."

For decades, Cuba held considerable sway in the Americas, but now Venezuela has taken center-stage in hemispheric relations. At her confirmation hearing, Rice thus characterized Venezuela "a negative force in the region."

Latin America stands poised at a historic crossroads. Left-leaning governments are consolidating power amid the hemisphere's evisceration by Washington-backed military and economic policies. The moment is ripe for a profound, continental transformation, and that Venezuela is trying to be the progressive locomotive driving this process makes Washington (and Wall Street) nervous.

Within the community of American governments, Venezuela has taken a prominent role in mapping out a future course for the Americas. President Hugo Chávez's words, and in many cases his actions, resonate deeply with Latin Americans struggling to escape poverty, inequality, exclusion and the yoke of neoliberal domination.

It is Chávez's efforts, along with those of neighboring leaders, to create a "counter-hegemonic bloc" that has more potential bite than bark. Although substantive steps toward greater and deeper regional economic and political integration have been largely led by Brazil, it is Chávez's emotive billing of integration under an anti-neoliberal banner that gives the process widespread support throughout the region. Helped by Brazil, he has also sought regional economic cooperation with Asian countries, particularly China, in an effort to diversify his country's U.S.-dominated trade and investment portfolio. Instead of perceiving Latin America's integration projects as sure-fire ways of ceding sovereignty, he understands regional integration, bloc-building and South-South solidarity as vehicles for attaining national sovereignty amid coercive U.S. power.

Undoubtedly, Chávez is attempting a state-sponsored transformation of Venezuela, and by extension the hemisphere. He has invited Venezuelans to join him in constructing "a socialism for the twenty-first century"—presumably as opposed to Cuba's. But in today's context, what the Venezuelan government is carrying out is almost as radical as what the bearded revolutionaries achieved in the Caribbean. In both cases, immediate efforts focused on the radical inclusion of the nations' poor, darker-hued majorities and the chipping away of elite power.

Much ink has been spilled about Chávez's "Bolivarian Revolution," his policies, his ideas and his style—especially by those questioning his "democratic credentials." It seems the stagnation of the Cuban predicament has given way to a new crucible of debate and critique around questions of social justice, anti-imperialism, neoliberalism, socialism, democracy and, ultimately, the liberation of a hemisphere.

Peter Lambert

Paraguay's Enigmatic President

When Nicanor Duarte, the candidate of the ruling Colorado Party, won the Paraguayan presidential elections in April 2003, few observers felt there was much to celebrate. The Colorado Party had, after all, been in power for over 50 years through civil war, dictatorship and, more recently, constitutional democracy. The introduction of any significant changes seemed unlikely.

Since the beginning of Paraguay's democratic transition in 1989, four successive Colorado administrations have been characterized by inefficiency, economic mismanagement and rampant corruption. By the time Duarte came to power, economic stagnation combined with unemployment and the decline of public welfare services had led to an unprecedented rise in poverty, reaching almost 50% of the population. Meanwhile, according to the rankings of Transparency International, the escalation of institutionalized corruption had earned Paraguay its place as the most corrupt country in Latin America. And as if this were not enough, Paraguay faced an unmanageable fiscal deficit and was on the verge of economic collapse. The country had taken its place among the poorest, most corrupt and most socially unequal of Latin America's new democracies. Not surprisingly, public confidence in democracy was lower in Paraguay than in almost any other country in the region.

However, against this bleak panorama, resistance from civil society organizations has begun growing. Between June and

September 2002, the Democratic Congress of Paraguay (CDP), a broad coalition of over 60 peasant, union and community groups, organized unprecedented mobilizations against government policies and an IMF-backed economic austerity package of policies of the Colorado administration of President González Macchi. Following widespread protest and conflict, the government was forced to accept all of the CDP's demands, including an indefinite suspension of all the privatization plans included in the IMF package. Further demonstrations also led to the repeal of government legislation that sought to introduce more belt-tightening measures, including a price hike in public services. Faced with such a resurrection of civil society organiz-ation, it was clear that any incoming government would have to take on this deep-seated opposition to neoliberal reforms.

Clearly conscious of the widespread sympathy for the CDP's demands, Duarte surprised many in his first year by promising a revolutionary democratic project and pursuing a number of policies aimed at achieving sustainable development and improving governance, policies that were completely out of step with his party. Indeed, Duarte is far from being a traditional Colorado politician: he is of humble origins with a background in journalism and education. And, more importantly, he has no links to the dictatorship of Alfredo Stroessner (1954–89) or to either of the two traditionally powerful sectors of the Colorado Party—the military and the business sector.

With a discourse that is at times openly populist, he has portrayed himself as a progressive reformer and has declared himself vehemently opposed to "savage neoliberalism" and to the power of traditional elites, instead favoring social reform and poverty alleviation. He has also sought to promote regional solidarity, firmly allying himself with the left-leaning govern-ments of Lula in Brazil, Kirchner in Argentina and Chávez in Venezuela. On the domestic front, he has further distanced himself from the Stroessner dictatorship by establishing a Commission for Truth and Justice to investigate human rights violations committed during the 35-year dictatorship.

Duarte has also won widespread acclaim for his fight against corruption, which he has identified as a major obstacle to democratic economic development. In his first year he replaced a number of senior government officials, including the Minister of the Interior, the head of social security and the president of the state-owned oil company, as well as a number of high-ranking police officers, all on corruption-related charges. Moreover, with the support of Congress, he replaced six out of nine members of the Supreme Court following widespread allegations of corruption in April 2004. He also took on the customs service, previously a byword for corruption, by introducing greater transparency and placing it under the control of Margarita Díaz de Vivar, now known as Paraguay's own "Iron Lady."

Central to Duarte's reform policies was his Minister of Finance, Dionisio Borda, a respected independent, left-of-center economist. Not only did Borda manage to avoid major debt default, regain macroeconomic balance and reduce inflation, he was also instrumental in promoting public sector transparency. The Ministry of Finance quickly became known as an island of integrity in a state sector normally laden with corruption. Improvements in internal auditing, public transparency and public sector procurement, made the Ministry a model for future civil service reform. Furthermore, in its first year, a major campaign against the country's rampant tax evasion resulted in a 44% increase in fiscal revenues, allowing greater funds for social welfare projects.

Borda also managed to convince Paraguayans to accept income and property taxes for the first time. Although watered down by a fearful Congress, a law passed in August 2004 introduced an income tax of 10% for those earning over ten times the minimum wage—that is, the richest 20% of the population—as well as a rural land tax on properties of more than 300 hectares. Both measures aimed to reduce Paraguay's dependence on regressive indirect taxation, and force the wealthiest sectors, previously adept at avoiding such inconveniences, to contribute to Paraguay's development.

Duarte's approval ratings rose to as high as 70% in the first two years, but his popular support obscures the fact that he is in an isolated and vulnerable position, under criticism from all sides. His progressive reforms have incurred the hostility of powerful groups, including the privately owned media, the land-owning oligarchy, economic elites often operating outside the law and conservative sectors within his own party. With their interests threatened by the tax and land reforms as well as anti-corruption measures, conservatives stepped up efforts to block further reforms and calls to remove Finance Minister Borda grew.

While under attack from the right, Duarte has failed to generate widespread support among the political left, which remains highly suspicious and critical of his openly populist rhetoric, his Colorado Party affiliation and his autocratic style. Wide sectors of civil society, including campesino organizations, unions and civic groups, have been vocal in criticizing his prioritization of macroeconomic stability to the exclusion of pressing social problems. Even the Church, previously supportive of his anti-corruption measures, has shown concern not only over the lack of measures to relieve the growing rural crisis, but also, in the words of a communiqué from the Bishops' Conference, the "contradictory measures and duplicitous discourse of our authorities."

Successive Colorado Party governments have promised much, but delivered very little, a charge frequently leveled at Duarte's social reform efforts. "[The President] is a difficult politician to pin down," says Roberto Villalba, an analyst for the Asunción-based Center for Documentation and Study. "He talks of social reform, but what action has he actually taken? What significant reforms has he implemented? He is a self-proclaimed social democrat but with strong populist and authoritarian tendencies." Villalba considers Duarte "an opportunist who bends with the wind, who is portraying a progressive image at the moment simply because this is what he thinks will serve him best in the regional context."

Similar criticisms have come to the forefront amid the escalating conflict over the key issue of land. Paraguay has one of the greatest disparities of landownership in the world, with over 30% of the rural population lacking access to cultivable land. Although partly a legacy of years of dictatorship, the strength of land-owning elites and a sequence of corrupt governments, Duarte paid little attention to the issue early on in his term. Following repeated promises of reform alongside continued government inaction over the growing crisis, the patience of the two major peasant unions—the National Coordinating Board of Campesino Organizations (MCNOC) and the National Federation of Campesinos (FNC)—finally ran out. In September 2004, they organized a series of nationwide mass land occupations and protests, demanding immediate land reform.

Initially, security forces met the protestors with the usual heavy-handed response, but Duarte swiftly backtracked and entered into negotiations with the peasant unions, reaching a deal that promised significant reform to begin within two months. This provoked a furious response from the powerful landowners' association, the Rural Association of Paraguay (ARP), and the organization representing the business sector, FEPRINCO. Under increasing pressure from these traditional elites to adopt a hard-line approach, Duarte stalled, failing to comply with his part of the September deal. This in turn provoked the first general strike called against his administration, which lasted nearly two weeks in November 2004. Despite meager nationwide support, it led to the resumption of campesino occupations and protests, roadblocks, increasingly violent clashes with security forces and mass arrests, demonstrating that the conflict will not simply disappear, particularly in the context of growing rural poverty, landlessness and unemployment. According to the FNC's Secretary General Odilón Espínola, "Agrarian reform is desperately needed in Paraguay, and we can only put forward our demands through mass mobilization."

Duarte has found himself caught between threats of mass protest from an increasingly desperate peasantry on the one hand, and the outrage of landowners who already speak of betrayal, anarchy and violence, on the other. His response has been to pursue an indecisive policy, a delicate balancing act seeking to satisfy both camps to avert a social explosion. He has strongly condemned illegal campesino occupations, while still promising future reform. The land reform issue has been widely seen as a decisive litmus test for the Administration's self-proclaimed progressive nature and its commitment to social change. Faced with growing polarization and violence, Duarte finds himself with decreasing room to maneuver, and growing pressure to revert to repression.

Duarte's achievements in the economy and in the struggle against corruption have been widely recognized, and if they become coupled with long-awaited social reforms, his adminis-tration might manage to reduce inequality and poverty. He is the first president who has dared to challenge the power of economic and political vested interests. While there is little doubt that Duarte represents the greatest opportunity for progressive reform in Paraguay's recent history, he is under growing pressure from conservative forces—mainly within his own party—to refrain from further reform or face serious consequences.

Despite doubts expressed by many on the left, in August 2004 Finance Minister Dionisio Borda stated, "I have no doubt that Nicanor is committed to social reform. It is simply a question of strategy, timing and sequence. The key is that we must now move fast. If we do not maintain our momentum, powerful and conservative interests will regroup and regain initiative, and this window of opportunity for reform will be lost."

These words proved to be prophetic, but not in the way Borda might have hoped. Under increasing pressure from vested interests within the Colorado Party, Duarte finally opted to force Borda's resignation in May 2005. While Colorado traditionalists celebrated, many within and outside Paraguay who had seen Finance Minister Borda as the greatest hope for the introduction of long overdue social reforms to benefit the poor, suspected that this window of opportunity was fast closing and that the enigmatic president might well be returning to the traditional Colorado fold.

ABOUT THE AUTHOR

Peter Lambert is senior lecturer in Latin American studies at the University of Bath, UK. He lived in Paraguay from 1987 to 1991, where he worked as a political analyst and researcher at the Centro de Documentación y Estudios (CDE).

Emir Sader

Brazil Takes Lula's Measure

In Latin America, the visible crisis of the neoliberal model intersected with longstanding traditions of radical mass movements and political upheavals, ushering a new era for the Latin American left, one marked both by institutional practice and social resistance, within the framework of global liberal hegemony.

In some respects, the victory of Luiz Inácio Lula da Silva of the Workers' Party (PT) in Brazil's 2002 presidential elections has marked the high point of this process. The PT is generally judged the largest left party in the capitalist world. At the city level, PT administrations had already introduced path-breaking participatory budgets and hosted the Porto Alegre World Social Forum, a meeting place for the "movement of movements" of the globalized era. The direction taken by the Lula government would inevitably have a significant impact on the dynamics of Latin American politics.

Any assessment of Lula's record in power must start from an analysis of the origins and context of the PT's formation. Until a few decades ago, Brazil's left forces were relatively weak in comparison to those of other countries in the region. This trajectory is essential to understanding the significance of the PT's rise to power, as well as of its limits and contradictions.

Brazil's military coup of 1964 took place earlier than those of Latin American countries where the left was stronger, such as Chile, Argentina or Uruguay. Here the fragility of popular opposition, combined with firm support for the Army from the United States meant that the generals were able to topple the government of João Goulart with a lesser degree of repression than was later required in the Southern Cone. The judiciary and Congress were untouched by the dictatorship, but the unions were closed down and the left hit hard—making plain the class character of the coup.

The dictatorship brought to a close the historic period of Communist hegemony over the Brazilian left. Both the Brazilian Communist Party (PCB) and the union leaderships allied to it were blamed for the impasse of the mid-twentieth century popular movement and the failures of resistance to the coup. But the economic expansion of the late 1960s and early 1970s brought about a shift in the composition of the labor force, laying the basis for the emergence of a new left movement. Much as in Argentina, injections of foreign—above all American—capital had led to the establishment of an automobile industry centered in São Paulo. At the same time, in the wake of severe droughts in the northeast hundreds of thousands of northeasterners gravitated to the south-central region, and especially metropolitan São Paulo, now the country's economic and financial hub.

Much of the growth of the late 1960s was concentrated in automobile and domestic appliance manufacturing—which in turn increased the weight of working-class fractions in the "ABC" zone, consisting of the districts of São André, São Bernardo and São Caetano do Sul, on the periphery of São Paulo. It was here that a grassroots trade unionism developed during the 1970s, despite the military ban, and at the end of the decade—under the leadership of a new generation of trade-unionists, including Lula—carried out a series of strikes that broke the regime's wage policy.

The PT, founded in 1980, grew principally from a base in this new trade unionism, as activists in São Paulo's automobile industry were joined by unionists from the oil and banking sectors, and by a range of social movements and former militants from the armed struggle of the 1960s. The Catholic Church also played a key role, in community organizing inspired by liberation theology. Initially confined to São Paulo, the PT extended its influence into the countryside through the activities of the two largest social movements linked to it, the Landless Rural Workers' Movement (MST) and the Brazilian Workers' Central (known as the CUT, and the more dynamic and radical of the country's two major labor federations). Its heterogeneous origins notwithstanding, from the outset, the trade-union core largely conditioned the outlook of party's ideological identity. This cohort had been educated politically by the struggle against the dictatorship, which informed their anti-statist line. Indeed, the new union leaders had less antagonistic relations with business groups, than they did with the state, whose rigid national security doctrine labeled the strike movement "subversive."

Liberal ideology grew to dominate the opposition to the dictatorship after the defeat of armed resistance movements in the late 1960s. A leading role was played by the legal opposition party, the Brazilian Democratic Movement Party (PMDB), flanked by social and civil movements and NGOs of a liberal-democratic stamp. It was in this period that the Brazilian left began to seriously address the question of democracy, previously marginalized by the PCB in favor of national and social concerns. Yet the left's re-evaluation of democracy took place within the framework of the liberal hegemony over the anti-dictatorship opposition, which also affected the PCB. As a result, democracy was incorporated into left debates at the expense of its class nature; capitalism as a general historical scenario disappeared altogether.

The key ideological text of the Brazilian left in this period was written in Italy by the exiled PCB intellectual Carlos Nelson Coutinho. "Democracy as a Universal Value" was the most influential product of the PCB current, which had been brought into direct contact with Eurocommunist ideas.[1] Coutinho took his cue from Enrico Berlinguer's interpretation of the coup against the Popular Unity coalition in Chile as a demonstration of the need to incorporate Christian Democrat forces, in order to prevent them from destabilizing a socialist government. The emphasis was placed on preserving democracy, rather than on the anti-capitalist dimensions of the struggle.

Coutinho's text had broad repercussions on debates within the PCB, but its principal effect was on the eventual configuration taken by the PT. In a sense, he foretold the identity the party would adopt, when he affirmed that "Brazilian *modernity* demands the creation of a secular, democratic, mass socialist party, capable of taking up what is valid in the heritage of Brazilian communism, but at the same time of incorporating the new socialist currents originating from different political and ideological horizons."[2] Coutinho argued that Eurocommunism was the "contemporary representative of the best traditions of the communist movement," in search of a "third way" between "the bureaucratic method of the Stalinists and neo-Stalinists" and the "limited reformism of social democracy."[3] The PT would seek the same equidistance, and later even proclaimed itself the "first post-social-democratic party."

In contrast to Coutinho, liberal opposition currents stressed the relationship between democracy and liberalism, rather than democracy and socialism. The principal exponent here was sociologist Fernando Henrique Cardoso whose theory of authoritarianism became hegemonic during the transition from military dictatorship in the 1980s. In this version, democratization would consist of the "de-concentration" of economic power from around the state, and political power from around the executive. Brazil's first post-dictatorship civilian government in 1985, and new constitution of 1988, marked the onset of political de-concentration; Cardoso himself set in motion the economic component of the strategy, when he served as president of Brazil (1994–2002) and implemented a neoliberal program. The triumphant advance of liberalism on the international plane in the 1980s was echoed in Brazil, above all in the strictly institutional nature of the passage from dictatorship to democracy; there were no significant social or economic reforms. The PT opposed this conservative model of transition, calling for citizens' rights and social policies; but it did not put forward any alternative conception of democracy, or question the notion that "democratization" was the answer to the country's problems.

Symbolically, it was in 1989 that the PT began to emerge as a genuine alternative for national government, with Lula's near victory in that year's election—he obtained 44% of the vote in the second round, to Fernando Collor de Mello's 50%. It was also at this moment that the PT began the process of ideological and political transformation that would bring it to office in 2002. The international context for this conversion was the consolidation of neoliberal hegemony, with the collapse of the USSR, the first Gulf War and the sweep of market ideology across Russia and Eastern Europe followed by the "Third Way" governments of Bill Clinton and Tony Blair. In Latin America, the extent of neoliberal hegemony was revealed in the embrace of the prescriptions of the Washington Consensus by both "socialist" and nationalist forces. In Brazil, Cardoso translated the prescriptions into pegging the currency (the *real*) to the dollar, cutting tariffs and raising interest rates to attract foreign capital. The subsequent wave of privatizations, mergers and acquisitions of Brazilian firms by foreign multinationals resulted not only in the displacement of national capital, but a real measure of deindustrialization.[4]

The PT's traditional base was devastated by the reforms. Much of the automobile industry of São Paulo's ABC zone was dismantled, with car manufacturers moving elsewhere. Official unemployment figures for São Paulo, generally assumed to be flattering, rose from 13% in 1995 to over 20% in 2002. Informal labor expanded in all sectors of the economy, weakening trade unionism further. Yet Lula's charisma as an outspoken working-class presidential candidate, and the dynamism of PT militants, ensured the party's growing presence within the country's political institutions.

The character of the PT was altered by its progressive insertion into Brazilian institutional life. The weight of the social movements affiliated with it decreased as its parliamentary representation rose; by the end of the 1990s it was congressmen, municipal governments and an expanded national structure that had the decisive influence on its orientation.

The PT's attitude towards Cardoso's economic reforms also underwent a shift. Initially it tried to take an independent line, organized through the São Paulo Forum, which beginning in 1990 convened leftwing parties unaffiliated to neoliberal governments—namely, the PT, Mexico's Party of the Democratic Revolution and Uruguay's Frente Amplio. However, this grouping was not immune to the dominant ideas. It took part in the "Buenos Aires Consensus," which implicitly aligned itself with the Third Way in advocating fiscal adjustment and monetary stability, albeit adding social policies. The PT took part in drafting the document, and only withdrew from signing it at the last minute, but by this stage there were no essential differences between the PT and the Buenos Aires Consensus.

Cardoso had pushed through an amendment to the constitution in order to be able to stand for re-election in 1998, and was the clear favorite to win. Lula's campaign made no mention of the crisis of Brazil's bankrupt economy, nor of the impending devaluation of the *real*. The aim was to ensure that the eventual catastrophe did not taint Lula's image. After a campaign in which he put forward no alternatives, Lula was defeated in the first round. The incumbent had effectively been negotiating with the IMF during the campaign, and desperately needed to win in the first round, before the crisis burst into the open. In January 1999, less than three months after the elections, Cardoso began his second mandate by decreeing a massive devaluation of the currency, renegotiating IMF loans and raising interest rates to 49%.[5]

After the 1998 defeat, Lula and his advisers moved to set up the Institute of Citizenship, a think-tank outside PT structures. It enabled Lula to become increasingly independent of the PT—expressing, in organizational terms, the far greater public projection he enjoyed compared to the party. The Institute organized seminars attended by economists and specialists in social policy, environment and political reform, among others, in order to formulate Lula's campaign program for 2002. The program's final version, which would be ratified by the PT, stressed what were to be the two key themes of the campaign: the "priority of the social" and the resumption of development, as a precondition for the former. Reviving the economy was to be the major objective, presaging a slow, gradual exit from the neoliberal model. Campaign publicity emphasized "change" and the "priority of the social." There were no concrete indications of what was meant by this priority, but the forms it would take once the PT was in government could already be seen: the "Zero Hunger" campaign proposal echoed Lula's repeated statements in 2002, and in earlier electoral contests, that his aim was for "all Brazilians to eat three times a day." Mention was also made of the need to maintain monetary stability, a program that by implication included many of the Lula's government's subsequent proposals—such as the reform of social security.

Two factors helped to determine the outcome of the election. The first was the candidacy of Ciro Gomes, and the other was the strong speculative attack on the *real* carried out by finance capital in the summer of 2002, a few months before the vote. At the start of the campaign both Lula and Gomes found themselves behind in the polls, led at that stage by Roseana Sarney. Cardoso's man, José Serra, then-Health Minister, was a distant fourth, before he orchestrated a string of denunciations that effectively removed Sarney from the race. But Serra still faced elimination in the first round, and so he began a new round of denunciations, this time aimed at Gomes. The latter's standing in the polls dwindled, but Serra failed to close the gap on Lula who, in turn, remained unable to break through the PT's historic threshold of slightly over 30% of the vote. The attack on the *real* was a show of force on the part of finance capital, as if to underline both its potential stabilizing role and its ability to sabotage any new government to which it objected. The message was that the return of capital to the country would depend on the result. The "Brazil risk" began to be known as the "Lula risk," implying that in the event of a PT victory, monetary destabilization and uncontrolled capital flight would ensue. As a result, the value of the *real* took a dive in July 2002.

Condemning the speculative attack, Lula released a document entitled "Letter to the Brazilians," in which he pledged that, as president, he would keep to all the previous government's financial commitments. There would be no renegotiation of the external debt, nor any regulation of the movement of finance capital. The "Letter" altered the Lula campaign's relationship with finance capital and, in the process, changed its social character and relation to the neoliberal model. The features of the future Lula government began to take shape.

The transformation was apparent even during Lula's electoral campaign, when decision-making was transferred to the marketing chief Duda Mendonça, who had previously run the campaigns of a prominent right-winger, and Antonio Palocci, a former PT governor and the man behind Lula's economic program and the "Letter." Mendonça devised the slogan "Lulinha, Peace and Love" in an attempt to soften his candidate's combative image. The slogan and the "Letter" proved a winning combination. In addition, Lula picked textile magnate José Alencar as his running mate, and even counted on the support of some conservative parties.

This was the basis on which Lula won the presidency in the second round of the election, with 61% of the vote to Serra's 39%. In Congress, his government depended on a coalition that included the centrist PMDB, and later the right-wing Popular Party, as well as the smaller parties of the left. The official opposition thus consisted of the parties that made up Cardoso's coalition—the Brazilian Social Democratic Party (PSDB) and the Party of the Liberal Front. Lula's rupture with PT traditions became still clearer with the announcement of his first cabinet at the end of 2002. The most significant appointment was that of Henrique Meirelles as president of the Central Bank. Formerly head of the U.S.-based FleetBoston Financial Group, Meirelles put together a team of young neoliberal cadres who had already served in previous governments. Not a single economist from the PT or any other left force was invited to join the team.

The Lula government initially argued that, due to the "accursed legacy" of Cardoso, it would not be able to change course immediately on the economy. What was required was an economic policy of transition, in order to gain the "confidence of the market" and attract capital; interest rates could then gradually be lowered and development would resume. The discussion focused on two issues: the risks of default on external debt, and those of losing control over inflation. In the case of the former, there was indeed a marked deterioration in the external accounts under Cardoso.[6] The untrammeled opening of the country to overseas capital increased the country's dependence in strategic sectors—autos, banks, food, electronics—and put large amounts of prime national capital into foreign hands at low prices. Privatizations of state industrial services added to the trend.

But on the eve of Lula's assumption of power, the situation was much better than it had been a year before. There was nothing that would justify maintaining a policy of fiscal adjustment, still less the introduction of new measures such as raising the primary fiscal surplus target to 4.5% of GDP, above IMF-recommended levels. The second conservative argument concerned the risks of inflation, which would prevent the reduction of interest rates—raised in the first month of the Lula government from already high levels. The economy was stagnant and unemployment high, undercutting any justifications based on inflation of demand; there was nothing to indicate that inflation was out of control.

Cardoso's economic policy was not simply maintained but, with the hike in interest rates and the raising of the primary fiscal surplus, actually taken a step further. In order to show that this was a strategic choice, in its first year the Lula government gave priority to two reforms in the style of World Bank "packages" on social security and tax reform. The first had a clear privatizing slant. A new tax was levied on the retired— who had already been paying all their lives—to reduce the social security deficit; and public-sector workers' pensions were capped, forcing them to turn to private pension funds. The proposal met with strong resistance from the unions, and resulted in the expulsion of three PT deputies and one of its senators— indicating how far the PT was prepared to cut into its own flesh to advance the program. The tax reform, meanwhile, aimed to simplify and reduce the tax burden on private investment. If this had less directly harmful social consequences than the social security reform, its failure to address Brazil's staggering disparities in income distribution, regressive taxation system and large public deficit was cause for serious concern. The Lula Administration has effectively evolved into two main axes: ministries in the social sphere—education, agrarian reform, health, culture, cities—and the Ministry of Foreign Relations on the one hand, and the central economic team on the other. While some good initiatives have been proposed on social issues, these have largely been stymied by the Finance Ministry's rigid fiscal austerity; as a result, the government's social record has been disastrous. The PT, rather than Lula, has taken the blame. Ministers in these fields have occasionally spoken out against the government line, though tepidly, owing to Lula's insistence on cabinet discipline.

The Ministry of Foreign Relations, meanwhile, has been building a series of international alliances—both regionally, through Mercosur and the South American Community of Nations, and internationally, with the G-20 and links to China, India and South Africa as well as Arab countries—that have sometimes clashed with the Finance Ministry's desire for good relations with Washington and the global financial institutions.

But it is the Finance Ministry that has been consolidated as the government's center of gravity. At the beginning of 2005, Lula announced that he considered his economic policy to be "the best of his government." In April the same year he reaffirmed his "hand-in-glove" relation to the man principally responsible for it, Finance Minister Palocci. Other key figures in the economic sphere include Meirelles, the Central Bank president, and the millionaire ministers of industrial development and agriculture. Together with Palocci, these three men constitute the nucleus of the Lula administration, determining the resources available to all other branches of government. The dominance of this cabal was established early on, when it stamped its authority on discussions over the minimum wage and monthly decisions on the interest rate.

The Lula Administration has moved from initial suggestions that it was adopting a transitional policy to the assumption, by its second year, that the present economic course would be permanent. Vice was turned into virtue. At the beginning of 2005, Lula triumphantly announced that "the predicted catastrophe did not take place," stressing that his government had "reversed a process that was leading us to the abyss." Despite all evidence to the contrary—and the admissions of his own finance minister—Lula insisted that "we are not continuing the policies of the previous government . . . we are rebuilding the economy, strengthening institutions and, above all, gaining credibility in the country and abroad."

The 2004 municipal elections were the first electoral test for the Lula government and the PT since winning the presidency two years earlier. Overall, the PT obtained an increased number of votes—as one might expect for a party fresh from success in a presidential contest. But there were also qualitatively significant defeats, including the loss of the mayoralties of Porto Alegre, Belém and São Paulo, which had been run by the party for 16, 8 and 4 years respectively. Both the city and state of São Paulo were lost to José Serra, Lula's opponent in 2002; the country's political and economic center of power is now in the hands of the PSDB.

If the first year of the Lula government was marked by opposition from the Left—and in particular from social movements mobilizing against the reform of social security—the second saw a resurgence of right-wing antagonists. This is not the corollary of any leftward shift on the government's part, but rather a sign of its political weakening—itself the consequence of a string of other reverses. It has failed to enact effective social policies, to significantly raise the minimum wage or reduce unemployment. Agrarian reform has ground to a halt and the government's environmental policy—including concessions to firms planting genetically modified crops—has been strongly opposed by environmental movements. The PT has been unable to consolidate and broaden its support base. Corruption allegations against members of the government—increasingly frequent since January 2004—have also taken their toll, as did the defeats in municipal elections later that year.

For the Right has realized that, though it is quite capable of living with Lula—since it recognizes his economic policy as its own—it is not condemned to do so. The focus of their criticism is the government's supposed "excessive spending," which they hold responsible for the country's high interest rates. They have attacked the progressive aspects of the PT's tenure, demanding repression of the MST, resisting all attempts at regulation contained in the government's media and cultural policies, and denouncing as "out of control" any social policies aimed at helping the poor.

The Brazilian left faces a serious dilemma with regard to the Lula government. In power, the PT has not fulfilled any of its historic aspirations, and cannot even be described as a government of the left. The municipal elections of 2004 brought significant defeats for the Party's left wing. There was a marked decline in social mobilizations, too, except in the case of the MST, which maintained pressure on the government with marches, land occupations and media campaigns. Overall, however, the left suffered an increasing tendency towards fragmentation. After the expulsion of the four PT representatives who voted against the social security reform in 2003, several militants left the party and founded the Socialism and Freedom Party (PSOL).

Those on the left still in the PT are in a no less difficult position. Critical of the federal government, they nonetheless belong to the party in power, share its general orientation and feel a sense of loyalty to its leader. They are hence unwilling to pursue an open political and ideological struggle within the PT or social movements, and members of the government are under pressure to keep quiet about their differences.

The youngest of Latin America's left parties, the Brazilian PT has also made the swiftest transition to economic orthodoxy. Formed under the liberal ascendancy of the 1980s, against the current of world political developments, the party was institutionalized during the 1990s even as Cardoso's reforms were eroding its industrial working-class base. Nevertheless, even bearing in mind the stranglehold mercantile relations have on states—the movements of the market, as Noam Chomsky has observed, now taking the place of military coups—the fact remains that on his election, Lula enjoyed a degree of domestic and international support that would have enabled him to create the conditions for a departure from the neoliberal model, inaugurating a transition to a system in which social priorities were central, as he had promised during his electoral campaign. He could have renegotiated Brazil's debts, subordinating financial targets to the need to tackle the social deficit—citing, as justification, his own manifesto's commitment to ensure that all Brazilians can eat three times a day.

But the transformation of the PT into a party capable of government—and in particular the compromise with finance capital in the "Letter to the Brazilians" that helped him secure victory at the fourth attempt—blocked off that possibility. In effect, Lula governs in accordance with the "Letter" and not his campaign commitments, still less in line with the original promise of his party. The result has been to deepen the insecurities and inequalities of Brazilian society. Toward the end of his mandate, the Lula government has lost its way politically and is plagued by allegations of corruption.

In June 2005 further corruption charges, coming at the same time as declining economic indicators and diminishing popular support, have brought about the Lula's government's worst crisis so far. They center on the resources of the postal service, run by one of the PT's coalition allies. The government is accused of buying Congress deputies' loyalty with a monthly stipend. The Congress has set up a commission of inquiry, with considerable press coverage, putting the government further on the defensive. The process has polarized the PT, with the CUT, MST and other social movements demanding a break with conservative coalition partners in Congress and a shift away from neoliberal economic policies. The likelihood, however, is that the latest crisis will only serve to strengthen Lula's Bonapartist tendencies as he distances himself still further from the party, governing entirely on the opposition's policies. It is the PT that will pay the price for Lula's accursed legacy.

ABOUT THE AUTHOR

Emir Sader is a Brazilian sociologist and a long-time analyst of Latin American social and political movements.

NOTES

1. Carlos Nelson Coutinho, *A democracia como valor universal* (Rio de Janeiro, 1980).
2. Coutinho, *Democracia*, p. 13. Coutinho identified the PT as this force, and along with other PCB militants joined it in 1989. He was to leave it in the first year of the Lula government.
3. Coutinho, *Democracia*, p. 114.
4. See Geisa Maria Rocha, "Neo-Dependency in Brazil," *New Left Review* 16, July/August 2002, pp. 14–15.
5. On the unraveling of Cardoso's economic strategy, see Rocha, "Neo-Dependency," pp. 20–25.
6. See especially Leda Paulani, "Brasil delivery: razões, contradições e limites da política econômica nos primeiros seis meses do governo Lula," in João Antonio de Paula, ed., *A economia política da mudança: Os desafios e os equívocos do início do governo Lula* (Belo Horizonte, 2003).

Raúl Zibechi

The Uruguayan Left and the Construction of Hegemony

In only three decades, the Uruguayan left has gone from a marginal political player, to a hegemonic political force. This astounding progression of the Frente Amplio (Broad Front), a coalition of leftist forces created in 1971, continues to gain momentum.

Fragmented, the left never achieved more than 5% of votes, but when it joined together in 1971, it gained 18%, cracking open what had been an exclusively two-party system. Since that moment, it has not stopped growing; according to recent polls, it enjoys 52–55% support. The factors explaining this growth are varied and explaining them requires casting a wide historical net that takes into account sociopolitical changes, culture and, above all, the failed neoliberal model, which destroyed a relatively equitable social fabric that had provided the most robust levels of well-being in all of Latin America.

The British historian Eric Hobsbawm sustains that at the beginning of the twentieth century, Uruguay was the only "real democracy" in Latin America.[1] Indeed, it's often referred to as the "Switzerland of the Americas." Prominent Uruguayan historians largely concur that part of what differentiates Uruguay from other countries of the region is that here there was never an all-powerful ruling oligarchy, because dominant economic groups quickly delegated the administration of the state to professional politicians.

The left bank of the Uruguay River, which forms part of the gigantic estuary of the River Plate (Río de la Plata), was destined to become a province of Argentina, something thwarted by the meddling of the British Empire. Instead, an independent state was created so that it would act as a "buffer state" between the two regional giants of Argentina and Brazil. The new country created in 1825, with the unusual name of the Eastern Republic of Uruguay, lacked the mineral wealth of its neighbors. In fact, the land was a vast, deserted albeit fertile plain, really only suited for cattle grazing, which remains the prime source of the country's wealth. The opening act for the new republic was the extermination of the few indigenous people that had not yet fled to neighboring Paraguay.

Serious problems mired the young republic. From the outset, conflict erupted between the rural landowning class and urban elites. These two factions were aligned with their respective political parties: rural landowners had the National Party, also called the *blancos* (Spanish for the color white), while the urban class had the Colorado Party (*colorado* is Spanish for the color red). After 1904, when the civil wars ended between the *blancos* and the *colorados*, the country's subsequent governments were either centrists or social-democrats in a broad sense. Even at this early stage, the country maintained an unusual climate of tolerance for the region and passed laws providing worker protections, democratic rights and political liberties. The fact that Uruguay suffered little social conflict in the 1900s was also helped by the country's sparse demographic landscape—two and a half million by the middle of the twentieth century, and just over three million at the beginning of the twenty-first. The density of the population was concentrated on the coast of the country around the capital city of Montevideo and composed mainly of European immigrants.

At the beginning of the twentieth century, the *colorado*

presidencies of José Batlle y Ordóñez, who served two inconsecutive terms, strengthened the state in a period relatively marked by cultural and political social peace. There were, of course, some localized labor conflicts, but these reinforced the centralization of the state and solidified mediation as the principle form of solving political and social disputes. After World War II, mid-size industry was given impetus by import substitution strategies, which protected national industries through state regulations. With state-ownership of enterprises—railroads, mail, electricity, telephone, oil and others—the state enjoyed a relative economic bonanza in the post-war period.

The environment of stability made it hard for the left to gain firm footing. Unlike most of the other countries of the region, Uruguay was for the most part socially and ethnically integrated, and had a strong, culturally hegemonic middle class made up of professionals, specialized workers and a mass of public sector employees. In this context, the Colorado Party, drawing support from Montevideo and other prosperous cities, and the National Party (*blancos*), with its rural roots, dominated the political landscape. It was not until the U.S. and European economic recovery after the war that helped bring on a crisis of Uruguay's industrial model and the related application of the International Monetary Fund's conservative economic prescriptions at the end of the 1950s that the left began to gain new relevance.

It was at this time that the union movement began opening new spaces amid the economic decline. It was not until 1964 that socialists, communists, anarcho-syndicalists and Christians were able to overcome their mutual mistrust and form the National Convention of Workers (CNT). A year later they convoked a People's Congress that brought together more than 700 grassroots organizations—including, union, neighborhood, church, professional and student groups. The Congress proposed an anti-imperialist program of agrarian reform, nationalist economic policies and a moratorium on debt payments. Meanwhile, the state at this time was controlled by new social sectors—mainly, large landholders and bankers—that began dismantling the welfare state, opening the economy, closing industry and limiting democratic liberties. What emerged, was a new country characterized by two antagonistic social forces set on a collision course.

Amid the growing destruction of the social fabric, which had been sown by the security of social mobility through education and specialized work, workers and progressive social sectors became increasingly radicalized, giving rise to social conflicts and eventually the leftist urban guerrilla movement of the Tupamaros. Within this storm of crisis, the left found unity, being joined, too, by the Christian Democrats and runaway progressive groups from the *blancos* and *colorados*. The space that had been first opened by the unions gave way to the recovery of the program put forth by the People's Congress. And in 1971, the two-party system suffered its first fissure, but mainly only in Montevideo, where the left garnered 30% support. In the countryside, however, the left remained marginal with support languishing at 10%.

The military coup and the subsequent dictatorship (1973–85) froze Uruguayan politics. But despite the harsh repression and massive emigration, a culture of the left was preserved at the micro level where it retained strength and was recreated with strong solidarities at the base. From its creation, one of the most unique and enduring aspects of the Frente Amplio—and a reason for its penetration over the years—was the creation of "Base Committees," which consisted of militants and activists from all currents that made up the constitutive parts of the movement. The dense network of the Committees became a space for socialization and for the forging of a *frenteamplista* identity that subsumed the existing identities making up the broader movement. Indeed, this is one of the peculiarities of the Uruguayan left that distinguishes it from other familiar models and experiences in Latin America: unity for the left in Uruguay was much more than the sum of all parts, it was the creation of something entirely different.

The Frente Amplio came out of the dictatorship legitimized, and, importantly, so did its longtime leaders. After a decade of imprisonment, General Liber Seregni, one of the founders of the coalition, was recognized by all of the country's political sectors. The guerrilla leader of the Tupamaros, Raúl Sendic, who valiantly endured 13 years of torture and prison, also came out of the dictatorship as a key political figure. It was during the dictatorship that a collective leftist identity was consolidated among the leadership, which had essentially made an oath forged in blood beneath the intense repression of the military. Indeed, loyalties were sealed at this time despite the vast differences among them in strategy and methods.

In the first post-dictatorship elections the left garnered 21% of votes, but its leaders had gained a reputability that transgressed partisan boundaries. More important, however, was the growth of political activism during the transition to democracy. By 1985, some 500 Base Committees existed in the country (that's about one for every 5,000 people), reaching every corner of society although the interior of the country maintained its distance from the left. Being a *frenteamplista* or of the left, meant much more than voting every five years, something that, in part, it picked up from some of the best socio-political traditions of the social democratic sector of the Colorado Party known as *batllismo*—named after José Batlle y Ordóñez, the party's most celebrated leader.

A watershed moment for understanding the growth of the left was the passage in 1986 of what's been called the "law of impunity." Approved by *blancos* and *colorados*, the law abrogated the trial and punishment of those in the military implicated in gross human rights violations. For the right, it was the beginning of the end. For the majority of the population, which was accustomed to living in a country in which all were equal before the law, it was a punch in the gut. The law resulted in the birth of an impressive social movement seeking to annul the impunity law, resulting in the formation of some 300 neighborhood organizations that were joined not only by *frenteamplistas*, but also by progressive *blancos* and *colorados*.

The annulment campaign lasted two years, and it became a truly grassroots social dialogue. In order for an annulment referendum to be convoked, 25% of the electorate's signatures were needed. To achieve this, neighborhood activists combed the country, going house-to-house, to dialogue with neighbors and explain what the law was about and to ask for their signatures. Some 30,000 activists participated in the door-to-door campaign. They visited 80% of Uruguay's households; spoke with over one million people; and in some cases had to return two, three and even seven times to obtain a signature.[2]

The campaign gave activists a much more profound understanding of their country, and they made notable headway in the outer reaches of the interior and in the marginal urban neighborhoods, where neither social movements nor left parties had previously ventured. Despite the fact that it became Uruguay's most significant social movement and that it changed the face of the country, the initiative failed in April 1989: 42% voted to annul the law and 52% voted to maintain it. Nonetheless, the medium-term outcome of the campaign was that the social and political left surpassed some its historical limitations, particularly in rural areas. Shortly thereafter, the left presented a divided electoral front. Still, its overall support increased: the Frente Amplio won 21% and the splinter party, Nuevo Espacio

(New Space) got 10%. What's more, the left won the mayoralty of Montevideo, the country's capital, with 35% of votes; a key office it has successfully administered and held to this day.

The left's seemingly unstoppable ascent was clinched as a result of the neoliberal crisis of the 1990s. In 1992, the concerted effort of the social movement and the political left managed to halt a key aspect of neoliberal policy: a referendum against the privatizations passed with 70% approval. The defense of the welfare state by the left legitimated its position against neoliberalism, because its agenda resonated deeply with the cultural and historical underpinnings of *batllismo*, which was geared toward an active state presence in social and economic life. In the 1994 presidential elections support for the Frente Amplio climbed to 30%, while Nuevo Espacio gained only 5% of votes. Seeing the undeniable rise of the left, the right obtained a constitutional reform for the next elections that implemented a run-off system, which it thought would make it more difficult for the left to win the presidency. In 1999, support for the Frente Amplio rose to 44% in the second round of voting, but the *blancos* and *colorados* joined together to defeat the left.

The brutal crisis of 2002, dealt another blow to the traditional parties, especially the Colorado Party, which had essentially founded the Uruguayan state and had ruled the country on and off for more than a century.[3] The economic recession hit in 1999 and plummeted with the stagnation of neighboring Argentina. Between January and July of 2002, the "risk factor" of the country determined by financial institutions went from 220 to 3,000 points; the financial run on bank accounts took with it 45% of all deposits; the price of the dollar doubled; and the gross domestic product (GDP) was cut in half compared to 1998 levels. Unemployment climbed to 20% and the portion of the population living below the poverty line skyrocketed to 40%.

As in much of Latin America, the neoliberal model had entered into a definitive crisis of legitimacy. In Uruguay that crisis did not generate a movement of social protest, instead it was channeled into the electoral field, leading to the ultimate triumph of the left led by the Frente Amplio. At the end of October 2004, after three decades of methodical electoral growth and social formation, the coalition of the Encuentro Progresista–Frente Amplio (EP-FA) led by Tabaré Vázquez won the presidential elections in the first round.

Only two months after Vásquez assumed power, the left won what was perhaps an even greater victory with the municipal elections of May 2005. It was a far less publicized victory, but it may after all prove to be more profound. Before the municipal elections in 2005, the left only controlled Montevideo, but in the elections it won eight of the 19 departments (provinces) of the country, making up two-thirds of Uruguay's population and comprising almost 80% of its GDP. The elections confirmed the strong and broad social base of the left, a strength that is unmatched by any political force on the horizon. In sum, the left has assured itself a high degree of maneuverability for at least the next five years, since it counts on absolute majorities in the parliament and does not need to enter into compromising alliances to implement its program.

Although in the first year or so of a left government the continuities with previous regimes have outweighed the changes, the Vázquez Administration maintains high levels of support. The most criticized aspects of the Administration are the continuation of neoliberal macroeconomic policies—which inevitably reduce the portion of the budget destined to social areas—the support its given to the construction of two contaminating paper mills on the Uruguay River and its timidness in confronting one of the worst inheritances of the dictatorship on human rights policy. The leftist government essentially decided not to annul the impunity law on a constitutional basis, leaving those accused of violating rights, of disappearing prisoners and of stealing the newborn of women in captivity remain unpunished.

Nonetheless, there are important achievements that should not be overlooked. A space of honest dialogue has been created between workers, business owners and the state that seeks to resolve labor conflicts and rollback some of the most grievous consequences of neoliberalism, such as labor flexibility and the loss of workers' rights. Moreover, despite budget limitations, funds are being allocated to alleviate the most pressing necessities of the unemployed and the most poverty stricken through the "Emergency Plan," which attends to the needs of some 40,000 families. But the most significant change has been the new social climate brought on by the government. Direct avenues for dialogue have been opened between the government and the social movements, stimulating the growth of civil society. And the new climate has certainly allowed the formation of new trade unions in areas that until now were impossible to unionize due to the harsh repression of bosses. Indeed, all of society has been infused with a sense of social activism; albeit, it's true, this could fizzle if real changes are lagging.

Although the right has become an increasingly louder critic, its exhortations have little resonance among the public, which may still be on a bit of honeymoon with the government. If the left's methodical construction of hegemony avoids unraveling due to generalized corruption or to domination, as has happened in other Latin American countries, it's possible that the Uruguayan left, despite its traditional moderation, will be able to rule as many decades as did the traditional parties.

ABOUT THE AUTHOR

Raúl Zibechi, a member of the editorial board of the weekly *Brecha de Montevideo*, is a professor and researcher on social movements at the Multiversidad Franciscana de América Latina and adviser to several grassroots organizations. He is a monthly contributor to the Americas' Program of the International Relations Center (IRC), www.americaspolicy.org. Translated from Spanish by Teo Ballvé.

NOTES

1. Eric Hobsbawm, *Historia del siglo XX* (Barcelona: Crítica, 1995), p. 118.
2. Maria Delagdo, Marisa Ruiz and Raúl Zibechi, *So the People Can Decide: The Experience of the Referendum Against Impunity Law in Uruguay, 1985-1989* (International Human Rights Internship Program, Washington, 2001).
3. In 1966, the two traditional parties (the Nacional, or Blanco Party, and the Colorado Party) received 90% of votes, nowadays they aspire to obtain 45%, but the Colorados went from a historical average of between 40–50%, to now scraping by with only 8%.

Luis A. Gómez

Evo Morales Turns the Tide of History

It was exactly 13 minutes after 2 p.m. in La Paz on January 22, 2006, when Evo Morales shed his first tears of the afternoon, and with him, cried all of Bolivia. In that instant, the new Vice President of the nation, Alvaro García Linera, was laying upon him the Medal of the Liberator, the maximum symbol of republican power in this country. The medal hung over the presidential sash and, with that, it was done: the first indigenous president of the century was ready to govern his country. But first, there were chapters to close, accounts to square.

"Mister president of the National Congress," said Evo to García Linera, who as Vice President is charged with presiding over the legislative branch, "I want to ask for a moment of silence to remember our fallen heroes." Thus began the speech of Bolivia's new president: asking a bit of peace and quiet to remember the dead. In a stirring run through the centuries, Evo mentioned, among others, leader of the eighteenth century anti-colonial rebellion Tupaj Katari, Che Guevara, dozens of indigenous leaders and, finally, the citizens of the city of El Alto that were massacred in October 2003, his *cocalero* (coca grower) companions and all the anonymous heroes of this country.

In recalling Bolivia's rebel lineage, the old republican-era building of the nation's Congress probably lived the longest minute of its history. The only sound heard in those 60 seconds was the deep lament of a *pututu* (a traditional wind instrument made from a bull's horn); that is, until the faltering voice of Evo Morales loudly interjected, asking for glory onto the martyrs of liberation.

It was with that dark thread woven with fallen heroes and defeats that the new president began his speech: "Because that is our history . . . we had been condemned to extermination and now here we are . . . precisely to change our history." Taking a breath, Evo launched into an explanation of how Bolivia's indigenous have been subjugated and humiliated for centuries, but that his government marks a definitive break with this past, and it will seek to "resolve this historical problem."

After coursing through the recollection of offenses against the country's indigenous population, Evo Morales left one thing absolutely clear, echoing what had been said at the archeological ruins of Tiwanaku the day before: 500 years of resistance had come to an end, and that they, the indigenous peoples of the Americas, should be ready to "take power for the next 500." But without enmity, he insisted, "Because we indigenous people are not rancorous."

Before the teary eyes of his brothers and sisters, such as the *cocalera* leader Leonilda Zurita—who stood in a balcony and cried the entire ceremony—Evo described what it meant to be indigenous, mixing it emotively with the strength of Che Guevara. He also situated the historical moment of his presidency as a continuation of the revolt led by Tupaj Katari, who encircled this city for months in 1781 and almost managed to put an end to colonial domination under the Spanish Crown.

"I say this with all sincerity and humbleness," said Evo of his historical account, affirming that only under a government of indigenous peoples would things ever change, because "we indigenous peoples are the moral reservoir of humanity." To which a standing ovation erupted, one of several that interrupted his inauguration speech. He went on to outline his ideas, his proposals, interspersed with more direct complaints and questioning.

The end has come to capital being amassed in the hands of the few, emphasized Morales, raising one dark finger straight into the air. "This has to change in a democracy," he said. And he announced that this was the job of his government, but without humiliating or mistreating others, as they had done to him.

He recalled that one afternoon in March 2005, he was walking from the Congress to the executive's office to dialogue with then-President Carlos Mesa during a conflictive period, when he was assaulted by a group of people on the street. "They wanted to hang Evo Morales," said the new president. But that offense by Mesa's sympathizers (the former president was in the audience) only emboldened the awakening of people's consciousness, he said.

"Ex-presidents, understand this: one shouldn't do that, one shouldn't marginalize people," lashed out Morales, looking up to the balcony, where the three invited ex-presidents sat with calm looks but visibly clenching their jaws. And it is because of all this, continued the indigenous president, that we have to "put an end to the colonial state."

Morales continued with a complete summary of what he has always said about racism and discrimination. In this part of the speech, during which the crowd interrupted with repeated applause and calls of support, the few right-wing congressmen maintained a serene attitude without applauding until Evo announced that democracy was the best way to decolonize the state, and thereby end corruption.

Then began the political explanation . . . .

Without taking off his jacket, which was adorned with Andean embroidery, Evo began recounting the historical looting of Bolivia's natural resources, something tolerated and encouraged by previous governments and legislators. "There was no love of country when this looting began," said Morales. "Politics is the way to better the economy for the people . . . and this has not happened in our country."

Water, he emphasized, should on principle be a public service, explaining that the privatization of the resource was an absurd notion that will be scrapped by his administration. In fact, said the Bolivian president, the previous policies over natural resources, such as "water, coca and gas," were what sparked "the consciousness of the Bolivian people."

And he spoke about land redistribution, appealing to large landholders to revert unproductive lands to the state. Morales said it cannot be that "a cow is given 40 or 50 hectares to live." Then adding, "It's not possible that one has to be a cow to get 40 or 50 hectares."

He expressed similar incredulity about industry and productivity, reminding the audience, for example, that since August 6, 1825—the date of the country's republican founding—nothing in Bolivia has been industrialized. Indeed, for more than a century and a half Bolivia has remained an exporter of raw materials, and without much benefit.

"All our natural resources should pass through the hands of the Bolivian people, be it water, coca or gas," said the new president of this country, which counts on the second-largest gas reserves of South America. "The challenge for all Bolivians is to industrialize our natural resources so that we can climb out of poverty."

But he also reaffirmed that the recovery of these natural resources should be carried out "responsibly." He underlined that negotiations would soon begin with the foreign energy companies—including Repsol, Total and Petrobras—to rework contracts in a way that would establish full state control over the industry and increase state income from gas and oil exploitation.

With a few words about the necessity of improving Bolivia's health and education programs, Evo concluded, "This economic model does not work." He entertained the possibility that perhaps it works in Europe or in some African country, but "in Bolivia," he said, "the neoliberal economic model just does not go." And since it was precisely the belief of the Bolivian people about the uselessness 'of neoliberalism that brought him to power, Morales said that his mandate would have to be respected.

Morales, single and 46-years-old, put forth that there would be respect for "those want to live better," but not under anyone's exploitation.

Evo directed himself forcefully various times to the former heads of state seated in the balcony up to his left. But it was when speaking about legal security—something demanded by transnationals and various countries to keep investing in Bolivia—that Morales made his toughest and clearest directive. Assistant Secretary of State for Western Hemisphere Affairs Thomas Shannon "came to visit us last night," said Morales, adding that he made clear that U.S. policies and values will no longer be accepted submissively.

"No to the importation of policies," was Morales' slogan, invoking by extension the entire international community. Immediately, he clarified that for development and growth to occur the necessary policies and laws must be created domestically. With this, Morales began weaving history together with his own personal political trajectory.

"I remember when I arrived to this building in '97," said Morales in reference to his first term as congressman. He described that back then, only four campesinos served with him in the Congress, and all of their legislative proposals were blocked. Looking over to the section of the Congress where the politicians from the opposition were seated, the President said, "Don't get nervous, we are not going to do what you did to us."

Instead, Evo called on them to get back to work, because of the many pending tasks ahead.

He clearly stated the need to convoke a Constitutional Assembly in June 2006 to re-write the Constitution, telling the audience that it was necessary to create a new form of organizing the government of Bolivia. To create this new form of government, which will undoubtedly include indigenous and regional autonomy, Evo asked for the Congress to work together, saying it should convert itself into "an army for the second independence of Bolivia." If Congress does not, or cannot, warned Morales, the task will be left in the hands of the social movements and the indigenous, who will surely mobilize and keep struggling. Because these measures and processes, Evo made clear, will serve "to deepen democracy, which is not only the right to vote, but also the right to live well."

The President returned to the theme of productivity, toughing on industrialization and about his government's economic austerity program, which begins by raising the minimum wage (currently at $60 a month) and cutting the salaries of state functionaries. For everything, of course, he appealed for support and backing from the people, the professionals and on a few occasions from the presidents of other countries—specifically, Cuba and Venezuela.

Evo mentioned a few more projects, including a literacy program (with Cuba's support), healthcare, official document provision to all Bolivians, support to microenterprise and small industry, and the eradication of corruption. "This country used to be the runner-up in the corruption championship," said Morales. And without missing a beat, he asked ex-President Jaime Paz Zamora how he could have permitted Bolivia to gain this title, since it was under his administration that Transparency International, which tracks corruption worldwide, declared Bolivia the second-most corrupt country on the planet.

Seeing that his speech had already ran long, Evo said that he would cut himself off, so that "you don't think I caught something from Fidel or Chávez"—a reference to the Cuban and Venezuelan presidents, respectively, and their long-winded speeches. The joke drew laughs and applause from Chávez and the rest of the audience, which then quieted down as Morales turned to the thorny issue of coca (the plant can be processed to make cocaine).

Evo Morales lamented the harm that drugs and narcotrafficking have done to the world. "These are harms that were imported here," he added. With the United States, he proposed to strike a genuine agreement against the drug trade. And, as he said several times on the campaign trail, he wants a deal that amounts to "zero narcotrafficking," but not to "zero coca."

In the last section of his speech, Evo greeted Ricardo Lagos, the outgoing Chilean President, recognizing that his counter-part's government meant a new era in relations between the two countries, which have long clashed over landlocked Bolivia's demand for an outlet to the sea. Morales announced he would attend the inauguration of newly elected President Michele Bachelette, adding that Bolivians "are not afraid" of what is ahead in the bilateral relations.

He also spoke of reactivating the mining industry and putting an end to the external debt, asking the international community and the financial institutions to definitively cancel Bolivia's entire debt. Only by producing "is it possible to get out of poverty," he assured, but reversing the debt and inequalities are important aspects of this path.

Moreover, he added, "Countries are equally entitled to the right for dignity and sovereignty." With some brief words in the native languages of Aymara and Quechua, Evo Morales called on all the indigenous people of his country to stand united, because in his new cabinet there will be no nepotism or corruption.

Finally, in reference to Mexico's Zapatistas, Evo ended by explaining his manner of governing: "Like Subcomandante Marcos says: rule by obeying the people. . . . Thank you very much." And with that, he left.

ABOUT THE AUTHOR

Luis A. Gómez is author of *El Alto de pie: Una insurreción aymara en Bolivia* (La Paz, 2004), an intimate account of the Bolivia's 2003 "Gas War."

Indigenous Movements

Teo Ballvé

¡Bolivia de pie!

By most accounts, the opening salvo in Bolivia's ongoing revolutionary cycle occurred in 2000.[1] Mothers, unionists, campesinos, students, in fact, citizens of all kinds seized the streets and plazas of Cochabamba to take back their water. Management of city's waterworks had been privatized in September the year before, and within weeks household water bills had skyrocketed by 200%.[2]

A coalition opposing the water contract and rate hikes nicknamed *La Coordinadora* led intermittent protests and strikes in the first months, but then declared an all-out "final battle" for April. The battle broke out as announced and, while under martial law, the people of Cochabamba fought armed troops throughout the tear gas-choked city. In about a week, the government succumbed and announced it had canceled the contract. The city's walls were still scrawled with the then-victorious rallying call, "*¡El agua es del pueblo, carajo!*" ("The water belongs to the people, damn it!").

It's fitting that the current cycle of struggle began by reclaiming such a basic and symbolic element of life. Since then, through similar mobilizations, Bolivia stands as the only country in Latin America—and perhaps the world—that has successfully rolled back some of the key impositions of dominant military, economic and political paradigms underlying current patterns of globalization. What's more, the social movements have done so by attacking, weakening and in some cases circumventing the power structure within its borders and beyond that determines what's "permissible" under conditions of Empire. Bolivia's rich histories of tightly knit campesino communities (called *ayllus*), workers' unions, campesino unions, neighborhood associations and many other forms of collective organization have long made it one of Latin America's most organized societies. "Hence when Bolivians began the latest cycle of resistance and insurgency in 2000," write historians Forrest Hylton and Sinclair Thomson, "their radical traditions of organizing provided unexpected reserves of strength. Revolutionary forces and aspirations, only recently thought to have been buried, suddenly resurfaced with surprising energy and creativity, albeit in new forms and under new circumstances."[3] These conditions make Bolivia uniquely poised to resist and overturn reigning global economic, political and military arrangements, and it has begun to do so with stunning success.

The early 1980s were desperate times for Bolivians. The widespread food shortages, astronomical hyperinflation and general instability led the government to call early elections in 1985. Víctor Paz Estenssoro of the Nationalist Revolutionary Movement (MNR) party won a fourth term as president. Paz had been a leader of Bolivia's Revolution of 1952, which in its early years had instituted broad reforms: nationalization of key industries, land reform, universal suffrage, education programs, subsidies and other social protections.

In a dramatic reversal from his more radical past, after the 1985 election, Paz enlisted the help of his U.S.-educated Finance Minister Gonzalo "Goni" Sánchez de Lozada to map out an economic strategy. Under the tutelage of Harvard economist Jeffrey Sachs, it took Goni and his team just 17 days to cobble together what they called the "New Economic Policy." Three weeks after his inauguration, Paz signed "Supreme Decree No. 21060," initiating the radical neoliberal transformation of Bolivia and the systematic dismantlement of the state built by the Revolution.

"Rather than a strictly economic program," explained Goni, "the New Economic Policy is a political plan. . . . Its aim is to recover the basic principles of republican life without which we run a serious risk of national disintegration." The next part of his analysis, an ominous warning, would later prove tragic: "The first political task consists of restoring the state's authority over society at large."[4] State-oriented economic policies were reversed, industries and services were privatized, government spending was cut, hyperinflation was stopped, the unions and labor laws were weakened and the financial sector was deregulated. The country was open for business.

"Using the contemporary tools of economic power—holding up loans, aid, and debt relief—the [World] Bank and IMF influenced and outright coerced the Bolivian government into selling or leasing its public enterprises into corporate hands," says Jim Shultz of the Cochabamba-based Democracy Center. In debt negotiations with the government in the 1990s, for example, the World Bank made $600 million in debt relief contingent on the privatization of Cochabamba's waterworks.[5] Eventually the cash-strapped government complied, awarding a 40-year contract to the sole bidder—the consortium Aguas del Tunari, whose majority owner was the U.S.-based Bechtel corporation. During this same privatization push by the Bank, the government also privatized the joint water system of El Alto and neighboring La Paz, awarding it to the private consortium Aguas del Illimani, mostly owned by France-based Suez.

This January, five years after residents of Cochabamba won

back their water and reestablished a public utility company with mechanisms for citizen participation, the Neighborhood Associations (FEJUVE) of El Alto won a similar battle. Illimani pegged El Alto's rates to the U.S. dollar and water bills shot up by 35%, while water and sewer hookup fees reached $445. According to the latest census, 53% of El Alto residents still lack these basic services.[6] After negotiations over the water crisis stalled, FEJUVE called a general strike on January 10. Protests paralyzed the city and shut down the international airport; some residents even seized Illimani offices and facilities. Two days later, the government was forced to scrap the contract.

Aguas del Illimani will likely bring charges against the government for canceling the contract at the International Center for Investment Settlement Disputes (ICISD), an arm of the World Bank. Bolivia already faces a pending $25 million suit at the ICISD for canceling Tunari's contract in Cochabamba. An ICISD case brought by Illimani, however, would have the added irony that the International Finance Corporation, which is also an arm of the World Bank, happens to be a shareholder in Illimani. In the contorted logic of global capitalism, this means that the World Bank Group, which demanded and funded the privatization in the first place, and was then a partial owner, will also decide whether the government complied with the "deal."

The International Monetary Fund (IMF), often working in concert with the Bank, has also played an insidious role in determining economic policy. In early 2003, the IMF recommended budget targets for Bolivia and suggested taxation as the best way to reach those goals. Then-Vice President Carlos Mesa told Jim Shultz of the Democracy Center that the first option, which was raising the taxes levied on private oil and gas companies, was immediately ruled out. "The great alibi, the great argument of the multinational corporations, is legal security," said Mesa.

"The moment that you change your tax rules, you are changing the rules of the game that establish the possibility that those companies will come and invest in Bolivia."[7]

The only way the government could meet the IMF's requirements was by raising income taxes. At first, the government considered only raising the income tax of the richest Bolivians, but budget projections showed the country would still fall short of the IMF's target. Finally, in early February 2003, Goni, who had recently been elected to a second presidential term, decided on a tax structure that included Bolivians earning only twice the minimum wage. The country erupted in protest, especially La Paz, where already-striking policemen joined the demonstrations and eventually had a daylong shootout with military forces in front of the Presidential Palace. Days later, the government was again forced to comply with the public's demands and repealed the tax.

Álvaro García Linera, the newly elected vice president of Bolivia, notes that the water revolts in Cochabamba and El Alto along with other localized mobilizations—against coca eradication, for example—have been mostly reactive and defensive.[8] Although the tax revolt fits this characterization, it differed in that it was national in scope. The so-called "gas war" in September–October 2003 that toppled the Goni Administration and its continuation in May this year was profoundly different from these previous uprisings. Instead of a responsive rearguard action, the movements—led by the insurgent communities of the altiplano (highland plateau) and the FEJUVE of El Alto— preempted the sale of the country's vast natural gas reserves by foreign corporations. Moreover, the social movements—in an unprecedented alliance—united around a common set of demands that eventually included the unequivocal nationalization of the country's hydrocarbons industry. "This constitutes a qualitative leap in the social movements' construction of an alternative political project," writes García Linera. "They have gone from the defensive and the local, to a position that is national and on the offensive."

The ongoing battle over the fate of the nation's gas reserves had the adverse effect of destabilizing long-standing fault lines in Bolivian society: between the indigenous peoples of the impoverished highlands and elite groups from the resource-rich eastern and southern lowlands of the country. These elites and their well-heeled civic and business groups are intimately tied to private energy companies. They argue that the future of the gas reserves should not be held hostage by what they see as extremist indigenous movements. Most of these rightwing groups also advocate for greater regional autonomy and some even call for the resource-rich regions to secede from the western highlands.

When President Carlos Mesa was forced to resign last June, the movements scrambled to prevent a surrogate of these elites, Senate President Hormando Vaca Díez—the next in succession for the presidency—from taking office. Protestors traveled across the country from La Paz to Sucre—where Congress had met to escape the La Paz demonstrations—encircled the colonial city and managed to block Vaca's appointment. In a dramatic development, the movements even counted on the tacit support of the military. At a press conference the military high command warned Congress "to listen to the voice of the people" and "popular demands." Despite the military's bloody history and Vaca's overtures for repression, even the Armed Forces sought to prevent "a confrontation at all costs between brothers," as one commander stated. (Juan Coro, a miner en route to Sucre, was killed, but reports indicate it was police that shot him, not the Armed Forces.) This restraint is all the more noteworthy because the U.S. Embassy had shown support for Vaca, and the military has a long-established history of bending to the will of the Embassy, which provides it with generous funding, weapons and training.

The Embassy forged this dependency of the military through the U.S.-sponsored Drug War. The protracted low-intensity conflict in Bolivia over U.S.-mandated coca eradication has led to widespread human rights abuses and the death of at least 33 *cocaleros* (coca growers) between 1998 and 2003. Under this violent repression, however, *cocalero* unions and the Movement Toward Socialism (MAS) party of recently elected President Evo Morales have scored important, yet partial, victories against the bellicose imposition of the Drug War.

Most recently, cocaleros reached an agreement with the government in October 2004 that allowed the marginal expansion of government-sanctioned coca in the Chapare, where most of the country's "illicit" crop is grown. Perhaps more significantly, in 2002 the U.S.-trained and -financed Expeditionary Task Force (ETF), a paramilitary counterdrug unit, was disbanded due to widely publicized abuses. Using their primary pressure tactic of road blockades—which effectively shut down the entire country with military precision—the cocaleros have won government reprieves on coca eradication and the construction of more military bases.

The social movements, particularly when acting in concert, now wield a veritable extra-governmental veto over government policy; a veto that was once the exclusive preserve of the U.S. Embassy and transnational capital. Among their many accomplishments, Bolivians have blocked a sweetheart deal with private energy companies, reestablished public companies, raised the debate of nationalization, thwarted rightwing efforts to take over the state and gained support for a new Constitution. Despite seemingly insurmountable obstacles cemented by reactionary forces within Bolivia and abroad, the social movements have succeeded at the very least in moving the goalpost: whether the issue is overturning facets of the neoliberal model, resisting the cycle of violence of the Drug War (increasingly subsumed by the War on Terror) or disregarding the strictures of Wall Street.

Official pronouncements of organizations in the social movements allude to the strategic assumption that the power of local elites and the more nebulous global networks of power are not merely symbiotic, but one and the same. The day after Vaca was forced to step aside, *La Coordinadora*, which remains one of the country's most vibrant and active social movement organizations, released a revealing communiqué stating:

> Through the enormous mobilization of Bolivians and the indigenous people throughout the country we have temporarily averted a grand maneuver by the transnational corporations, the U.S. government, the Santa Cruz oligarchy and the traditional Bolivian political parties. . . . This, compañeros, is no small thing: all the power of global capital was brought down against us yesterday, and we managed to stop it.[9]

Under conditions of Empire, which makes the already-limited spaces of political maneuverability even more contested, the current state of affairs in Bolivia brings to sharp focus some core, familiar questions for the Latin American left: what is the most effective path for national self-determination and social justice? Would a broader alliance, including less politically progressive forces, widen the appeal and viability of a transformative project, or would such an approach be doomed by compromise and stagnation? Broadly stated, the two competing left currents in Bolivia are generally associated with Evo Morales, on the one hand, and radical Aymara leader Felipe Quispe and his allies on the other.

Since the 2002 elections in which Morales lost by less than 2%, he and his *cocalero*-based party, the MAS, focused on local elections as the springboard for winning the presidency. Quispe leads the much smaller Indigenous Pachakutik Movement (MIP) party and is closely linked to the militant Aymara communities of the *altiplano*. When asked about his relationship with Morales and the MAS, Quispe charged, "Evo Morales wants the presidency; we want our autonomy. . . . While we're fighting in the streets, they are there, happy, on the balconies watching us, and then at the last minute when we're about to overthrow the government they join us."[10]

At the June 17, 2005, meeting of the MAS, its bases called for an allegiance, "principally, with other sectors of the social movements."[11] Morales subsequently began constructing an "anti-neoliberal coalition" for the December 2005 elections. But in an effort to gain middle class support, Morales' first move was to ally with the Movement Without Fear (MSM) party, which opposes the nationalization of the hydrocarbons industry. It seemed like the beginning of a now-familiar Latin American story.

Morales won the presidency with an unprecedented margin in the first round on December 18. The country's first-ever indigenous president now faces the challenge of walking the tightrope between transnational capital, a hostile U.S. regime and the far-reaching demands of the movements for a profound national transformation. Still, the social movements will continue to be a dominant, oppositional force whichever the government in power. Moreover, the all-or-nothing ties between political parties and the social movements are much more fluid and flexible in Bolivia than in other Latin American countries. But for now, the country's fate is sealed in the outcome of the constituent assembly that is slated to convene in August 2006 to rewrite the Constitution. Only then will it be seen if the new country that emerges from that process will be capable of translating the demands from the street into the actions of government.

NOTES

1. Title from a popular Bolivian protest chant heard frequently in El Alto: *"El Alto de pie, nunca de rodillas!"* ("On your feet, El Alto! Never on your knees!). Also borrowed from Luis A. Gómez's authoritative blow-by-blow account of the 2003 "Gas War": Luis A. Gómez, *El Alto de pie: Una insurreción aymara en Bolivia* (La Paz: Self-published, 2004).

2. For a comprehensive account of Cochabamba's "Water Revolt" see the information compiled by Jim Shultz of the Cochabamba-based Democracy Center, http://www.democracyctr.org/bechtel/.

3. Forrest Hylton and Sinclair Thomson, *Revolutionary Horizons: Indigenous and National-Popular Struggles in Bolivia, 1781–2005*, (New York: Verso, forthcoming).

4. Sonia Dávila, "In Another Vein," *NACLA Report on the Americas*, "Bolivia: The Poverty of Progress," Vol. 25, No. 1 (1991), p. 12.

5. See http://www.democracyctr.org/bechtel/.

6. "Bolivia: Privatized Water Company Defeated," *NACLA Report on the Americas*, "Social Movements: Building from the Ground Up," Vol. 38, No. 5 (2005), pp. 41–43.

7. Jim Shultz, "Deadly Consequences: The IMF and Bolivia's 'Black February'," (Cochabamba: Democracy Center, April 2005), http://www.democracyctr.org/publications/imfreport.htm.

8. Álvaro García Linera, "La segunda batalla por la nacionalización del gas," *El Juguete Rabioso* (La Paz), Vol. 5 No. 131, p. 6.

9. "Comunicado de la Coordinadora de Defensa del Gas," June 10, 2005, posted on The Narcosphere: <http://narcosphere.narconews.com/story/2005/6/10/165054/060>.

10. "Evo Morales quiere la presidencia; nosotros, nuestra autonomía: Felipe Quispe," Interview, *Crónica* (Mexico), June 10, 2005.

11. Walter Chávez, "El MAS y el MSM optan por un frente tradicional," *El Juguete Rabioso* (La Paz), Vol. 5, No. 132, June 25, 2005, p. 8.

Forrest Hylton and Sinclair Thomson

The Roots of the Rebellion: Insurgent Bolivia

The great anti-colonial indigenous insurrection of 1781 has haunted republican Bolivia since its founding in 1825. From their military encampment in El Alto overlooking the colonial city of La Paz, Aymara leaders Túpaj Katari and Bartolina Sisa laid siege to the ruling Spanish elite from March to October 1781. Lacking urban allies, they were ultimately unable to seize the city, yet the aspirations of that uprising have taken on new life at the beginning of the 21st century.

In October 2003, popular classes of Aymara descent living in El Alto spearheaded what became a broad-based movement to overthrow the increasingly repressive and illegitimate regime of then-President Gonzalo Sánchez de Lozada. They too laid siege to the capital and brought it to a virtual standstill. Unlike Katari and Sisa, the latest insurgents successfully overtook the urban center, occupying all but a few blocks around Plaza Murillo where the Presidential Palace is located. Waving the Aymara flag (the *wiphala*), and the Bolivian flag side by side, the crowds swelled to as many as 500,000 on October 17, the day a heavily guarded Sánchez de Lozada fled to Miami. The stunning turn of events—dubbed by journalists the "gas war"—brought the era of neoliberal domination in the country to a close. It also confirmed that Bolivia has entered a new revolutionary cycle in which indigenous actors have taken the leading role. It is a time of great promise, but one whose outcome remains unforeseeable.

A powerful tradition of popular urban mobilization has been evident in earlier historical moments, as when "national-popular" forces overthrew the dictatorship of Col. Alberto Natusch Busch in 1979 or brought the Democratic Popular Unity (UDP) government to power in 1982. Yet the profile and organization of these previous mobilizations were different. In the 1970s and 1980s, workers, students and members of the progressive middle classes organized themselves through left parties and the national Bolivian Workers' Confederation (COB). The politically emergent indigenous peasantry mobilized as well during this period, but almost entirely at the behest of the COB and as a junior partner in the national-popular bloc.

However, in October 2003 the progressive middle classes stirred only belatedly and the COB was a relatively minor player. More importantly, these groups were essentially backing demands previously launched by Aymara insurgents, organized mainly through their community, union and neighborhood organizations. Ultimately, though, all sectors converged around the same demands: the resignation of Sánchez de Lozada and his ministers, a trial to punish those responsible for state violence against the unarmed civilian population, a national referendum on how to develop the country's natural gas reserves, the formulation of a new Hydrocarbons Law and the convening of a Constitutional Assembly.

In contrast to the proletarian character of the national-popular struggles that ended the phase of military and narco-dictatorships in the early 1980s, the powerful movement in 2003 displayed an indigenous centrality in synch with the current demographic, sociocultural and political realities of Bolivia, where 62% of the population claims indigenous identity, according to the 2001 census.

If we are to understand the October insurrection, however, it is not enough to point out Aymaras' currently assertive historical agency. We must first note that the keen sense of Aymara identity is itself a product of recent political struggle, and that the entire context for the revolutionary cycle that opened in 2000 has been shaped by forceful and fluid processes of ethnic formation. The galvanization of indigenous identity is especially striking among the subaltern actors of October's events.

Members of mobilized rural communities on the *altiplano* (highland plateau) have gradually adopted a self-conscious cultural and political identity as "Aymaras" since the late 1970s. The rise of militant peasant unionism and the emergence of radical indigenous leaders criticizing ongoing forms of colonial hierarchy and racism within the country are largely responsible for this ethnic affirmation.[1] The trajectory of Aymara leader Felipe Quispe—known as *"El Mallku,"* an Aymara term meaning both condor and traditional authority—reflects this process.

One of the most arresting features of the 2003 uprising was the expression of Aymara ethnic identity and solidarity among the urban residents—especially young protestors—of El Alto, an impoverished yet dynamic city of 900,000 outside La Paz. According to the 2001 census, 82% of *alteños*, as the city's residents are known, identify as indigenous. In La Paz, laborers from the hillside neighborhoods of Munaypata and Villa Victoria, a proletarian stronghold during the Revolution of 1952, actively supported the insurgent *alteños*. Although not all these neighborhood residents would overtly identify themselves as Aymaras, they share with *alteños* a history of multi-generational migration from the Aymara countryside and insertion into the ethnically segmented urban social hierarchy.

Bolivian miners have traditionally identified and organized themselves on a class basis. When mineworkers traveled from the mining center of Huanuni to join the protests in El Alto, they revived the memory and symbolic power of earlier proletarian struggle in the national-popular tradition. However, on this occasion they also surprisingly affirmed their own indigenous roots.

Cocaleros—cultivators of the coca leaf, which has been consumed for millennia by indigenous groups as a mild stimulant, is also the base ingredient of cocaine—are another important sector in the contemporary popular movement, and agrarian colonizers from the Yungas recognize their own Aymara origins, although their collective identity is more closely tied to grassroots union organizations than to the traditional Andean community, or *ayllu*. In the Chapare, the country's principal coca-growing region, the majority of residents are from the Quechua-speaking regions of the Cochabamba valleys. Others, like *cocalero* leader Evo Morales, are Aymara migrants from the highlands or Quechua-speaking former miners.

The *regantes* (small-scale coordinators of regional water distribution) who are best known for their role in the 2000 "water war" in Cochabamba also played their part in the "gas war." They have their roots in the region's Quechua-speaking mestizo peasant culture. Other actors in the uprising, like the peasant communities from Potosí and Chuquisaca, are organized through *ayllus* and are of mixed Quechua-Aymara background. All of these groups contributed to the insurgent movement that expressed itself so boldly, and with such a strongly indigenous accent, in 2003.

The point to emphasize, however, is that the insurrectionary energy of the 2003 uprising stemmed initially from the Aymara heartland of Omasuyos, on the *altiplano* around Lake Titicaca, and later from the Aymara city of El Alto. Likewise, indigenous communities and neighborhoods were the first to put forth the basic demands around which so many others eventually converged in October.

Historically, indigenous movements have sought to build ties with other popular and middle class opposition forces in cities and mining districts. Such tentative efforts took place during the indigenous mobilizations against Spanish rule in 1780–81, the insurgent federalist movement led by Pablo Zárate Villca in 1899, the regional revolutionary movement led by Manuel Michel in 1927, the uprisings that began in Ayopaya in 1946 and the general strike of 1979. But relations between indigenous movements and their potential national-popular allies have generally been marred by mutual suspicion, misunderstanding or plain racism.

Political theorist René Zavaleta Mercado pioneered the idea of "national-popular" forces in Bolivian history. Zavaleta posited that the insurrectionary "multitude" opposing oligarchic elites and their foreign, imperialist allies was formed through the political unification of normally divided subaltern subjects.[2] National-popular struggles of this sort can conceivably be traced back to the wars of independence against Spain. The active consolidation of this mode of struggle on the national political stage, however, began during the Chaco War (1932–35) and culminated in the Revolution of 1952.

National-popular struggles were behind the nationalization of Gulf Oil under Gen. Alfredo Ovando Candia in 1969, the Popular Assembly government of Gen. Juan José Torres in 1971, as well as the overthrow of the Col. Alberto Natusch Busch and Gen. Luis García Meza dictatorships and the rise to power of the center-left UDP between 1979 and 1982. Throughout this period the left and the union movement held, at best, a condescending view of indigenous participation in national political organization. These groups privileged a schematic vision of class consciousness over cultural identity as the basis for political action. They also shared with elites a "whitening" ideology of national progress through mestizaje. More recently, however, this began to change. The political fortunes of the left and the COB went into decline with the onset of neoliberalism in 1985, but indigenous political and cultural organization gained increasing momentum in the 1980s and 1990s. During this same period, coca producers acquired a strategically crucial political importance through their opposition to U.S. militarized drug intervention. Then in 2000, a new revolutionary cycle was ushered in with indigenous protests on the altiplano and the water war in the Cochabamba valley. Finally, the events of October 2003 revived the tradition of Aymara community insurrection in one of Latin America's largest indigenous cities. The latest insurgency constitutes a major challenge to Bolivian society's internal colonialism and may lead to the formation of a new national-popular bloc representing the social majority.

The national revolutionary tradition, symbolized by the overthrow of oligarchic rule in 1952, seemed definitively vanquished by neoliberal ideology after the structural adjustment of 1985. The government set out to privatize state tin mines and to "relocate" mining families to the outskirts of Oruro, Cochabamba, El Alto and the lowland frontiers of the Chapare. The union movement, which the government deemed an outmoded corporatist institution, came under relentless attack. Technocrats, ideologues and mainstream party functionaries— former middle class dissidents prominent among them—recited neoliberal mantras: competitivity, governability, efficiency, deregulation, decentralization, direct foreign investment. Globalization, they argued, afforded unprecedented opportunities for indigenous peoples to reap the benefits of modern capitalist democracy.

Though economic growth was sluggish and state revenues plummeted as a result of privatization, the discourse of neoliberalism appeared hegemonic. During Sánchez de Lozada's first administration (1993–97), international financial institutions signaled Bolivia as a model of "reform" and demo-cratization for other developing countries. Harvard economist Jeffrey Sachs, an architect of Bolivia's free market "shock treatment" in 1985, hailed Sánchez de Lozada as one of the most creative politicians of the era. The southern Andean nation became a shining star in the neoliberal firmament, and its militant popular movements appeared to have suffered a historic defeat.

As part of the wave of privatizations, Sánchez de Lozada drafted a Hydrocarbons Law in 1996 that dismantled YPFB, the state energy firm, setting the stage for the transnational takeover of Bolivia's rich oil and natural gas resources. A year later, just two days before the end of his first term, he signed another decree effectively forfeiting constitutional sovereignty over the reserves. An official report released by the Bolivian government in December 2003 revealed that the Bolivia-based operations of British-owned BP Amoco and Spain's Repsol YPF enjoyed the lowest operating costs for oil and gas production and exploration in the world.

The sweetheart arrangement for these oil corporations was an eerie—and not unnoticed—repetition of the oligarchy's sell-off of Bolivia's mineral reserves to Anglo-Chilean capital following the War of the Pacific in the late 1800s. Bolivians have had a long and bitter experience with the expropriation of their mineral wealth for the benefit of oligarchs connected to foreign capital. The monetary system in early modern Europe thrived on the export of Bolivian silver from Potosí, now one of the country's poorest, most desolate regions. In the nineteenth and twentieth centuries, tin extracted from the area near Oruro was smelted in the U.S. and Britain. Today, the working conditions and technology in most of Potosí's mines recall those of the colonial era, while Oruro is a landscape of post-industrial devastation where residents make superhuman efforts to survive. The protestors in the gas war were unwilling to see the old pattern repeated with natural gas since, according to many, only sovereign control over Bolivia's gas reserves—the second-largest in Latin America—could underpin a viable political and economic future for later generations.

A deal to export gas through a Chilean port to California was negotiated between San Diego-based Sempra Energy and the Spanish-British-U.S. energy consortium Pacific LNG under the watch of one-time dictator and then-President Hugo Bánzer. During his administration (1997–2001), Bolivia ranked as one of the most corrupt countries in the world. With state violence and social protest on the rise, and the legitimacy of neoliberal political parties eroded, Sánchez de Lozada narrowly won the 2002 elections. His attempt to close the gas deal in 2003 sparked massive opposition to which he responded with blunt force. On September 20, the day after some 500,000 people marched throughout the country to defend national economic sovereignty, security forces killed three civilians in Warisata and one in Ilayata as part of an effort to "liberate" a group of tourists stranded by a road blockade. The center of conflict spread to El Alto on October 8 when the Federation of Neighborhood Associations (FEJUVE) and the Regional Workers' Federation (COR-El Alto) declared a general strike. Members of the insurgent communities of Warisata and Achacachi, like their kinfolk in the *alteño* neighborhood of Villa Ingenio, conceived of themselves as patriots and their rulers as traitors to the Bolivian nation.

Once the massacres began, first in the countryside and then in the city, the relatives and friends of the deceased dubbed their dead "martyrs fallen in the defense of gas." The repression intensified and 31 died on October 12, the anniversary of

Columbus' incursion into the Caribbean. Simultaneously, urban Aymara insurgents and their allies in the neighborhood of relocated miners known as Santiago II began to develop autonomous institutions for self-government similar to those developed in Warisata after September 20. More than 150,000 people marched from El Alto to downtown La Paz on October 13. After several days of mourning, and once the insurgent communities from Omasuyos arrived, rebels set out to overrun the capital.

Prominent middle class personalities and politicians organized hunger strikes on October 15 that spread with remarkable speed to every major city in the republic. But by that point what had once seemed impossible had already become likely: Sánchez de Lozada—also known as "El gringo" because of his heavily accented Spanish (he was raised in the United States)—would have to go.

In retrospect, the ideological hegemony of the Washington Consensus, embodied in Bolivia by Sánchez de Lozada, appears to have been a mirage. Contrary to neoliberal common sense, Bolivia's revolutionary past was not obliterated after 1985, but rather reconfigured. Contemporary indigenous radicalism grows out of a long, largely underground history, yet its irradiating effects since 2000 have reanimated aspirations for social and political change, harkening back to earlier moments of inter-ethnic, interregional and cross-class alliance.[3]

In the aftermath of the Days of October, traditional parties and the right retreated to their regional base in the Santa Cruz lowlands. In 2005, however, they began to exert more strength, successfully cornering Sánchez de Lozada's successor, former Vice President Carlos Mesa, and positioning themselves for a right-wing constitutional coup. With Mesa's ouster, the executive mantle was to pass to the head of the Senate, Hormando Vaca Díez, a man with longstanding ties to Santa Cruz and traditional parties. Faced with mounting pressure from social movements in La Paz, Vaca Díez moved parliament to Sucre in order to guarantee his own succession.

A new wave of popular insurrection in May and June 2005, even larger in geographical scope than that of 2003, blocked this outcome and posed more forcefully than ever the demand for nationalization. Once again, a diverse array of subaltern social forces mobilized, but this time the initiative moved from El Alto and La Paz to the provinces and the countryside, as indigenous peasant communities and miners played the decisive role. In the end, Mesa resigned, and Vaca Díez was forced to renounce presidential office in favor of Eduardo Rodríguez Veltzé, whose task it was to call new elections. The underlying issues in this struggle were not lost on anyone, and polls in June 2005 indicated that over 75% of Bolivians favored some form of nationalization.

The October insurrection, followed by that of June 2005, thus represents an exceptionally deep and powerful, though not unprecedented, convergence between two traditions of struggle—indigenous and national-popular. Earlier mobilizations, and some of their gains—notably the nationalization of mines in 1952 or petroleum in 1969—left a more enduring legacy than had been supposed. Self-consciously building on earlier revolutionary cycles, especially those of 1780–81, 1899 and 1952, the current cycle since 2000 will leave its own legacy. The upcoming Constitutional Assembly, demanded by indigenous peoples and secured by the intervention of popular forces, offers the most immediate possibility for social reform, or even national transformation.

The Assembly could help redraw state-society relations to reflect Bolivia's new historical conditions. It could recognize the enduring non-liberal forms of collective political, economic and territorial association by which most rural and urban Bolivians organize their lives. It could democratize the political relations that throughout the republican era have limited the participation of indigenous peoples in national political life, forcing them to resort to costly insurrectionary struggles. It could also redirect the future exploitation of the country's coveted resources in a way that benefits most Bolivians. Political and economic elites will undoubtedly continue to sabotage the current process. However, as long as they have no alternative agenda to offer, their attempts to stonewall the process are likely to only further radicalize the opposition. These elites may try to construct a more visionary new hegemonic project but there are no signs of this as yet.

Meanwhile, popular sectors continue to engage in effervescent debate and are formulating their own visions of the future. What would Bolivia look like with sovereign control over its territory and natural resources, with forms of regional and ethnic self-determination, with meaningful national political representation for popular movements or with true majority rule? Whatever the future brings, there will be no return to the neoliberal status ante. The current conjuncture in Bolivia is marked by seasoned political skepticism, yet also measured hope, and has helped galvanize other struggles in the Andes and Latin America more broadly. As indigenous insurgents of previous centuries proclaimed in moments of anti-colonial and autonomist insurrection: *"Ya es otro tiempo el presente"* ("The present is a new time").

ABOUT THE AUTHOR

Forrest Hylton is a PhD candidate in history at New York University and author of *An Evil Hour: Colombia in Historical Context* (Verso, forthcoming). Sinclair Thomson teaches Latin American history at NYU and is the author of *We Alone Will Rule: Native Andean Politics in the Age of Insurgency* (University of Wisconsin, 2002). They are coeditors of *Ya es otro tiempo el presente: Cuatro momentos de insurgencia indígena* (Muela del Diablo, 2003).

NOTES

1. See Silvia Rivera Cusicanqui, "Aymara Past, Aymara Future," *NACLA Report on the Americas*, Vol. 25, No. 3, December 1991, pp. 18–23; and Rivera's article in this volume.
2. See René Zavaleta Mercado, *Las masas en noviembre* (La Paz: Juventud, 1983), *Lo nacional-popular en Bolivia* (Mexico: Siglo XXI, 1986); and Luis Tapia's, *La producción del conocimiento local: historia y política en la obra de René Zavaleta* (La Paz: Muela del Diablo, 2002).
3. See Rivera, this volume; Forrest Hylton, Felix Patzi, Sergio Serulnikov, and Sinclair Thomson, *Ya es otro tiempo el presente. Cuatro momentos de insurgencia indígena* (La Paz: Muela del Diablo, 2003).

Silvia Rivera Cusicanqui

The Roots of the Rebellion: Reclaiming the Nation

The U.S. government allows the Bolivian government only the minimal amount of wiggle room required to keep the masses at bay: a shred of maneuverability to neutralize the demands of the indigenous and working population. But Washington's serious miscalculations created an explosive situation in which the government in La Paz is hostage to contradictory policies that the country's social movements constantly challenge. The result is an unprecedented crisis of the Bolivian state, which has effectively lost its legitimacy and territorial control. Consequently, political spaces have emerged that are organized, maintained and occupied outside the dominant state system.[1] Indeed, since 2000 indigenous and popular uprisings have completely changed the face of Bolivia's political system.

The crisis of the state in Bolivia has actually been incubating for quite some time, but it only received international attention with the uprisings of February and October 2003, or perhaps earlier with the "water war" of Cochabamba in April 2000. After decades of invisibility and silence, our country again astonished the world with the vigor and radical nature of its popular mobilizations, which were surely seen from abroad as spasmodic, irrational convulsions, product of an accumulated, latent discontent.[2] In reality, however, they were remarkably coherent expressions of a collective consciousness with deep historical roots, announcing an alternative vision for Bolivian society. Bolivians have periodically asserted similar alternate national visions in the past at critical junctures when the exclusionary state has fallen into crisis.

Indeed, there are strong threads connecting recent episodes of social mobilization to the period of social turbulence that produced the "State of 1952". Many of the same social actors, propelled by the same history, traditions and grievances, have arisen again now, and their upsurge stems in large part from the deterioration and collapse of the unstable social pact established through the Revolution of 1952.

The political configuration known as the "State of '52" defused and contained the radical momentum of the 1952 national revolution, a popular insurrection that threatened to overturn the then-reigning social order. Despite introducing important structural changes that produced substantial social gains—universal suffrage, greater labor rights, nationalization of the mining industry, agrarian reform—the State of '52 inaugurated an enduring system of control and cooptation that long forestalled the renewal of independent political action by the popular and indigenous masses. Many Bolivians have subtly resisted or subverted the precepts of this system; on occasion, oppositional movements have challenged it directly. But until the recent crisis, this system of governance had managed to precariously sustain itself and keep a lid on challenges from below. But no longer: the stopgap State of '52 has crumbled, and today's popular-indigenous movements are resuming the unfinished insurrections of the past.

The post-1952 state system was first destabilized somewhat in the mid-1960s by union militancy in the mining sector, but various military governments salvaged it through the so-called "Military-Campesino Pact." The pact was used by the regime of Gen. René Barrientos (1964–69) to turn campesino unions against the radical autonomous miners' unions. During this time the state subordinated indigenous-campesino organizations to its own authoritarian and clientelistic apparatus, manipulating these organizations as instruments to quell the miners' activism.[3]

The crisis of the state began in earnest in 1974 during the dictatorship of Gen. Hugo Bánzer with the massacre of unarmed campesinos at a demonstration in Cochabamba. The "Massacre of Tolata" left 80 dead and hundreds injured. The legitimacy of the state eroded and an oppositional indigenous movement arose. This movement articulated indigenous-campesino unionism with an ideology inspired by the anti-colonial uprisings of the eighteenth century, especially the 1780–81 rebellion led by Túpaj Katari and Bartolina Sisa. This "Katarista-Indianista" reawakening among the indigenous-campesino unions of the *altiplano* (highland plateau) and the Aymara-Quechua valleys resulted in the founding of the independent Confederation of Bolivian Campesino Workers (CSUTCB) and several indigenous political parties. This reemergence of a popular, indigenous-based political and ideological countercurrent to the state anticipated and informed today's movements.

The subsequent tumultuous era of dictatorships and brief democratic interludes (1978–82) gave way, finally, to a period of representative democracy monopolized by traditional parties of both the right and the left. These parties entered into alliances among themselves to reaffirm control of the state apparatus by a minority of Creole Spanish background.

Under this arrangement, the legitimacy of the political order continued to dissolve. And the deep contradictions of Bolivian "democracy" became more and more apparent and increasingly subject to challenge. Bolivia's representative democratic system is characterized by a rampant clientelism that creates an insidious façade of mass participation while reinforcing colonial mechanisms of exclusion and fragmentation. The system is dominated by a racist elite culture that renounces and denies the discourse of the popular and indigenous multitudes, which ultimately express themselves most forcefully through collective action. Already during the early 1980s, their strikes, mass mobilizations and marches became increasingly confrontational, testifying to the exclusionary nature of formal democracy. Bolivian democracy, as it currently exists, is incapable of processing indigenous and popular demands unless forced to do so by insurgent action.

The crisis of the state reached a critical point with the policies of structural adjustment introduced in 1985, and the commencement in 1988 of the militarized campaign to eradicate coca. Structural adjustment measures privatized state enterprises; deregulated markets, salaries and prices; eroded the negotiating power of unions; and dismantled traditional agriculture. All of which created unprecedented migratory waves to cities and centers of industrial agriculture. The few legitimizing vestiges of the State of '52—high public employment, a degree of labor protection (albeit through controlled unions), a measure of economic sovereignty, partial protection for domestic industry and agricultural producers—were wiped away almost in a single stroke. The U.S.-directed "War on Drugs" represented a further ceding of sovereignty to the colonial masters of the North. Not only is coca a valued cultural asset, but it also constitutes one of the few viable economic pursuits remaining to many Bolivians.

Urban and rural indigenous movements created their own strategies of resistance to these processes. Their strategies were not only anchored in the memory of the anti-colonial battles of the past, but also in the more "recent memory" of their incorporation to the political arena with the Revolution of 1952, which extended a de facto citizenship to sectors previously excluded and negated. This citizenship, however, came at a cost: the westernization of their practices of representation and way of life. In this sense, the political and economic system created a precarious hegemonic model of a *mestizo* citizen: a consumer and producer of merchandise, a speaker of Spanish and an aspirant to a western ideal of civilization.

Nevertheless, behind this veneer of seeming conformity, indigenous communities and their unions expressed their own identity and demands to mold hope for an "other" democracy: one that speaks Quechua or Aymara and that is communitarian and participatory (*asambleísta*). This is the form of democracy that was activated in full force during the road blockades of 2000–03, and on a regional scale with sector-specific demands during the water war and during mobilizations against coca eradication and against the marginalization of the indigenous population more generally.

It would be wrong to perceive these incidents of resistance as lacking in overriding collective vision or will. Behind these regional mobilizations are nodes of popular action: the *altiplano* of La Paz and Oruro, and the coca-growing regions of Cochabamba and the Yungas. These nodes, as Aymara sociologist Pablo Mamani Ramirez has shown, have generated a set of repertoires for common action that reveal a functioning collective memory as indigenous people, rather than fragmented regions or communities.[4] The conscious, political use of shared symbols of indigenous identity, like the *wiphala*—the rainbow-checkered Aymara flag—and the coca leaf, exemplify this. Like the Katarista-Indianista mobilizations of the 1970s and 1980s, today's social actors articulate indigenous-campesino demands with dimensions of ethnicity, citizenship and anti-colonialism towards the state.

The modalities of contemporary struggle also differ from past, more corporatist forms. Various present day movements are no longer simply making demands of the state; they are entering the state arena directly. Both the CSUTCB and the *cocalero* movement have shifted their emphasis from advocacy and unionism to political action. The *cocalero* movement catapulted itself into national politics in the elections of 1997 when it put four congressional deputies in the lower house of the Bolivian Congress. In the following municipal elections, leaders who reached prominence through the *cocalero* unions won five municipalities in the Chapare, while dozens of leaders throughout the country began entering municipal politics by way of popular and union organizations.

With this groundwork laid, the elections of 2002 brought a fundamental rupture in the caste-based, restricted democracy that was beginning to actively reconstitute itself after the cooptation of indigenous demands in the 1980s. With more than half a million votes and a third of all parliamentary seats, the Movement Towards Socialism (MAS, the new *cocalero*-based party), became the country's second most important political force. Although it was favored in the departments of La Paz and Cochabamba, its success did not only stem from *cocalero* support. It was also the preferred party in the departments of Oruro and Potosí, which do not produce coca. For its part, the Indian Pachakuti Movement (MIP), lead by militant Aymara leader and CSUTCB head Felipe Quispe, won six seats—more than were won by some of the traditional parties.

Such a drastic political change had been unthinkable in 1985 when the Democratic Popular Unity (UDP), a center-left coalition of Creole parties, ended its administration by giving way to the policies of structural adjustment and other doomed reforms. That a majority indigenous electorate would place its confidence in "one of their own"—the first language of both Morales and Quispe is Aymara—instead of a suit and tie from the "gentry" was completely unforeseen. After decades of disciplined clientelism, it became clear that the electorate was no longer a submissive flock without political free will. This, too, revealed the post-1952 system of state control to be decidedly moribund. In the end, the system's ability to absorb demands or neutralize frustrations was proven tremendously limited by the lack of foresight of the political class, which, as historian Sergio Almaráz described it, "felt itself the owner of a country it despised."[5]

A nationwide pattern of exhausted clientelism determined that the mobilizations of the new millennium would be articulated from below, and would no longer obey commands from above. Indeed, party politics in Bolivia—even the most radical—have proven incapable of articulating or representing the most essential broad-based collective demands. No matter how well crafted, parties usually succumb to suicidal factionalisms or are simply incapable of integrating the myriad struggles of Bolivia's diverse social actors. With their innumerable rural-urban networks, Bolivia's social actors are capable of sustaining denser and more democratic structures of collective political action with a richness and diversity not easily contained within a party structure. That is why it is so extraordinary that these diverse networks, each with its own perspective and particular social demands, are able to converge on common platforms of vast national reach, outside of the political party system.

During the water war (February–April 2000), the prolonged war on coca (since 1988, with a peak during January 2003) and the gas war (September–October 2003, May–June 2005), demands were no longer union-specific, nor did they include requests for inclusion into the political system, as were typically made by the Katarista mobilizations of the 1980s. In fact, the indigenous majority is already in de facto possession of the public space in which public opinion is formed on issues of concern to all Bolivians: sovereignty, natural resources, militarization and economic policy.

And the combative resiliency of the Aymara, Quechua and

lowland indigenous peoples is proof that the long arm of the Empire has not definitively triumphed. This tenacity is all the more admirable considering the onslaught of "modernization," a falsehood that has only created poverty and truncated processes of political and productive autonomy in vast expanses of the Bolivian territory. But Bolivia's indigenous have clung to the root of their power: the simple fact of being the occupants of a space for thousands of years, of naming it and converting it into a cultural and productive space through the force of their own fiestas, communal work, cultural resourcefulness and autochthonous technology.

Today these histories explode with a fury accumulated over centuries. The colonial plunder of its riches, the squandering of the creative and productive energies of its people and the consignment to indigence of those responsible for creating its wealth, have relegated Bolivia to the status of colonial backwater. The so-called War on Drugs being directed from Washington has the same effect. It seeks to liquidate the coca leaf, one of the first forms of modern indigenous merchandise and a pillar of the internal market. The coca leaf is not only fundamental to indigenous identity and to a vast set of cultural practices, but it also forms part of an indigenous modernity rooted in the past, comprising what Indian historian Partha Chatterjee would call "Our modernity."[6]

Bolivia's converging popular networks have launched the struggle for "Our modernity," a modernity based on organically structured internal markets; one that combines market relations with traditional practices of reciprocity; and one that is founded on this emergent indigenous citizenship that continues to conquer political and economic spaces. This modernity offers its own "other" form of democracy, drawing on practices and values of the indigenous past, and it conceives of Bolivia as a holistic territorial unit that is the birthright of the productive communities that occupy it—from the topsoil down to the resources beneath.

The era of state crisis that began in the 1970s, or perhaps even before in the 1950s, seems to have reached its definitive climax. Liberal promises made by the Revolution of 1952— citizenship for women and the indigenous, economic sovereignty, the domestic production of basic goods—have been rift by fissures or exposed as fallacies. This utter failure has denuded the internal colonial structures of the Bolivian state, and laid bare its acquiescence to new forms of external colonial domination. Unveiling this was precisely what the Katarista-Indianista mobilizations of the 1970s did for the first time in the post-1952 era. The indigenous mobilizations of the new millennium, whose demands and projects are permeated by the same majority consciousness of that earlier movement, have only reaffirmed this bankruptcy of the state.

Structural adjustment policies and the dismantling of the country's productive and industrial base were only the culminating factors that brought this long-developing crisis to its breaking point. They strained the existing cracks and contradictions in Bolivian society until the whole flawed structure shattered into an outburst of general questioning. Now Bolivia's masses are demanding an inclusive and pluralistic renovation of the country, where to govern is not merely to "administer Indians" or to serve as a transmitter for decisions made in the North.[7] Instead, the indigenous majorities of the country are demanding that power be returned to them, breaking the centuries-old monopoly of the oligarchs, who mistakenly believe they inherited the country as if it were a feudal hacienda.

ABOUT THE AUTHOR

Aymara sociologist Silvia Rivera Cusicanqui is professor emeritus at the

Universidad Mayor de San Andrés in La Paz. She is a founding member of the Andean Oral History Workshop (THOA) and the author of several books. Translated from the Spanish by Teo Ballvé.

NOTES

1. See Pablo Mamani Ramírez, *El rugir de las multitudes. La fuerza de los levantamientos indígenas en Bolivia-Qullasuyu* (La Paz: Aruwiyiri y Yachaywasi, 2004). Also, Félix Patzi Paco, *Sistema comunal. Una propuesta alternativa al sistema liberal* (La Paz: Comunidad de Estudios Alternativos, 2004).
2. Edward P. Thompson, "La economía 'moral' de la multitud en la Inglaterra del siglo XVII," in *Tradición, revuelta y conciencia de clase: Estudios sobre la crisis de la sociedad pre-industrial* (Barcelona: Crítica, 1979), pp. 62–134.
3. Silvia Rivera Cusicanqui, *Oppressed but not Defeated. Peasant Struggles among the Aymara and Quechua in Bolivia, 1900–1980* (Geneva: United Nations Research Institute for Social Development, 1987).
4. See Mamani Ramírez, *El rugir de las multitudes*.
5. Sergio Almaráz, *Réquiem para una república* (La Paz: Universidad Mayor de San Andrés, 1969).
6. Partha Chatterjee, *Our Modernity* (Rotterdam and Senegal: SEPHIS-CODESRIA, 1997).
7. Eduardo L. Nina Qhispi, *De los títulos de composición de la corona de España. Composición a título de usufructo como se entiende la excención revisitaria. Venta y composición de tierras de orígen con la corona de España. Títulos de las comunidades de la república. Renovación de Bolivia. Años 1536, 1617, 1777, 1825 y 1925*. La Paz, ed.

Chris Jochnick and Paulina Garzón

A Seat at the Table

In the fall of 1997, a tiny indigenous community deep in Ecuador's Amazonian interior was engaged in fierce negotiations with a team of environmentalists posing as oil executives. The "oil men" were eager to sign an agreement that would allow them access to indigenous lands and were willing to offer almost anything the community desired: a short-wave radio, motors for their canoes, solar panels, a health clinic. With hundreds of millions of dollars at stake, the negotiators could afford to be generous. But the indigenous leaders—all of them teenage boys—were skeptical: They complained about potential harms, and insisted on more time, more information and more access to lawyers. The elders in the back of the room could not understand the Spanish, but they were clearly agitated by the rising emotions and tension.

Suddenly, commotion erupted just outside the hut as three real oil workers arrived by chance. The environmentalists watched in dismay as the teenagers ran outside to greet the visitors, eager for information about possible jobs and gifts. On this day, concerns about oil development, so evident in the mock negotiations, were little match for the real material promises of this wealthy industry. It would take more than technical training to overcome the vast economic, social and cultural factors working against these marginalized communities threatened—and tempted—by oil.

The petroleum industry, perhaps more than any other, has long been surrounded by conflict and protest. Local communities have played an increasingly important role in these protests and have forced significant changes on the industry. Once dispatched as meddlesome provocateurs, the affected communities are now often considered essential "partners" in oil projects. Ecuador is one of the smallest oil-producing countries, but its conflicts are a case in point. In particular, the Ecuadoran experience highlights new forms of activism provoked by oil, and shows how that activism has forced change upon the government and industry. Ecuador's experience also illustrates the tensions and struggles within the rapidly expanding field of corporate responsibility.[1]

Ecuador shares problems common to all oil-producing countries in the South: high levels of government corruption, social inequality, poverty, external debt and political instability. It also suffers from a weak judiciary, growing ethnic and regional tensions, and an authoritarian government with an active military role. In early 2000, indigenous groups and sympathetic members of the military overthrew the government—ushering in Ecuador's sixth president in a tumultuous five-year period. An expanding narco-military conflict along the Colombia-Ecuador border, fueled by the U.S. counterinsurgency/"drug war" military package "Plan Colombia," has only aggravated social and political turmoil.

Ecuador's "oil boom" has brought billions of dollars into the country, accounting for roughly half of the national budget since the early 1980s. However, the lack of effective government control has allowed a tiny group of elites and foreign companies to capture the benefits, while leaving the most vulnerable populations to shoulder the burden. The oil boom has tended to exacerbate economic dependency, structural inequities and political instability that date to the country's colonial past. The statistics are telling: Before oil development, the country had a negligible foreign debt of $200 million, a poverty rate below 50%, unemployment and under-employment of 15%; meanwhile, the poorest 20% of the population controlled 6.7% of the country's resources. In 2002, after 30 years of oil production, with an estimated half of the country's reserves depleted, Ecuador per capita was the most highly indebted country in Latin America. The poverty rate was over 67%, under-employment and joblessness ran at 65%, and the poorest fifth of the population controlled only about 2% of the country's wealth. The precise role of oil in these grim statistics is impossible to measure, but its influence has been overwhelming in skewing resources, corrupting politics and creating enormous dependency on a volatile industry.

Ecuador's oil boom began in 1967 when Texaco discovered oil in the eastern Amazon region (the "Oriente"). The Oriente covers 32 million acres of pristine rainforest considered one of the most biologically diverse areas on earth. It is also home to eight distinct indigenous groups with a total population of 100,000, as well as 250,000 recent immigrants. The oil industry has focused on the northern part of the Oriente, where it has had devastating impacts on local communities and their environment. Socioeconomic conditions within this region have been described by the World Bank as "calamitous," with poverty rates close to 90% and little or no basic infrastructure— sanitation, potable water, or paved roads.

Oil development in Ecuador—particularly relations between the industry, government and local communities—has gone through three overlapping stages: an initial period of widespread neglect by the state and abuses by the industry; a second one of conflict, organizing and protest; and a third era of dialogue. At the time of Texaco's discovery, the Amazon was a largely neglected frontier that supported indigenous peoples, church missionaries and a dwindling cacao industry. Few indigenous groups had legal title to their lands, and they were almost completely ignored by the state, which hardly considered them citizens. The Ecuadoran government had neither the resources nor experience to develop oil and instead allowed Texaco to exploit the region as it saw fit. The military quickly assumed a share of national oil revenues, and its presence in the Amazon, where tensions with Peru ran high, became intermingled with the task of providing security and support to the oil industry.

Texaco built a vast network of roads into the rainforest, and a pipeline running the length of the country, as well as refineries and hundreds of wells. The government encouraged colonization of the Amazon to relieve internal land pressures, offering legal title to any person who cleared and planted crops in the jungle.

Texaco's unrestrained development and the colonization rush were devastating for local communities, causing widespread deforestation, loss of land and wildlife, cultural disintegration, disease and a host of new social problems, including alcoholism and prostitution. Traditional indigenous groups like the Cofan, the Secoyas and the Huaorani, once numbering in the tens of thousands, were reduced to a few hundred each, and the Tetetes disappeared completely. To save costs, Texaco dumped its toxic wastes directly into the environment—an estimated four million gallons a day—causing massive contamination of land and rivers and an array of health problems among local communities, including increased rates of cancer. Texaco paid little heed to these communities, at best compensating them at the company's discretion for specific property losses.

The 1980s brought rising concerns about oil development, alongside community organizing and protests. Much of the interest in oil was sparked by the government's decision in 1985 to license millions of acres of new Amazon territories to private companies. The impacts of Texaco's operations were just beginning to reach a national audience, and newly organized indigenous groups joined with environmentalists to oppose further exploration and development, particularly in indigenous territories and national environmental preserves.

The Confederation of Indigenous Nationalities of the Ecuadoran Amazon (CONFENAIE), established in 1980, was a critical force in helping organize smaller indigenous groups to obtain land titles and build opposition to oil development. At the turn of the decade, CONFENAIE pressed the government to undertake a first-of-its-kind impact study of oil operations, and protested the World Bank's role in promoting oil development. CONFENAIE joined with the other major indigenous organization, Ecuarunari, representing the central region of the country, to form the Confederation of Indigenous Nationalities of Ecuador (CONAIE), a national indigenous organization that has since become a critical political and social force.

Environmental groups with a traditionally conservationist focus began to work more closely with communities in the Amazon to strengthen campaigns for sustainable development. This coming together at the local level was mirrored and supported by an international initiative between Northern NGOs and indigenous federations in the nine Amazon countries, who established the Amazon Alliance in the early 1990s. The natural target of these initial efforts was Texaco, the company responsible for the infrastructure and 90% of all oil produced in the 1970s and 1980s. A local NGO, Acción Ecológica, led protests aimed to raise awareness about environmental and social harms, to block further development and to ensure clean up and compensation. The actions included demonstrations, marches, takeovers of government offices, shareholder protests with U.S. NGOs, media campaigns and meetings with a range of government and industry officials. Texaco refused to be moved by the demonstrations and negative press, and assumed some responsibility for clean-up only under pressure from a later lawsuit.

In the early 1990s, meanwhile, the U.S. oil company Conoco was negotiating exploration rights to a block of rainforest that included one of the most valuable national parks and was home to the Huaorani, an indigenous group hardly touched by Western contact. The project provided a new focal point for protests, joining CONFENAIE and local environmentalists. These groups targeted not only the company, but also the U.S. NGO, Natural Resources Defense Council (NRDC), which was trying to broker an innovative scheme that would impose stricter environmental and social policies on oil drilling activities. At the international level, the Sierra Club Legal Defense Fund (now Earthjustice) filed a petition with the Organization of American States (OAS) on behalf of the indigenous communities, and Rainforest Action Network campaigned in the international media to raise awareness about the conflict. The pressure drove Conoco (and NRDC) out of the country, and provided one of the first concrete (though short-lived) victories for activists.

In 1993, U.S. lawyers filed a ground-breaking suit against Texaco in U.S. federal courts on behalf of some 30,000 Ecuadoran plaintiffs. Accompanying the lawsuit, a U.S. NGO, the Center for Economic and Social Rights (CESR), undertook water testing with a team from Harvard University, and compiled a report providing scientific proof of the contamination and evidence of widespread human rights violations. The lawsuit, scientific data and human rights report attracted national and international media coverage and sparked a wave of organizing in the Amazon, particularly among non-indigenous communities who had come to represent a majority of the Amazon population. The Amazon Defense Front, which grew up around the Texaco lawsuit, now comprises 26 communities with 10,000 people, and provides the most active regional voice against irresponsible development.

The protests had a tangible impact on the Ecuadoran government. The Congress initiated hearings and an investigation of Texaco, and threatened to impeach several government ministers because of their role in oil industry abuses. In 1994, under pressure from Congress and NGOs, the Minister of Energy and Mines organized an unprecedented trip of oil executives, indigenous leaders and environmental activists to witness the damage done to the Amazon. At the first site, a clearly surprised minister waded into the oil wastes and publicly lambasted the Texaco representative. The government followed with new environmental regulations and regular meetings with indigenous groups and NGOs. These steps had little practical impact, but they were evidence of the growing influence of civil society protests.

For their part, oil companies took pains to distinguish themselves from Texaco and began touting their commitment to the environment and communities. As a result, a new company ethic emerged that replaced Texaco's neglect with an equally questionable paternalism. In the absence of public resources and state intervention, private companies were implicitly or explicitly charged with providing for the local population. The short-sighted practice of offering gifts and small projects created a so-called "worship of begging" described by one anthropologist: "If an oil base is situated in the traditional hunting grounds of the population, it is treated like a new tree [with] large quantities of food that legitimately belong to the local population" and which "has to be harvested quickly and completely, like the fruit that goes bad after a few days."[2] Laments one indigenous leader: "The people are always thinking about how to take immediate advantage of the relation with the company, without thinking about environmental impacts or long-term development. . . . The idea imposed by the company is that everything comes down to money. Sucres [the local currency] begin to appear in the mind, and the whole world thinks about how to collect indemnification."[3]

The tremendous leverage exercised by the industry over impoverished communities often succeeded in quelling protests and frequently divided and even corrupted local leaders. In one of the more brazen examples of this dynamic, Texaco undermined indigenous protests against the company shortly after the lawsuit was launched, by offering certain communities $1 million in "compensation." Texaco also funded a phony environmental company run by indigenous leaders who used the money to finance their successful congressional bids, putting Texaco in probable violation of the U.S. Foreign Corrupt Practices Act and removing these leaders and their organizations from the protest movement.[4]

A third stage in Ecuador's oil development now prevails, characterized by dialogue and negotiations. Companies chastened by the protests and wary of provoking local communities (some of whom had taken to kidnappings and sabotage), have sought to build more lasting good will.[5] At the same time, the economic and social pressure mounted by the industry, the government, and to a smaller extent the military, have undermined most attempts to resist oil, and communities have widely opted for dialogue with the companies. Over the course of a decade, negotiations and agreements between companies and indigenous groups have evolved from a limited focus on short-term benefits to addressing company operations, long-term development and the actual process of negotiations.

A growing awareness of and support for indigenous rights has provided an important backdrop to these agreements. An OAS human rights mission visited the Amazon in 1997 and issued a report strongly critical of the government and oil industry. A new Constitution in 1998 and the ratification of an international treaty protecting indigenous rights greatly strengthened community rights to consultation and participation in development as well as environmental, land and social rights.[6] While the state retains control over all subsurface minerals and the judiciary remains extremely weak, awareness of community rights has played a role in mobilizing protests and strengthening negotiations.

Many of the early agreements were mere formalities intended to provide cover for oil operations. Companies pushed these agreements through with material promises on the one hand and legal, political and even military pressure on the other. Communities had little understanding about the oil industry or likely impacts, no outside support and certainly no experience with Western-style agreements or negotiations. Additionally, it was most often the young males who represented the communities, as they spoke Spanish and had the most contact with the outside world. These young "leaders" were more likely to be swayed by the promise of Western-style development and goods than were community elders and women.

Early agreements between Occidental Petroleum and the tiny Secoya community provide a case in point. The Secoyas are an isolated group of approximately 300 members living according to their traditions and entirely dependent upon the rainforest. An independent consultant hired by Occidental to measure potential impacts on the Secoyas warned that development would be culturally and socially devastating, and recommended that it not be undertaken in their traditional lands.[7]

Notwithstanding that report, in 1996, Occidental representatives with military escort pressured community leaders to sign an agreement giving the company multi-year access to Secoya lands in return for solar panels, water pumps and medical kits.

According to leaders of the Secoya Indigenous Organization of Ecuador (OISE) who signed the agreement, the community had no information about the company's plans or likely impacts, no outside advisors, no time to consider the issue and were threatened with expropriation of their lands by the military official accompanying the oil representatives.

After discussing the agreement with NGOs, OISE formally rejected it as unfair. Occidental then flew the leaders to a luxury hotel on the Ecuadoran coast, where they signed another agreement that merely modified some of the material benefits for the community. Occidental officials justified the agreements and process by noting that the community drew up the list of benefits, the company had provided general information about their plans, and the community had no need for outside advisors.

Similar negotiations were conducted between Maxus (successors to Conoco) and the Huaorani, and were actively promoted by Ecuador's president following the Conoco scandal. Maxus funded a Huaorani organization, then negotiated a number of projects and material benefits with the organization in exchange for access to their territories. At the official signing of the agreement, the President's daughter was caught on tape comparing Ecuadoran and U.S. approaches to pacifying indigenous communities with "trinkets and beads."

Some companies recognized that superficial agreements like these would provide little protection against future conflict and public criticism. In 1994, the Organization of Indigenous Peoples of Pastaza (OPIP), assisted by Oxfam America, negotiated an agreement with Arco Petroleum that included a number of novel provisions, including local participation in the environmental impact study as well as an environmental management plan for the region, and sharing benefits from oil production in order to finance projects under the management plan. The follow-up has been mixed: OPIP succeeded in establishing a technical team and taking part in the environmental impact study and environmental management plan, but Arco failed to provide funds for the expected projects and has created divisions in the community by funding a new organization and hiring irresponsible subcontractors.

After three superficial and short-lived agreements between Occidental and the Secoyas, the latter proposed a code of conduct to govern all future dialogue between the community and the company. With the assistance of CDES, the Quito-offshoot of CESR (with the same name in Spanish), the Secoyas negotiated a code that provides an array of rights, including information, consultation, collective negotiations, advisors, arbitration and resources to prepare the community for dialogue. The code is notable for having included a statement from the oil company promising to respect international human rights treaties and the constitutional rights of the community, and for its focus on the process and conditions of dialogue—including resources, mediators and transparency.

Another indigenous organization succeeded in enforcing the principle of "collective bargaining" through a lawsuit. In 1999, the Shuar Federation (FIPSE) brought an unprecedented injunction against Arco, challenging the oil industry's traditional divide-and-rule tactics. Arco had discovered that they could more easily enter Shuar territory by ignoring FIPSE and negotiating agreements with individual families and leaders. The local court decision (later ratified by the Supreme Court) held that this practice violated the communities' right to cultural integrity and prohibited the company from negotiating with anyone outside the elected and representative body.

While dialogue increasingly prevails in Ecuador, it is not the only option. A number of groups continue to seek a halt to oil development at least in parts of the Amazon. One of the more successful efforts involves the Achuar, who have established a thriving eco-tourism business and are pursuing different forms of sustainable development, while holding oil companies at bay. Two years ago, a larger-scale NGO-indigenous campaign supported by the Catholic Church pushed the government to designate 2.5 million acres of Amazon lands as "off limits" to industrial development. One area was inhabited by an "uncontacted" indigenous population, and the other was considered particularly fragile from an environmental perspective. While the territories cover less than 10% of the Oriente, they set an important precedent both nationally and regionally.

Along similar lines, CDES and CONAIE have promoted an ambitious "debt-for-Amazon" swap based on the fact that Ecuador and its public creditors have far more to gain from preserving the rest of the nation's rainforest as a global environmental asset than from continuing oil development. Ecuador's external debt drives the frenetic search for oil, and the interest on the debt alone consumes almost all oil revenues. In 2000, the government adopted the proposal as part of its negotiating position with public creditors through the Paris Club, and now there is hope for smaller-scale swaps with individual creditor countries. The Achuar have drawn up one such proposal, which would include carbon trading rights to offset lost oil earnings.

Despite these alternatives, the rush to development and dialogue continues, spurred by an international movement to overcome community and NGO hostility to multinational corporations. Through multi-stakeholder initiatives like the Voluntary Principles on Security and Human Rights, environmental and human rights groups are lining up to work with yesterday's corporate villains. Northern governments are strong proponents of such collaboration; as one U.S. State Department official explains: "There is no arena in which corporate conduct and human rights have come under a harsher spotlight than in the extractive industries of oil and mining, in part because of their massive impact on the communities and countries where they operate. . . . These are problems for U.S. foreign policy."[8]

The World Bank and Latin American Organization of Energy have stepped into this fray with an ambitious set of initiatives aimed at promoting community-oil industry negotiations throughout South America. These two institutions, in partnership with the Confederation of Amazonian Indigenous Peoples (representing indigenous organizations from the nine Amazon countries) and the Weatherhead Center for International Affairs at Harvard, have undertaken a series of trainings for indigenous leaders. And the Bank is currently funding efforts in countries like Ecuador and Bolivia to establish national regulations for community consultation and negotiations.

Two important issues are often lost in the single-minded focus on dialogue and conflict resolution. First, hurdles to "fair" negotiations are almost insurmountable, given the vast power and resource imbalances between the Goliath multinational corporations and the marginalized and impoverished Amazon communities. Good faith on the part of companies will never be enough. Fair negotiations and real guarantees relating to environmental, social and cultural impacts are next to impossible without the more active and progressive intervention of the state and civil society. New laws and technical training for indigenous leaders are a step in the right direction, but they must be supported by public oversight and continued activism by others.

Second, even assuming a perfect process, dialogue aimed at facilitating oil development inherently raises larger national and global questions. The most progressive treaties, laws and codes have never contemplated the communities' right to refuse oil in their territories, and negotiations always presume that development will take place. Beyond the immediate environmental, social and cultural impacts dealt with in some of the more promising agreements, oil development, in and of itself, is in many areas a questionable pursuit. Countries like Ecuador are ill-suited to take advantage of the short-term wealth generated by oil. Instead, the industry has fomented corruption, inequality and political instability, caused irrevocable damages to priceless rainforest and discouraged the pursuit of more sustainable development paths. By channeling concerns into a narrow set of issues, dialogue risks obscuring the costs of oil development at the national level, and—as in the case of global warming—at the international level as well.

Amazon communities and NGOs have thus made important gains in challenging industry practices in Ecuador, but they still face daunting odds. As oil expands deeper into the rainforest, the increasing attention to corporate responsibility and dialogue bring new opportunities and risk. If communities and NGOs can somehow take advantage of these opportunities without losing their vigilant and activist edge, there may still be hope for finding a sustainable compromise. Ecuador is on the frontlines of these changing dynamics, and its fate will foretell the destiny of conflicts throughout South America.

ABOUT THE AUTHORS

Chris Jochnick is Legal Director, Centro de Derechos Económicos y Sociales (Quito), co-founder of the Center for Economic and Social Rights, and former editor in chief of the Harvard Human Rights Journal. Paulina Garzón, executive director of Centro de Derechos Económicos y Sociales, has organized over 50 workshops in the Amazon and led various campaigns around oil and human rights.

NOTES

1. For additional information about oil and indigenous protests in Eduador, see Natalie Wray, *Pueblos Indígenas Amazónicos y Actividad Petrolera en el Ecuador* (Quito: Oxfam/IBIS, 2000); Judy Kimmerling, *Amazon Crude* (New York: NRDC, 1991); Joseph Kane, *Savages* (New York: Knopf, 1995).
2. Laura Rival, "Huaorani y Petroleo" in Giovanni Tassi (ed.), *Naufragos del Mar Verde: La resistencia de los Huaorani a una integración impuesta* (Abya Yala/Confenaie, 1992) cited in Natalie Wray, p. 96.
3. Interview with Johnson Cerda, cited in Natalie Wray, p. 86.
4. The Act prohibits the payment of money to "any person while knowing that all or a portion of such money . . . will be offered . . . to any candidate for foreign political office, for purposes of . . . influencing any act or decision of such foreign official." (15 USCS 78dd-1(a)(3), 1998).
5. As the editor of one trade journal comments: "How the petroleum industry is perceived by the various publics and governments in the way it conducts its operations may well decide its future. There is already a battle for the hearts and minds of these stakeholders under way with groups whose agenda often is decidedly hostile to the industry. The front line of the battle is now in South America's rainforest, and even those companies without an investment in that region cannot afford to ignore the outcome." Bob Williams, Managing Editor-News, "Foreign Petroleum Companies Developing New Paradigm for Operating in Rain Forest Region," *Oil and Gas Journal*, Vol. 95, No. 16 (April 2, 1997).
6. Convention Concerning Indigenous and Tribal Peoples in Independent Countries (International Labor Organization Convention #169).
7. Andy Drumm, "Evaluación de Impactos Socioeconómicos y Culturales de la Siguente Fase de Exploración Sísmica en el Bloque 15." Unpublished study done for Walsh Environmental Scientists and Engineers, Inc., (1997).
8. Bennet Freeman, Deputy Assistant Secretary for State Bureau of Democracy, Human Rights and Labor, U.S. Department of State. Speech given at Conference on Corporate Citizenship, Royal Institute of International Affairs, London, England (November 8, 1999).

Jennifer N. Collins

A Sense of Possibility: Ecuador's Indigenous Movement Takes Center Stage

At about 9:45 on the morning of January 21, 2000, a thousand protesters, mostly indigenous people from the Ecuadoran highlands, burst through a military cordon and rushed the National Congress building. The soldiers who had placed large spirals of barbed wire fencing around the Congress the day before to protect it from the demonstrators had stepped aside, indicating that a faction of the military had shifted support from the government of Jamil Mahuad to the indigenous protesters. Wooden planks were placed over the barbed wire, and one by one the demonstrators scurried over these makeshift bridges to occupy one of the central seats of power in their crisis-ridden country. By mid-morning a large *huipala*, the rainbow-colored flag of the indigenous movement, could be seen hanging from the roof of the eight-story building as defiant protesters stood out in stark silhouette against the bright blue Quito skyline.[1]

As the protesters proceeded to install themselves in the Congress and inaugurate their own National Parliament of the Peoples of Ecuador, about 200 army officials, led by a high-ranking army colonel, filed through the middle of the euphoric gathering and officially threw their support in with the movement. A short time later, a three-member Junta of National Salvation was declared, composed of Army Colonel Lucio Gutiérrez, the president of the Confederation of Indigenous Nationalities of Ecuador (CONAIE), Antonio Vargas, and a former supreme court judge from the coastal region, Carlos Solórzano. As the morning wore on, other officers and their subordinates continued to arrive to demonstrate their support for this self-declared new government.

The rebellious army colonels and their new indigenous movement allies argued that these radical measures were necessary to put an end to corruption, which was seen as permeating all Ecuadoran political institutions and as the underlying cause of the very severe economic depression that the country was experiencing at the time.[2] In the words of one of the colonels: "We are here so that they [the corrupt politicians] don't pillage this country."[3] Addressing "all the people of Ecuador," Vargas, an Amazonian Quichua and second-term president of CONAIE, enthusiastically declared: "The people are now in power and we are going to triumph!"[4] While he spoke at times in his native Quichua, a language not understood by the majority of Ecuadorans, Vargas had clearly assumed the role of national leader. And yet this leader of the most powerful nonviolent social and political movement in Ecuador and the most well-organized indigenous movement in the Americas was also speaking as part of an unelected military-civilian junta.

The events of January 21 highlight the profound crisis of popular legitimacy of Ecuador's young democracy. Triggered and intensified by a year-long economic depression that showed no signs of abating, the crisis was characterized by a complete loss of faith in virtually all of Ecuador's political institutions. Only 7% of those surveyed in a national public opinion poll, for example, expressed confidence in Congress, and by December the President's popularity rating was also down to 7%.[5] As the economic crisis worsened during 1999, people increasingly perceived that the government, and in particular the President, as biased toward powerful banking interests to the detriment of the majority of poor Ecuadorans. This led CONAIE and its social movement allies to call for the removal of all three branches of government, a demand that was clearly unconstitutional. The events that began with this call and culminated in the January 21 takeover also reveal the contradictions and paradoxes that can emerge when social movements attempt to chart an alternative course and vision for social change in contexts where formal democratic institutions have failed to effectively address the profound structural problems of inequality and injustice.

Even as the new military-civilian junta was making its first public statements, it became clear that the chief institutional arbiter would be the military. Those who had joined the Indians in the Congress were high-ranking officers, but they were not members of the Joint Command, and it was unclear what the reaction of this highest echelon of the Ecuadoran military would be. Earlier in the day the Joint Command of the Armed Forces had publicly called on President Mahuad to resign, but had not made any statement regarding the self-appointed junta. Later that afternoon, Mahuad was informed that the security of the presidential palace could no longer be guaranteed, forcing him to abandon his post. In fact, it was later revealed, orders came down from above to break the protective police and military cordons and allow the protesters to occupy Congress and eventually the presidential palace. This has led many observers to suggest that high-ranking members of the military who wanted Mahuad out of office took advantage of the indigenous protests to move against the increasingly beleaguered President.[6]

For a few hours it appeared that the military high command was going to accept the new civilian-military junta. At midnight on January 21, after General Carlos Mendoza of the Joint Command met with the junta—referred to as the "Triumvirate"—it was announced that he would replace Colonel Gutiérrez as its head. But the next morning, the country awoke to the news that

Mendoza had resigned from the army and was withdrawing from the Triumvirate so that the constitutional successor to Mahuad, Vice-President Gustavo Noboa, could assume power. Mendoza claimed that he never had any intention of allowing the junta to remain in power, and that joining the Triumvirate was a ruse to avoid bloodshed and facilitate a peaceful return to the constitutional order.

Ironically, the indigenous/military takeover of January 2000, while symbolically potent, was immediately followed by a major defeat for indigenous and social movement interests in the area of economic policy, when, despite strident social movement opposition, the Ecuadoran economy was dollarized in March 2000. Mahuad's decision to dollarize the economy had been one of the immediate triggers for the protests that culminated in his ouster on January 21. While the protests succeeded in removing this unpopular president they failed to block the implementation of this controversial economic policy.

The rule of this unprecedented junta lasted less than 24 hours and the radical changes to the economic and political status quo promised by its members did not materialize. But the events of January 21, nevertheless, represented a major watershed in Ecuadoran politics, highlighting the fact that the indigenous movement had taken center stage within a complex array of forces. On that day, the indigenous movement declared unequivocally its desire to play a leadership role in national politics, even as its actions and those of its leaders brought to the fore unresolved and thorny strategic contradictions within the movement itself. Indeed, since its jump into electoral politics in 1996 with the formation of the Pachakutik political movement, the indigenous movement has been attempting to juggle—at times more successfully than at others—two parallel strategies. The first, related to its social movement origins, is one of opposition and protest from outside the system; the other is a more recent strategy of working within existing political institutions via the formation of an official political movement. On January 21 these two strategies collided head-on, and the impact of this collision on the future direction of the movement remains unclear.

The indigenous movement in Ecuador stands out among similar movements in Latin America due to its impressive mobilizational capacity and the fact that it has succeeded in uniting a variety of different ethnic groups throughout the country. These two characteristics—mobilizational capacity and unity in diversity—are key to explaining the prominent political profile that the movement now enjoys, as well as the significant gains it has made over the last 25 years.

While a social movement cannot be conflated to a single organization, the fact is that the vast majority of social movement activities carried out by indigenous peoples in Ecuador are led and/or coordinated by a single national-level organization, CONAIE, or by one of its member organizations.[7] CONAIE was founded in 1986 when two regional organizations, one representing highland indigenous peoples and the other Amazonian Indians, joined forces. CONAIE's organizational membership includes federations representing all 12 indigenous nationality groups, which, CONAIE organizers say, represent 70% of the country's total indigenous population.[8] This population is itself very diverse, with several million living in the Andean highlands, a smaller but still sizeable population living in the Amazonian lowlands and the smallest number located in Ecuador's tropical coastal region.[9]

Since its inception, CONAIE has consistently combined a strong emphasis on indigenous identity with efforts to address the pressing economic situation of the majority of the indigenous population as well as other marginalized groups.[10] One of the first identity-related goals achieved by CONAIE was the creation of a national bilingual education program, designed so that indigenous students could study in their native languages as well as in Spanish. Another achievement was winning the recognition of Ecuador as a "pluricultural" and "multi-ethnic" state in the first article of the Constitution. Another key CONAIE demand—that indigenous communities be granted some form of political and legal autonomy within the confines of the Ecuadoran national state—has been opposed by many non-indigenous politicians, who argue that such a proposal would dismember the country.

CONAIE has also worked together with its member organizations on the key question of land rights and aid to small farmers and campesinos. While the substantive issues related to land tenure and use are very different in the Oriente (the Amazonian jungle) and in the highlands, the land issue is of central concern to CONAIE constituents in both regions. Major achievements in this area include the legalization of territorial and land rights; obtaining legal recognition of land rights for several Amazonian groups; and blocking passage in 1994 of an agrarian reform bill which would have benefited agro-exporters at the expense of small peasant production for the national market.

Whether to obtain land rights, stop a concession to an oil company, or institute the bilingual education program, the principal goals and strategies of the movement have tended to center on effecting change at the level of national policy. The movement has been creative and flexible in its use of tactics, primarily direct negotiations with the national government. For example, the National Intercultural-Bilingual Education Agency, administered by indigenous educators under the auspices of the Ministry of Education, was established after President Rodrigo Borja agreed to negotiate with the movement after years of political pressure. Though the program held out much hope in its early years, it has since come under attack. Critics say that innovative pedagogical practices initially proposed have been stifled by bureaucratic control, and that instead of developing new holistic educational models, the program has tended to replicate the rigid scholastic methodologies used in the public education system that emphasize repetition and rote memorization.[11]

One of the main tactics employed by CONAIE to bring the state to the bargaining table has been the indigenous "uprising." The term harks back to a long history of spontaneous but isolated indigenous rebellions that occurred repeatedly in the colonial and republican eras. In contrast to the historical uprisings, these modern mobilizations are coordinated at the national level by CONAIE, and have involved the participation of tens of thousands of people throughout the country. Actions include roadblocks, marches and the refusal to bring food to market. These mobilizations have always been nonviolent and usually involve civil disobedience.

Despite its state-centered focus, until the mid-1990s the movement maintained a discourse that rejected the state in its existing form as "exclusionary, hegemonic, antidemocratic and repressive."[12] CONAIE program documents propose the construction of an alternative state—"A New Pluralist and Participatory Nation"—based on a utopian vision of a nation free from poverty and discrimination and in which the cultural values of all Ecuador's ethnic and cultural groups would be valued and respected.[13] The movement's rejection of the legitimacy of the existing state was most evident in its stance towards the electoral process. Until 1995 CONAIE's official position was to urge its members to boycott all elections and prohibit its leaders from running for elected office. "We were questioning the system," says Miguel Lluco, now National Coordinator of Pachakutik, "a system that did not offer any guarantee of responding to the interests of the whole, much less to Indian interests. So we said: 'invalidate your vote.'"[14]

In 1995, however, CONAIE made an about-face and helped form a political movement to run candidates for elected office. The Pachakutik Movement is a coalition with non-indigenous social movements and thus is not solely an indigenous party. In both the 1996 and 1998 elections Pachakutik candidates won seats at all levels of government, from town councils to Congress. Currently there are 53 indigenous politicians elected on the Pachakutik ticket holding local and provincial seats, and four holding seats in Congress.[15] With two mestizo deputies, there are a total of six Pachakutik members within the 123-member Congress. Pachakutik also won seven seats to the National Constitutional Assembly, established in 1998 to reform the Constitution.

Considered "the political wing" of the CONAIE and the non-indigenous Social Movement Coordinating Committee (CMS), Pachakutik maintains close ties to both organizations. At the same time, however, the lines of authority between Pachakutik and its parent organizations are not well stipulated, and the dynamics of a social movement as compared to a political party have generated tensions at different points over the years. Tensions were evident in the weeks before the January 21 uprising, as CONAIE insistently pressed its demand that all three branches of government be dissolved. Elected Pachakutik members agreed with CONAIE's analysis of the crisis facing the country, but were frustrated that they were being lumped together with all the other congressmen into the category of "corrupt politicians." They have also expressed disagreement with the CONAIE and CMS demand for a plebiscite in which one of the questions asks whether the Congress' mandate should be revoked.[16]

While this is not the first time that tensions have surfaced between CONAIE and Pachakutik, in the past they have been prompted primarily by disputes over candidate selection or

alliance strategies.[17] Today's tensions appear to be more fundamental in nature in that they revolve around two different political strategies that are difficult to reconcile, if not fundamentally
contradictory. While the indigenous movement's strategies have
always been eclectic and creative, the more radical strategy of
calling into question the legitimacy of the whole political system
cannot easily coexist with efforts to get out the vote for local
and provincial elections scheduled in May. Something will surely
have to give. To the movement's credit, the various actors are
approaching these differences in a spirit of dialogue, but the
outcome of these discussions remains uncertain.

The fact that the indigenous movement, which represents
primarily rural peoples and some of the poorest and most
marginalized sectors of Ecuadoran society, attained a degree of
political power such that their actions were instrumental in
bringing down a standing president is quite remarkable. Any
attempt to explain the movement's success must take into
account both external contextual factors and characteristics
particular to the movement itself.

A confluence of propitious factors at the international and
national levels at the time of the founding and the initial
building of the movement provided the necessary political space
for it to grow and make concrete gains early on. This space, in
turn, was wisely and adroitly taken advantage of by a mature
leadership that focused on the strengthening of a pan-Indian
identity as the symbolic glue to hold the movement together.
An imperfect but essentially democratic and participatory
decision-making structure has thus far prevented usurpation
by any one faction or leader.

At the international level, interest in and support for
indigenous peoples' struggles increased as the Cold War waned
and eventually ended. In 1982 the UN commissioned a working
group to develop a set of principles on indigenous peoples'

rights, which resulted in the UN Draft Declaration of the Rights of Indigenous Peoples. In 1989 the International Labor Organization (ILO) passed Convention 169, which stipulates a wide-ranging set of rights for native peoples, including collective rights, protection of languages and cultures, and the right to be consulted by governments when proposed laws will affect them.[18] These and many other actions, including the UN's decision to designate 1993 the International Year of Indigenous People, have drawn attention to native peoples' struggles and facilitated contacts between indigenous organizations around the world. This interest and concern at the international level has served to legitimate the identity agenda of the movement, as well as to provide it with important international contacts, solidarity and monetary support.

At the national level, three main factors have shaped the movement's evolution: a relatively non-repressive military, a divided and factionalized political elite, and an economically bankrupt state without the capacity to undertake large-scale populist projects. Compared especially to the Southern Cone and Central American militaries, the Ecuadoran Armed Forces have never been extremely repressive. This meant that between 1990 and 2000 the indigenous movement was able to carry out five uprisings that shut down roads and markets throughout the country for days and sometimes weeks at a time with no massive retaliation by the military.[19] Given that the "uprising" has become a central tool of the movement, both for bargaining with the state as well as for its symbolic impact, it is clear that the movement's success cannot be fully understood without taking into account the nature of the Ecuadoran military.

Ecuador's highly fragmented party system, exacerbated by deep regional divisions among the country's economic and political elites, has meant that the movement has not had to face a unified ruling class or a monolithic state. The fragmented party system also made it possible for a relatively small minority party like Pachakutik to wield a certain degree of political power at the national level.[21] The slow and piecemeal way in which neoliberal economic reforms were implemented in Ecuador was as much due to infighting and divisions at the elite level as to the indigenous movement's opposition to such measures.[20] Even so, as one of the most vociferous opponents of neoliberalism, the movement can claim at least partial credit for having stymied the neoliberal advance in Ecuador to a significant degree, even as it swept inexorably across the rest of Latin America.

Finally, the fact that this movement emerged onto the national arena in the 1980s—when statist populism and the co-optation of social sectors that this model often implied was no longer viable—meant that the risk of full-scale co-optation was much lower. Different governments have of course attempted to divide the movement and co-opt its leadership, but the lack of resources necessary to mount economic and social programs grand enough to draw grassroots allegiance away from the movement has stymied such efforts.

In terms of its own internal structure, CONAIE sits at the top of a pyramidal organizational network. At the base are local associations and cooperatives that began to proliferate in the countryside in the early 1970s.[22] These local organizations are linked together through provincial federations, which in turn belong to one of three regional federations, representing the highlands, the Amazonian lowlands and the coast.[23]

The fact that CONAIE was constructed upon a previously established network of organizations helps explain its relatively rapid institutional consolidation. All member organizations are guaranteed representation and voting rights in CONAIE and their leadership is consulted and included in all major policy decisions. For example, in the initial meetings held to set the ground rules for talks between CONAIE and President Noboa in the wake of the January 21 uprising, some 40 movement leaders participated, including the presidents of all member federations.[24] The pyramidal structure facilitates fairly fluid communication from the rank-and-file up to the national leadership, and a practice of "consulting the bases" has developed within the organization. While there are times when the "consultation" process can in practice become more of a means of transmitting directives or perspectives from above down to the grassroots, nevertheless it does serve to keep lines of communication open between different sectors and levels of the movement. One mechanism that has served to maintain unity between the two major regional groups—the Amazon and the highlands—has been the informal practice of striking a regional balance in the top leadership of CONAIE.[25]

The diverse make-up of the indigenous movement, including marked regional differences, concerns and interests, has led to occasional disagreements over strategy and internal elections. On the whole, the organization has been quite successful at resolving these differences internally and presenting a united front to the public. "Don't air our dirty laundry in public" has become an informal organizational norm.

Finally, it is important to take into account the movement's consistent and express avoidance of violence. The leadership has repeatedly reinforced this policy of nonviolence, which appears to have widespread grassroots support. This has bolstered the movement's legitimacy in the eyes of the rest of the population, despite the continued prevalence of racist attitudes within much of Ecuadoran society.

Popular support for the indigenous movement appeared to grow in the wake of the January 21 uprising. In a survey taken the day of the congressional takeover, 71% of those polled said they were in favor of the indigenous movement and 64% approved of the takeover. This, however, did not mean support for the continuation of the junta—fully 79% said they were in favor of maintaining the constitutional order.[26] What these figures do indicate is that as a protest action, the uprising struck a chord among most Ecuadorans.

One of the areas the movement needed to work on in order to responsibly assume its new mantle of popular leadership was the development of concrete and more realistic proposals for political and economic reform. For example, many of the economic proposals generated by grassroots popular consultations failed to take on the difficult task of finding ways to finance the government's budget, focusing almost exclusively on demand making.[27]

Continued flirtation with solutions falling outside the constitutional framework proved to be risky and was wisely largely abandoned by the movement by 2002. While the events of January 21 increased the movement's popular legitimacy, it came under attack from the press, the political establishment and international actors for its leadership role in what many referred to as an attempted coup d'état. Further actions like these could have seriously jeopardized the movement's international political clout. In the months immediately following the events of January 21, the CONAIE and CMS attempted to collect enough signatures to hold a national plebiscite that would have asked citizens to vote on whether or not to revoke the Congress' mandate. Beyond doubts about the constitutionality of the question itself, such a plebiscite raised the specter of a Fujimori-like "solution" to Ecuador's crisis, as the President could have used the results of such a referendum to justify the dissolution of Congress and the assumption of dictatorial powers.[28]

Popular support for continued brinksmanship of this kind did not materialize. Months passed before plebiscite organizers delivered their signatures to the electoral authorities, and after they did so, the plebiscite was tabled because electoral authorities accused organizers of forging and manufacturing signatures. This episode tarnished the reputations of some of the CONAIE and CMS leadership who had been pushing for the plebiscite, in particular Antonio Vargas, who in late 2000 was reprimanded at a CONAIE national meeting both for the scandal surrounding the signatures, as well as, for his lack of consultation with the broader organization in the days leading up to January 21.

On the morning of January 22, after nearly 24 dramatic hours in the National Congress building, the remaining 60 or so members of the People's Parliament and a couple hundred of their supporters obeyed the police order to abandon the premises. Once outside in the fresh morning air, Luis Alberto Bautista, one of the Parliamentarians, told me he had doubts about the whole process. "Yes, we took power," he said, "but would the Triumvirate really have worked? Would a coalition government with the military really have been a good idea?"[29]

The time was not yet ripe and the tactics were not the appropriate ones for the indigenous movement to assume the mantle of state power, but a glimpse was had, a memory created, a threshold crossed. "The right of Indians to protest and, yes, even to govern has been established," says Nina Pacari, long-time movement leader and congressional representative for Pachakutik. "Something very fundamental has emerged for us from this experience: a sense of possibility."[30]

Two years later possibility would again become reality when Pachakutik came into power as part of an electoral coalition supporting the winning presidential bid of Lucio Gutiérrez in 2002. While this passage into state power came via constitutional means and was longer than the 24-hour triumvirate, it also ended in disappointment as Gutiérrez reneged on his campaign promises to implement a more socially conscious economic agenda. After only six months in office Pachakutik withdrew from the governing coalition citing differences with Gutiérrez over economic policy and the President's unwillingness to fully involve the party in the policymaking process. Ultimately this departure proved to be a wise move, as Gutierrez was forced out of office in 2004 before the end of his term in the midst of a political crisis of his own making and charges of corruption. Since then the indigenous movement has maintained a lower, less dramatic profile as it has sought to strengthen its internal organization and rethink its strategies for change. Nevertheless it remains an extremely important political force on Ecuador's national stage.

ABOUT THE AUTHOR

Jennifer N. Collins is currently a visiting instructor at Colgate University and a doctoral candidate in the department of political science at the University of California, San Diego. Her doctoral dissertation examines the rise of social movement and indigenous political parties in Ecuador and Bolivia.

NOTES

1. The author is grateful to the Fulbright Commission for funding her research in Ecuador, and to Robert Andolina for his comments and corrections.
2. In 1999 Ecuador was in the 82nd spot out of a total of 99 countries surveyed in Transparency International's Corruption Perceptions Index; the higher the ranking the more corrupt the country is perceived to be by citizens of that country.
3. Colonel Fausto Cobo, Author's notes from Ecuavisa live television broadcast, Quito, January 21, 2000.
4. Antonio Vargas, Author's notes from Ecuavisa live television broadcast, Quito, January 21, 2000.
5. Poll was conducted by CEDATOS and reported on the February 6, 2000 broadcast of the television show, "La Televisión."
6. This view was expressed at the time in several newspaper articles and editorials, including: León Roldós Aguilera, "Quién y Cómo?" *El Comercio* (Quito), January 26, 2000; "Las Fuerzas Armadas: Una suma de conflictos sin resolver," *El Comercio*, January 30, 2000; and Enrique Ayala Mora, "Necesidad de amnistía," *El Comercio*, February 15, 2000.

7. There are two other national-level indigenous organizations—the Ecuadoran Federation of Evangelical Indians (FEINE) and the National Federation of Campesino, Indigenous and Black Organizations (FENOCIN)— which historically have had competitive and at times conflictive relations with each other and CONAIE, but neither of them can match the organizational strength of CONAIE.

8. While reliable estimates on the size of Ecuador's indigenous population have been hard to come by, a reasonable estimate is probably in the range of about one third of the total population, which in 2005 numbered over 13 million.

9. For movement estimates from the end of the 1980s of the size of regional indigenous populations see: CONAIE, *Las nacionalidades indígenas en el Ecuador* (Quito: Editorial TINCUI/CONAIE and Ediciones Abya-Yala, 1989), p. 37.

10. There have been efforts in the past to link the struggles of Afro-Ecuadoran peoples, who make up about 5% of the total population, with indigenous struggles. Some Afro-Ecuadoran organizations are official members of CONAIE, and campesinos in general have benefited from some of the gains made by the indigenous movement.

11. Carlos Viteri, "Ecuador un país fictício," *Ikonos*, No. 2 (May/July 1997), pp. 51–58.

12. Consejo de Gobierno de la CONAIE, "Proyecto Político de la CONAIE" (1994), p. 7.

13. Consejo de Gobierno de la CONAIE, "Proyecto Político de la CONAIE" (1994), p. 5–7.

14. Author's interview, Miguel Lluco, Quito, January 3, 2000. Voting is obligatory in Ecuador and so it would not have been realistic for CONAIE to have encouraged people simply not to go to the polls.

15. Fernando Garcia, "Presente y perspectiva del movimiento indígena ecuatoriano," Paper presented at the seminar on Movimientos Sociales, Democracia y Cambio Político en el Area Andina, Quito, Ecuador, November 22–23, 1999.

16. These comments are based on the author's interviews with three of the six Pachakutik Congressional representatives: Nina Pacari, Quito, February 3, 2000; Miguel Pérez, Quito, February 3, 2000; and Antonio Posso, Quito, February 1, 2000.

17. Kenneth Mijeski and Scott Beck, "Mainstreaming the Indigenous Movement in Ecuador: The Electoral Strategy," paper presented at the XXI International Congress of the Latin American Studies Association, Chicago, IL, September 24–26, 1998.

18. Ecuador's new Constitution contains a chapter on collective rights for indigenous people modeled after the ILO Convention 169. This was largely a result of the efforts of Pachakutik delegates to the 1998 Constitutional Assembly.

19. In 1994, one indigenous protester was killed and a building belonging to

214 / Dispatches From Latin America

an indigenous organization was burned down by unknown arsonists.

20. Jennifer Collins, "Not for Sale: Barriers to Privatization in a Non-Crisis Case, Ecuador, 1992–1996," Presented at the Joint Conference of the Canadian Association for Latin American and Caribbean Studies (CALACS) and the Canadian Association for Mexican Studies (CAMS), Vancouver, British Columbia, March 19–21, 1998.

21. For instance, despite having only six seats in the legislature, the Pachakutik congressional bloc was able to get one of their representatives, Nina Pacari, elected as the congressional vice-president.

22. For an analysis of the origin and evolution of these local organizations, see Anthony Bebbington, Hernán Carrasco, Lourdes Peralvo, Galo Ramón, Victor Hugo Torres and Jorge Trujillo, "De la protesta a la productividad: Evolución de las federaciones indígenas del Ecuador," Desarrollo de Base, Vol. 16, No. 2.

23. CONAIE was founded by the highland and Amazonian regional federations, ECUARUNARI and CONFENAIE. Coastal groups joined the organization later under their regional umbrella organization, the Confederation of Indigenous, Black and Campesino Organizations of the Ecuadoran Coast (COINCCE).

24. "Noboa y la CONAIE buscan fecha para una reunión," El Comercio (Quito), February 9, 2000, p. A3.

25. Though they are members of CONAIE, coastal organizations and leaders have never had a high profile within the organization. The indigenous and Afro-Ecuadoran populations on the coast are relatively small, and they are not as well organized as those in the highlands and Amazonian lowlands.

26. Poll conducted by CEDATOS and broadcast on the television show, "La Televisión," January 23, 2000.

27. This is evident in various unpublished documents coming out of recent meetings of the Popular Parliaments convened by indigenous and social movements in an effort to develop alternative government programs and proposals. This view was also expressed by Pachakutik legislator, Nina Pacari, Author's interview, Quito, February 3, 2000.

28. The question, as it was proposed at the time by the social movements, included stipulations that would presumably have precluded a presidential takeover. It was, however, almost certain that the solution contained in the proposed question—to give temporary authorization to the Popular Parliaments to come up with new electoral laws—would not have been accepted by the political establishment.

29. Author's interview, Luis Alberto Bautista, Quito, February 3, 2000.

30. Author's interview, Nina Pacari, Quito, February 3, 2000.

Richard Stahler-Sholk

Autonomy and Resistance in Chiapas

The people of Nuevo San Isidro watched warily as a helicopter appeared over the horizon, circled in over their seven thatched huts and landed somewhere on the far side of the Lacantún River. This Tzotzil indigenous community had migrated to the remote jungle near the Mexican-Guatemalan border in February 2001. They came from Chavajebal in Chiapas' central highlands, a region of land scarcity and paramilitary violence, and wanted simply to work the land peacefully. But in October 2004, when government agents came in and promised to help them relocate elsewhere in exchange for government aid, their small community was divided: six of the original 13 families started taking the aid and seven refused. Those who refused identified with the Zapatista Army of National Liberation (EZLN) and moved a few hundred yards upriver, establishing formal affiliation with the Zapatista Autonomous Rebel Municipality of "Freedom for the Mayan Peoples," part of one of the Zapatista regional *Juntas de Buen Gobierno* (Juntas of Good Government) called "Towards Hope." They now referred to the pro-government side of the village as the *priístas*, an old habit from the 71 years during which the Institutional Revolutionary Party (PRI) ruled Mexico.

While the Mexican government tries to uproot communities, freeing up more land and resources for the global market, the Zapatistas have continued to resist by constructing autonomous government. They began by building on community structures of local self-governance continually created since the 1950s by migrants from the highlands and other regions to Las Cañadas, the jungle canyons of the agricultural frontier of eastern Chiapas.[1] When government troops encircled this region in a military offensive in December 1994, the EZLN declared the existence of 38 autonomous municipalities, including many in the highlands and other areas outside Las Cañadas.[2] In July 2000, the EZLN grouped the Zapatista Autonomous Rebel Municipalities into regional autonomous government structures administered by five Juntas of Good Government based in governing centers called *Caracoles* (conch shells, an ancient Mayan symbol).

The helicopter that circled over the newly divided community of Nuevo San Isidro had brought 19 government agents. The wary Zapatista side gathered on the riverbank to see their pro-government neighbors ferry their benefactors across the river by *cayuco* in groups of four. Some time after the last cayuco had crossed, as the villagers continued talking among themselves at the riverside, an agrarian reform official appeared in the clearing escorted by two *priístas*. She was a wiry, thirty-something woman named Alejandra, sporting close-cropped brown hair with frosted highlights. With the overly chipper air of a kindergarten teacher, she greeted the assembled crowd and launched into a speech about how she and her colleagues were here to help; they were going to have a meeting at the pro-government cluster of huts, and they wanted to invite everyone on this side to come and hear a proposal about "how to make the best use of the land."

Gregorio (not his real name), who spoke the best Spanish, responded. "We are not with the government," he began, pointing to a hand-lettered sign nailed to a tree at the riverbank that read "Zapatista Army of National Liberation. Entry by government officials is prohibited." He continued, "We are a Zapatista community. We are in resistance. We don't want government people here."

Alejandra started to protest that she had only come to invite them to a meeting, and that it was about giving them land. "We already know that the government's word is pure lies," Gregorio replied. "Look what happened to the people in Santa Cruz. You promised them aid for three years and it ended after three months." Alejandra broke in again: "I recognize that some mistakes have been made. But I'm here to make sure the promises are kept. You can pick out the land you want. Look, these people have already chosen their land!"

Gregorio kept his composure. "This is the same government that is responsible for the massacre at Acteal in 1997," he said, "45 men, women and children massacred. The government also killed people from this community, on June 10, 1998, in Chavajebal. Why do they send soldiers from village to village to kill? Then they come with promises that are pure lies." He switched back and forth from Spanish to Tzotzil for the benefit of the *priísta* escorts.

Alejandra, visibly agitated but maintaining her forced smile, responded: "No, I agree, that wasn't right. I have nothing to do with what the soldiers do, I disagree with it, in fact, I have denounced it myself. But look, I just came to invite you to a meeting, so you can hear the proposal yourselves." Gregorio effectively ended the conversation: "If you want to invite us to a meeting you can present yourselves at Caracol Number One, to the Zapatista Junta of Good Government, and see what response they give you. I'll take you there myself right now if you want." Alejandra backpedaled. "No, no, I already know where it is. Anyway, that's all we came for. If you want to come, we'll be meeting over there." She said goodbye with a huge smile and a wave as she whirled around to disappear with her entourage.

The villagers lingered by the riverbank, chuckling that

Alejandra was afraid to take her proposal to the Zapatista regional autonomous authorities. But there was an underlying sense that the stakes were rising, and that the community would be even more isolated if their neighbors were spirited off to faraway lands.

Since the government's initial military response to the 1994 Zapatista uprising, the counterinsurgency has shifted emphasis toward state-sponsored paramilitary groups composed mainly of rootless young indigenous men who lack land and are given arms and money to attack communities of Zapatista supporters.[3] This allows the government to portray the killing in Chiapas as inter-communal violence, and its own troops as a stabilizing force. The most intense military/paramilitary operations have shifted over the years from the jungle canyons of east-central Chiapas, to the northern zone, then to the central highlands and now to this southeastern slice of jungle where the government had demarcated the vast "Montes Azules Biosphere Reserve" nearly 30 years before. The government has been waging a campaign to evict settlers from Montes Azules over the last two years, particularly targeting Zapatista settlements of indigenous people who have recently taken refuge here.[4]

Officially, the government invokes a conservationist rationale for evicting settlers from the biosphere reserve. Yet, the Echeverría Administration in 1972 had conceded 614,000 hectares (1.5 million acres), including much of what in 1978 was designated the Montes Azules reserve, to a group of 66 indigenous families it had inaccurately labeled the "Lacandón Community." The government gave them trinkets in exchange for exclusive lumber concessions to strip valuable hardwood from the forest. Over the decades, various communities of Tzeltal and Ch'ol people living within the overlapping Montes Azules and Lacandón Community boundaries also received recognition of their land rights under agrarian reforms. In the midst of all these overlapping concessions, the government only initiated evictions when communities of Zapatista supporters began to settle the southern fringe of the jungle reserve.

Another clue to the newfound interest in Montes Azules may be found in President Vicente Fox's much-publicized "Plan Puebla-Panamá" (PPP), a grand scheme to attract billions of dollars of investment to southern Mexico and Central America.[5] The PPP envisions port and railway facilities for expanded maquiladora plants and dams for hydroelectric power for the anticipated industrial boom. Part of the attraction of the region for foreign capital is the rich biodiversity found in this stretch of jungle. An exposé by local NGOs has already halted one bio-prospecting project by the U.S.-funded "ICBG Maya" consortium.[6]

Not far from the settlement in Nuevo San Isidro is the mysterious Chajul "ecotourism station," which locals say is a base for bio-piracy, run by former Secretary of Environment, turned entrepreneur, Julia Carabias. Her pseudo-NGO, ENDESU, began building another station in 2002 at Río Tzendales, where a billboard proclaimed a "conservation" project to be supported by the Ford Motor Company. In mid-2004 the legislative frame-work for bio-prospecting was drafted in a proposed "Law for the Conservation of Biodiversity and Environmental Protection for the State of Chiapas," denounced by human rights groups as a violation of indigenous rights to autonomous control of resources in their territories.[7]

Since the 1980s, the neoliberal agenda in Mexico has been implemented with the help of a series of programs designed to create new clientelistic mechanisms to divide and co-opt discontent. The prototype was the National Solidarity Program (PRONASOL), which selectively doled out benefits through local committees to compensate for the social impact of economic austerity (which far exceeded the payouts). A similar program called PROCEDE undermines the management of communal landholdings by offering individual titles to those who opt out of the collective agrarian *ejidos*. Resistance to the counter-reform is weakened as state resources are drained from this social property sector and the cheap products of U.S. agri-business flood the Mexican market. Another program, PROCAMPO, gave direct per-hectare compensation payments to producers as price supports for peasant agriculture were being dismantled.

The Zapatista movement had its roots in independent rural organizing initiatives that demanded rights rather than clientelistic privileges. The Zapatistas insisted not only on individual citizenship rights within a democratic national framework, but also collective ethnic rights for indigenous peoples, a departure from the atomizing ideology of neoliberalism.[8]

The Zapatistas also continued pressing at the negotiating table for recognition of indigenous rights and culture, something the government formally conceded with the signing of the San Andrés Accords in February 1996. Implementing legislation, however, was never passed, so the Zapatistas inaugurated a second phase of the autonomy movement by proceeding to implement it themselves. The Zapatista communities boycotted the municipal elections of October 1996, and instead elected parallel authorities through indigenous *usos y costumbres* (traditional customs and practices). Since they lacked official recognition and resources, the autonomous municipalities were supported through five Zapatista multiservice centers called *Aguascalientes*. For the most part, however, the municipalities relied on local resources to launch production and social service projects, drawing on the indigenous tradition of a community labor tax in which each family contributed a quota of person-days.[9]

Following the collapse of the San Andrés process, the Zapatistas began a third phase by further institutionalizing their de-facto municipal governments, often expelling the official government authorities. The federal government launched a series of joint police-military raids in April and May 1998, dismantling the two autonomous municipalities of Ricardo Flores Magón and Tierra y Libertad. The Chiapas state government, meanwhile, approved a redistricting scheme creating seven new municipalities aimed at undermining Zapatista autonomy claims.

A fourth phase of the movement began in July 2003, when the Zapatistas launched a regional structure of autonomous government in Chiapas. Each autonomous municipality now sends rotating representatives to one of the five regional *Juntas de Buen Gobierno* based in the Caracoles that replaced the old *Aguascalientes*. In a preliminary self-evaluation of the Juntas after one year, the Zapatistas celebrated advances in social-service provision, as well as the experience gained by community members serving one- to two-week shifts in the regional governments.[10] Yet they recognized problems of inefficiency and discontinuity caused by the frequent rotation; as well as serious under-representation of women in governing councils that are distant from their communities. There was also uneven ability to attend to dispersed settlements far from the Caracoles. In October 2004, one of the Zapatista Juntas de Buen Gobierno decided to consolidate eight beleaguered, isolated communities from Montes Azules, including Nuevo San Isidro, in order to better integrate them into the resistance offered by their new regional structures of government.[11]

A fifth phase was inaugurated in June 2005 with the Sixth Declaration of the Lacandón Jungle, which inaugurated a series of open meetings in the jungle communities of Chiapas between Zapatista leaders and various leftist sectors of Mexican civil society.[12] These forums were a prelude to "The Other Campaign," a schedule of visits by Zapatistas to activist groups around the country from January to June 2006. This was an apparent effort to avoid isolation in the Caracoles, and to put fundamental social justice issues back on a national agenda that was bogged down in election-year politicking.

As the Zapatista autonomy movement evolves, it offers potential alternatives to the neoliberal model, but autonomy is not without its dilemmas. One model of autonomy that predates the 1994 emergence of the EZLN in Chiapas is based on the concept of the Pluriethnic Autonomous Region (RAP).[13] The RAP model envisions autonomy as decentralization, and creates an additional representative layer for an indigenous territory within the existing structures of national government. A variant of this model can be seen in the North and South Atlantic autono-mous regions of Nicaragua. In essence, this created a fourth level of government, in addition to the federal, state and local. In the Nicaraguan case, implementation of a 1987 autonomy statute fell short of expectations due to problems of represent-ation and the under-funding of the autonomous government structures.

Skeptics of the RAP model cite the danger of regional "bossism," and the concern that it merely replicates the top-down structure of existing political institutions without developing new leadership capacity rooted in local communities. Some interpretations of a comparable experience in Ecuador suggest that a territorially bounded definition of autonomy might create a kind of self-policed homeland, limiting options for indigenous people whose subsistence and cultural identity depend increasingly on complex patterns of mobility.[14] The Zapatistas themselves, while preferring to build autonomy from the community level upward, nevertheless remained open to a pluralism of autonomy models.

Another dilemma is presented by a version of autonomy without resources, i.e. the potential for the neoliberal state to pass off responsibility for the unprofitable provision of public goods to "autonomous," but underfunded units. The market paradigm tends to privatize gains while socializing costs and risks. The apparent recognition of autonomous spaces in society could create new mechanisms for division and cooptation, as social sectors and regions compete with each other for a share of the shrinking pie. This could leave them vulnerable to clientelistic politicians or even paternalistic NGOs moving into the breach.

A third potential trap is what an analyst in the Guatemalan context called "managed neoliberal multiculturalism."[15] It is noteworthy, for example, that the 1991 agrarian counter-reform, which modified Article 27 of the Constitution and eroded the communal agrarian *ejido*, was coupled with reforms to Article 4 that for the first time explicitly recognized the multiethnic character of the Mexican nation.[16] Both reforms were imposed from above without grassroots consultation, and taken together, they reflect the neoliberal model's recognition of a plurality of indigenous identities, as long as those identities do not become the basis for collective organization around substantive rights. This allows entrepreneurial ecotourism and bio-prospecting ventures in the Lacandón jungle to pick and choose partners among the "diverse" indigenous peoples, while celebrating the Disneyesque concept of a multiethnic "Selva Maya."

The limits of working within the neoliberal legal framework of individual property guarantees and corporate prerogatives are illustrated by the struggle over the San Andrés Accords. After the March 2001 Zapatista caravan to Mexico City demanding implementation of the Accords, the legislature passed a sham "indigenous rights law" that actually reneged on key provisions of the agreements.[17] The original Article 4 of the indigenous rights law drafted by the congressional peace commission, COCOPA, affirmed that "indigenous peoples have the right to free determination and, as expression of that, to autonomy." Its replacement begins with the affirmation that "the Mexican

Nation is one and indivisible," and adds that "the right of indigenous peoples to free determination will be exercised in a constitutional framework of autonomy that assures national unity. The recognition of indigenous peoples and communities will be done in the constitutions and laws of the federative entities."

Rights of indigenous communities to elect their own authorities, in the revised version, would only be granted "within a framework that respects the federal pact and the sovereignty of the states." In other words, the right to have rights will be at the discretion of the existing authorities. Crucial language guaranteeing indigenous peoples access and use of resources in their territories was replaced. Access would be decided "with respect for the forms and modes of property and land tenancy established in this Constitution and relevant law, as well as rights acquired by third parties or by members of the community, to the use and preferential enjoyment of the natural resources of the places inhabited and occupied by the communities, except those corresponding to strategic areas."

Article 26 of the original COCOPA law requiring "the necessary mechanisms so that development plans and programs take into account the indigenous peoples and communities in their cultural needs and specificities" was eliminated along with a clause that "the State will guarantee them their equitable access to the distribution of the national wealth." Indigenous identity was to be recognized, but stripped of collective rights.

When this "indigenous rights" legislation passed the Congress in a "fast-track" deal between the National Action Party (PAN) and the PRI, it was denounced by indigenous rights groups and rejected in all the states with large indigenous populations but ratified in enough states to pass. The Supreme Court rejected all 320 constitutional challenges to the law, claiming it had no jurisdiction over such matters, and the law took effect.

Meanwhile, since their inauguration in August 2003, the Zapatista *Juntas de Buen Gobierno* have been offering to serve both Zapatista and non-Zapatistas, and the Fox Administration has had to reluctantly concede that they are probably not unconstitutional. To overcome the dilemma of autonomy without resources and the danger of losing decision-making control to outside NGO funders, the Juntas have set up mechanisms for reviewing NGO development proposals and taking a 10% tax to redistribute to communities within each region.[18]

The juntas do not preclude other authority structures or autonomy models, but they do exert a greater discipline over who gets to claim the "Zapatista" label within a given region. This, in effect, means greater control over the movement by the Zapatista communities themselves, represented in the Juntas, rather than the insurgent structures of the EZLN. In some of the Caracoles, there are already signs of local acceptance of the legitimacy of the Juntas, even by non-Zapatistas, who turn to them for dispute resolution and other governance functions. But the October 2004 Montes Azules evacuation and regrouping of communities of Zapatista supporters illustrates the continued conflictive negotiation of space between the state as broker for global capital and the rebels representing community autonomy.

ABOUT THE AUTHOR

Richard Stahler-Sholk is an associate professor of political science at Eastern Michigan University. He has served as a human rights observer in Chiapas on numerous occasions since 1994.

NOTES

1. Xóchitl Leyva Solano, "Regional, Communal, and Organizational Transformations in Las Cañadas," pp. 161–84 in Jan Rus, Rosalva Aída Hernández Castillo and Shannan L. Mattiace, (eds.), *Mayan Lives, Mayan Utopias: The Indigenous Peoples of Chiapas and the Zapatista Rebellion*

(Lanham, MD: Rowman & Littlefield, 2003). The other chapters of this book provide an excellent picture of the many facets of the Zapatista autonomy movement.

2. The Zapatistas based the right of self-government on Mexico's 1917 revolutionary Constitution. For the text, see EZLN, "Third Declaration of the Lacandón Jungle" (January 1995), www.ezln.org/documentos/1995/199501xx.en.htm.

3. See *Global Exchange, Always Near, Always Far: The Armed Forces in Mexico* (San Francisco: December, 2000), Chapters 9–10; and "The Wars Within: Counterinsurgency in Chiapas and Colombia," *NACLA Report on the Americas*, Vol. 31, No. 5, March/April 1998.

4. Maderas del Pueblo del Sureste, "Breve historia de la llamada 'Comunidad Lacandona'" (San Cristóbal de Las Casas, Chiapas: December 2002), and "¡No al desalojo!: El caso de la Reserva Montes Azules en la Selva Lacandona, Chiapas" (San Cristóbal de Las Casas, Chiapas: April 2003); CIEPAC (Centro de Investigaciones Económicas y Políticas de Acción Comunitaria), "Nuevos Desalojos en los Montes Azules," Chiapas al Día, No. 393, February 3, 2004, www.ciepac.org.

5. See: CIEPAC, "El Plan Puebla Panamá (PPP)," www.ciepac.org/ppp.htm.

6. Andrés Barreda, "Biopiracy, Bioprospecting, and Resistance: Four Cases in Mexico," in Timothy A. Wise, Hilda Salazar and Laura Carlsen (eds.), *Confronting Globalization: Economic Integration and Popular Resistance in Mexico* (Bloomfield, CT: Kumarian Press, 2003), pp. 101–25; and "Mexico Biopiracy Project Cancelled," November 9. 2001, www.etcgroup.org/documents/news_ICBGterm_Nov2001.pdf.

7. CIEPAC, "El Pukuj Runs Loose in Montes Azules," *Chiapas al Día*, No. 409, April 29, 2004; and "La Red de Derechos Humanos de Chiapas rechaza el proyecto de ley de biodiversidad para el Estado de Chiapas por ignorar a los pueblos indígenas," *Chiapas al Día*, No. 418, June 30, 2004.

8. See Neil Harvey, "Resisting Neoliberalism, Constructing Citizenship: Indigenous Movements in Chiapas," in Wayne A. Cornelius, Todd A. Eisenstadt and Jane Hindley (eds.), *Subnational Politics and Democratization in Mexico* (La Jolla, CA: U.C.-San Diego Center for U.S.-Mexico Studies, 1999), pp. 239–65. For a comparative discussion of this reframing of indigenous rights in the region, see: Deborah Yashar, *Contesting Citizenship in Latin America: The Rise of Indigenous Movements and the Postliberal Challenge* (New York: Cambridge University Press, 2005).

9. For examples of implementation of community-level autonomy, see: Richard Stahler-Sholk, "Massacre in Chiapas," *Latin American Perspectives*, Vol. 25, No. 4, July 1998, pp. 63–75; Jeanne Simonelli and Duncan Earle, *Uprising of Hope: Sharing the Zapatista Journey to Alternative Development* (Lanham, MD: AltaMira Press, 2005); June Nash, "Indigenous Development Alternatives," *Urban Anthropology and Studies of Cultural Systems and World Economic Development*, Vol. 32, No. 1, Spring 2003, pp. 57-98; and Maya Lorena Pérez Ruiz (ed.), *Tejiendo historias: Tierra, género y*

poder en Chiapas (Mexico City: Instituto Nacional de Antropología e Historia, 2004).

10. Subcomandante Insurgente Marcos, "Leer un video," August 2004, http://www.ezln.org/documentos/2004/leer_un_video_1.es.htm.

11. Hermann Bellinghausen, "Comenzó la reubicación de poblados zapatistas en el sur de Montes Azules," *La Jornada*, October 29, 2004; and "Reubicaciones de la SRA propician confrontaciones en la selva Lacandona," *La Jornada*, September 15, 2004.

12. EZLN, "Sixth Declaration of the Lacandón Jungle," http://www.ezln.org/documentos/2005/sexta1.en.htm (June 2005). For analysis of the declaration and the subsequent "Other Campaign" of outreach, see Neil Harvey, "Inclusion through Dissent: Zapatistas and Autonomy," *NACLA Report on the Americas*, Vol. 39, No. 2, Sept./Oct. 2005.

13. For a balanced assessment of the RAP model in Chiapas, see Shannan L. Mattiace, *To See with Two Eyes: Peasant Activism and Indian Autonomy in Chiapas, Mexico* (Albuquerque: University of New Mexico Press, 2003). For a positive presentation of the territorial decentralization model including the Nicaraguan case, see Héctor Díaz Polanco, *Autonomía regional: La autodeterminación de los pueblos indios* (Mexico City: Siglo XXI, 1991). For a critical view of this model from a Zapatista advisor, see Gustavo Esteva, "The Meaning and Scope of the Struggle for Autonomy," in Rus et al. (eds.), *Mayan Lives, Mayan Utopias*, pp. 243–69. On the political prospects of autonomy claims, see Donna Lee Van Cott, "Explaining Ethnic Autonomy Regimes in Latin America," *Studies in Comparative International Development*, Vol. 35, No. 4, Winter 2001, pp. 30–58.

14. Rudi Colloredo-Mansfeld, "Autonomy and Interdependence in Native Movements: Towards a Pragmatic Politics in the Ecuadoran Andes," *Identities: Global Studies in Culture and Power*, Vol. 9, No. 2, April–June 2002, pp. 173-195. For interesting analysis of the changing definitions of indigenous community in Chiapas in the context of globalization, see Jan Rus, "Local Adaptation to Global Change: The Reordering of Native Society in Highland Chiapas, Mexico 1974–1994," *European Review of Latin American and Caribbean Studies*, No. 58, June 1995, pp. 71–89.

15. Charles R. Hale, "Does Multiculturalism Menace? Governance, Cultural Rights and the Politics of Identity in Guatemala," *Journal of Latin American Studies*, Vol. 34, Part 3, August 2002, pp. 485–524.

16. On the impact of the agrarian counter-reform in Chiapas, see: Neil Harvey, "Rural Reforms and the Question of Autonomy in Chiapas," in Wayne A. Cornelius and David Myhre (eds.), *The Transformation of Rural Mexico: Reforming the Ejido Sector* (La Jolla, CA: UCSD Center for U.S.-Mexico Studies, 1998).

17. For a textual comparison of the initial November 1996 compromise language for an indigenous rights law drafted by the Congressional peace commission (COCOPA), the executive's December 1996 modifications, and the bill introduced in April 2001, see: EZLN, "Reformas a la Iniciativa de Ley de

Derechos y Cultura Indígena," http://www.ezln.org/san_andres/cuadro010430.html. See also Luis Hernández Navarro and Laura Carlsen, "Indigenous Rights: The Battle for Constitutional Reform in Mexico," in Kevin J. Middlebrook (ed.), *Dilemmas of Political Change in Mexico* (London: Institute of Latin American Studies, 2004) pp. 440–65.

18. Subcomandante Insurgente Marcos, "Chiapas: La treceava estela," seven-part communiqué (July 2003), available at www.ezln.org. English translation in *¡Ya Basta! Ten Years of the Zapatista Uprising* (Oakland: AK Press, 2004), pp. 589–625.

R. Aída Hernández Castillo

Zapatismo *and the Emergence of Indigenous Feminism*

One thing I am clear about is that since I realized, at the age of 13 or 14, that something is not quite right with being a woman, I had a change of conscience. That was when I discovered that there were injustices done towards women. Why didn't anyone ask me if I wanted to be married at that age? Many things that seemed unjust happened to me because of the fact that I chanced to be born a woman. And I started to be aware that changing one's consciousness meant an important step for indigenous women themselves. To change one's consciousness is not easy, nor is it something that happens all the time—it is achieved little by little. At the same time that I realized that the life we were living as women was unjust, I developed a restless desire to work directly with women I wanted to find ways, spaces, places, something that had to do with our rights. Why don't women have the right to education? Why didn't we have birth certificates? Why couldn't I go out on the street without being persecuted or harassed? Why are so many things made difficult for us? . . . These were my worries in the 1970s. It was difficult to find women's spaces then. . . . Ever since I began to look for spaces that would allow me to directly tackle the problems of women, I started to work freely and openly on women's rights. . . . I discovered that there are independent organizations, civil associations and collectives that work with women. I discovered that there are other visions, other alternatives and many hopes that there will be change. That is how we began talking with other women of this state [Oaxaca, Mexico] and from other states. We began to realize there were other indigenous women who thought the same way—they wanted something different. And we have also found the new spaces, which in 1997 came together to form the National Coordinating Committee of Indigenous Women [CNMI].

> Marta, Mixtec woman from the organization,
> Et Naaxwiihy (The Space We Live In) [1]

As an indigenous feminist I intend to recover the philosophical principles of my culture and to make them fit into the reality of the twenty-first century. That is to say, to criticize what I don't like about my culture while proudly accepting that I belong to that culture. Indigenous feminism is to me part of a principle—women develop and make revolution to construct ourselves as independent persons who become a community that can give to others without forgetting about themselves. The philosophical principles that I would recover from my culture are equality, complementarity between men and women, and between men and men and women and women. That part of the Mayan culture currently doesn't exist, and to state the contrary is to turn a blind eye to the oppression that indigenous women suffer. The complementarity is now only part of history; today there is only inequality, but complementarity and equality can be constructed.

I would also recover the double vision, or the idea of the *cabawil*, the one who can look forward and back, to one side and the other and see the black and white, all at the same time. To recover this referent, as applied to women, implies knowing one's self with all the sad and terrible things that are part of my reality as a woman and to reconstruct myself with all the good things I have. It means to recognize that there are women different from me, that there are *ladinas* and indigenous women, that there are black, urban and *campesina* women.

Alma López, Quiché woman, councilmember of the City of Quetzaltenango, Guatemala.[2]

Marta and Alma are not alone in their search for new consciousness and organizing spaces. Many indigenous women like them have started to raise their voices in the public sphere, not only to demand cultural and political rights for their communities, but to signal that the construction of a more just society must begin within the family itself. Some of them, like Alma, have opted to self-identify as feminists. A minority (but very important part) of indigenous women have made women's rights the principal demand of their organizations.

To speak of indigenous feminisms would have been unthinkable 15 years ago. Nevertheless, whether they identify as feminists or not, beginning with the 1990s we have seen the emergence of indigenous women's movements in different Latin American countries that are struggling on different fronts.[3] In Mexico, organized indigenous women have joined their voices to those of the national indigenous movement to denounce the economic and racial oppression that characterizes the insertion of indigenous communities into the national project. At the same time, these women are struggling within their organizations and communities, to change those "traditional" elements that exclude and oppress them.

An analysis of indigenous women's demands and strategies in their struggle points to an emergence of a new kind of indigenous feminism. Although in some ways their demands coincide with those of urban feminists, they have substantial differences as well. The economic and cultural context in which indigenous women have constructed their gender identities marks the specific forms that their struggles take, as well as their conceptions of "women's dignity" and their ways of building political alliances. Ethnic, class and gender identities have determined their struggle and they have opted to incorporate themselves in the broader struggle of their communities. But at the same time they have created specific spaces to reflect on their experiences of exclusion as women and as indigenous people.

The public appearance of the Zapatista National Liberation Army (EZLN) in 1994 served as a catalyst in the organization of indigenous women in Mexico. Zapatista women became some of the most important advocates of indigenous women's rights, through the so-called Women's Revolutionary Law. This charter, created in consultation with Zapatista, Tojobal, Chol, Tzotzil, and Tzeltal women, was made public on January 1, 1994, and has been of great symbolic importance for thousands of indigenous women who are members of peasant, political and cooperative organizations. It contains 10 articles, which enumerate a number of rights of indigenous women. These include the right to political participation and to hold leadership posts within the political system; to a life free of sexual and domestic violence; to decide how many children they want to have; to a fair wage; to choose a spouse; to an education; and to quality health services. Although many indigenous women are not aware of the detailed contents of the charter, its mere existence has become a symbol of the possibility of a fairer way of life for women.[4]

Since the emergence of *Zapatismo*, a movement of indigenous women from different regions of the country has not only voiced their support for the demands of their *compañeros* and the interests of their communities, but also pressed for the respect of their specific rights as women. Parallel to their participation in the struggle for land and democracy, this wide sector of women has begun to demand the democratization of gender relations within the family, the community and the organization. The emergence of this new movement is the expression of a long process of organizing and reflection involving Zapatista and non-Zapatista women.

Although *Zapatismo* played an important role in the creation of national spaces for organizing and reflection, thus making indigenous women's movements' demands more visible, it is impossible to understand the force of these movements without considering the experience of the indigenous and campesino struggles of the last two decades. Beginning in the 1970s, an important indigenous movement in Mexico began to question the official discourse stating the existence of a homogeneous, mestizo nation. Indigenous women incorporated themselves into these emerging spaces for collective reflection. Together with the demands for land, they voiced cultural and political demands that later became couched in the general demand for the autonomy of indigenous peoples.

Much of the academic research on indigenous movements of this time, however, does not mention women's participation. But we know from testimonies of women participants that they were in charge of the "logistics" of many of the marches, sit-ins and meetings that those studies document.[5] This "supporting role" excluded them from the active participation and decision making in the organizations, but still allowed them to come together and share experiences with indigenous women from other regions.

At the same time that women actively participated in the campesino mobilizations, important changes in the Mexican economy pushed them into the informal sector, selling agricultural products and handicrafts in the local markets. The "oil boom" of the 1970s, together with the scarcity of arable land, caused many indigenous men from Chiapas, Oaxaca,

Tabasco and Veracruz to migrate to the petroleum zones, leaving the women to deal with the family's economic matters.[6] Indigenous women's entry into the money economy has been analyzed as making their domestic work evermore dispensable to the reproduction of the labor force and thus reducing women's power within the family.[7] Nevertheless, at the same time that their position within the family was restructured, they entered into contact with other indigenous women and mestizas in the informal sector, and they began to organize spaces for women's collective reflection outside the home.[8]

The Catholic Church, through priests and nuns influenced by liberation theology, also played a very important role in the promotion of women's spaces, especially in the diocese of San Cristóbal (in Chiapas), Oaxaca and Tehuantepec (in Oaxaca) and Tlapa (in Guerrero). Even though the liberation theology that guided the work of these dioceses did not promote a gender-based analysis, its workshops and courses on social inequality and on mestizo society's racism led indigenous women to also question gender inequalities they experienced in their own communities.

Parallel to this, feminist nongovernmental organizations (NGOs) began to take their work into rural areas to support development projects for women and gender consciousness-raising among indigenous women. In this line, the feminists of Comaletzin A.C., an organization founded in 1987, were pioneers in working with indigenous women of the states of Morelos, Puebla, Sonora and Chiapas.[9] The Center for Research and Action for Women (CIAM) and the Women's Group of San Cristóbal de las Casas, both founded in 1989, initiated work against sexual and domestic violence and in support of organizing among indigenous women of the Chiapas highlands and Guatemalan refugee women. Women for Dialogue, working with women of Veracruz and Oaxaca, and the consultants of Women in Solidarity

Action (EMAS), who work with Purépecha women of Michoacán, were also early promoters of indigenous women's rights. The Church's discourse on the "dignity of women" was in some regions replaced by a discourse about women's rights and claims for gender equality, which indigenous women appropriated and gave new meanings in their dialogue with feminists.[10]

Migration, religious groups, feminist NGOs, government development programs and the experience of organizing itself, have all influenced indigenous men and women in such a way that they have restructured their relations within the family and are rethinking their strategies for struggle. But it was starting in 1994, with the public debut of the EZLN, that indigenous women began to raise their voices in the broader public sphere, not only to demand indigenous rights, but also to make claims for the respect of their specific rights as women. Under the influence of *Zapatismo*, a national movement emerged in Mexico—although incipient and full of contradictions—articulating different local efforts to incorporate gender demands into the indigenous movement's political agenda.

Nevertheless, indigenous women have paid a high price for this political participation. They are the ones most affected by the militarization of society and by the paramilitary attacks against the autonomous regions. The establishment of military bases and military patrols in their lands has disrupted their everyday lives. They denounce drug and alcohol sales as corollaries of the military's presence in their communities. "We want the military to leave. They use our houses as brothels; the few classrooms we have for our children are used by soldiers. They use sports fields to park their tanks, helicopters and the bad government's armored cars."[11]

Paramilitaries are using rape as an instrument of repression and intimidation in the communities that are trying to establish autonomous government or communities allied to the EZLN.

The 1994 rape of the three Tzeltal sisters Méndez Sántiz by the Mexican military, the rape of three nurses in San Andrés Larraínzar by paramilitaries, the rape of Chicana activist Cecilia Rodríguez in 1995, and the December 1997 massacre and mutilation of 32 Tzotzil women in Acteal by paramilitaries are only a few examples of the specific way that women are experiencing the low intensity war in Chiapas.[12] This violence against organized women is both a "punishment" for their activism and a message aimed at the men in their families and organizations. Nevertheless, the repression, harassment and terror sown by the military and paramilitaries in different indigenous regions have not been able to stop women's struggle for democracy inside and outside the home.

In 1997, during the National Meeting of Indigenous Women titled "Constructing Our History," with the attendance of 700 women, the National Coordinating Committee of Indigenous Women (CNMI) was formed. This national-level organization includes women from approximately 20 indigenous communities from Mexico City and the states of Chiapas, Michoacán, Morelos, Guerrero, Hidalgo, Jalisco, Puebla, Querétaro, San Luis Potosí, Sonora, Veracruz and Oaxaca. Their mission statement says that they aim to "strengthen indigenous women's leadership from a gender perspective; establish a communication network of indigenous women at the national level; provide skills training for indigenous women at the national level; raise funds to implement regional development, training and service projects for indigenous communities; sensitize indigenous peoples on indigenous women's human rights, utilizing a gender analysis."[13]

Although the members of the CNMI have not publicly declared themselves feminist, their gender-based demands and their interest in struggling against indigenous women's subordination allow us to speak of the emergence of a new indigenous feminism.[14] We can say that even if women's participation in the indigenous and campesino struggle is not a new phenomenon, and even precedes the Zapatista movement by centuries, what is new is the creation of a space within the national indigenous movement for indigenous women to organize and struggle for their specific demands as women.

Contrary to the urban feminist movement in Mexico, indigenous women have maintained a double militancy, linking their gender-specific struggles to struggles for the autonomy of indigenous communities, while continuing to be part of the National Indigenous Congress (CNI). This double militancy has nevertheless confronted resistance from both the feminist movement and the indigenous movement.[15] Yet both movements have benefited from this double militancy; feminists benefited by incorporating cultural diversity into its analysis of gender inequality and the indigenous movement benefited by incorporating gender into its perspectives of the ethnic and class inequality experienced by indigenous peoples.

The members of the CNMI have maintained a double militancy as members of the CNI, the most important national-level independent indigenous organization in Mexico. Since its creation in 1996, the CNI has enjoyed the active participation of women in its various areas of work. Women leaders in the CNI have tried to include a specific agenda for women. At the CNI meeting in Nurío, Michoacán in March 2001, with the Zapatista leadership present, indigenous women activists achieved the creation of a women's panel. Despite the commitment by the CNI leadership, when the discussion began, many indigenous leaders insisted that this space be opened to the participation of men. Purépecha, Mixtec, Zapotec and Chocholtec women patiently explained to their male compañeros that their initiative did not intend to divide the CNI, but rather to provide a strategy for creating a supportive context in which indigenous women, who are mainly monolingual, could express their feelings. A male Purépecha leader interrupted the discussion by abruptly grabbing the microphone from the coordinator of the panel and insisting that the audience turn to "more serious issues." The panel ended up mainly being made up of women. This apparently unimportant incident shows the difficulty that indigenous women face, even within the CNI, to democratize internal relations.

The incident also shows men's and women's different styles of discussion within the CNI. Women tended to focus on daily problems, the specific ways that they experience racism and exclusion, while the men made political pronouncements. Indigenous women nevertheless took advantage of this space to declare that the way to strengthen the CNI is by democratizing it, permitting the active participation of women in the leadership of the movement and working to develop a gender perspective within the organization.

These new processes of organization for gender rights are also taking place in other parts of Latin America, and new networks are being built with the participation of indigenous women. Since 1995, these women have chosen to construct their own independent spaces apart from those of the national indigenous movements and from the feminist movements of their respective nations. The first Continental Encounter of Indigenous Women took place in Quito, Ecuador, the second in Mexico (1997) and the third in Panama (2000). The Summit of Indigenous Women of the Americas took place in Oaxaca, Mexico in 2002, and the fourth Continental Encounter was in Peru in 2004. The participation of indigenous women from other continents has grown. From these events there has emerged a Continental Coordinator of Indigenous Women, an organization formed by activists from Latin America, the United States and Canada.

These transnational organizing spaces have become important for women's struggles on many fronts. Organized indigenous women have joined the Latin American indigenous movement to denounce the economic oppression and racism that marks the place of indigenous peoples in national projects. At the same time, these women are developing their own political practices and discourses based on culturally situated gender perspective that question both the sexism and the essentialism of indigenous organizations, as well as the ethnocentrism of hegemonic feminism.[16]

In some contexts this struggle for the social justice of indigenous peoples and women's equality has happened through the appropriation of transnational discourses on human rights; in others, however, these discourses have combined with the argument that reclaims the indigenous worldview as a more holistic way of relating to nature and society. In many cases the discourses have been dismissed as essentialist by academics and non-indigenous activists, who fail to consider that a strategic essentialism might offer potential for peoples whose cultures and identities have been rejected by the colonization process. Some feminist academics have been particularly critical of this discourse, pointing out that some factions of the Latin American indigenous movement have used the concept of complementarity to make an idealized representation of their cultures and societies, thus denying the power relations that exist between the sexes. However, from another perspective, indigenous women are reclaiming the concept of complementarity to question and contest the way in which indigenous men are reproducing the power relations of the colonizer and abandoning the principle of duality of the Mesoamerican cultures.

Although it is still premature to speak of a consolidated movement of indigenous women in Latin America or of an indigenous feminism, the Zapatista women, together with other organized indigenous women, have made us recognize that the struggles against racism, sexism and economic exploitation, can and should be complementary and simultaneous struggles. The ethnocentrism of Mexican feminism is being questioned and the movement is being challenged to re-examine the importance of ethnicity and class in understanding the processes of women's identity in multicultural Mexico. The contributions of indigenous women, whose voices we can find in the documents produced in their congresses, meetings, workshops and essays and interviews in feminist journals, tell us of the necessity to construct a more inclusive feminist practice based on the recognition of diversity. It is up to us to learn to listen to the claims made by these dissident voices.

ABOUT THE AUTHOR

R. Aída Hernández Castillo is a researcher-professor in the Center for Advanced Studies in Social Anthropology (CIESAS) and her latest books are *Histories and Stories from Chiapas: Border Identities in Southern Mexico* (University of Texas Press, 2001); *The Other Word: Women and Violence in Chiapas* (ed. IWGIA, 2001); and is co-editor with Lynn Stephen and Shannon Speed of *Dissident Women: Gender and Cultural Politics in Chiapas* (University of Texas Press, 2006). Translated from the Spanish by NACLA.

NOTES

1. Patricia Artía Rodríguez, "Desatar las Voces, Construir las Utopías: La Coordinadora de Mujeres Indígenas en Oaxaca," MA Thesis in Social Anthropology, 2001, CIESAS, Mexico City.
2. Interviewed by Ixtic Duarte for Estudios Latinoamericanos de la Facultad de Ciensas Políticas de la UNAM.
3. For the experience of Guatemalan women, see Morna McLeod (ed.), *Identidad: Rostros sin máscara. Reflexiones sobre Cosmovisión Género y Etnicidad* (Guatemala City: Oxfam-Australia, 2000) and "Algunos colores del arcoiris: Realidad de las Mujeres Mayas," document by Fundación para la Democracia "Manuel Colom Arqueta" and Grupo de Mujeres Mayas Kaqla, Guatemala, November 2000. For the experiences of indigenous women in different countries of Latin America see Martha Sánchez (eds.) *La Doble Mirada: Voces y Experiencias de Mujeres Indígenas Latinoamericanas* (México City: UNIFEM-ILSB, 2005)
4. For a description of the ways the EZLN has appropriated gender demands

through the Revolutionary Women's Law and its impact on the organizing processes of indigenous women, see R. Aída Hernández Castillo, "Reinventing Tradition: The Women's Law," in *Akwe Kon: A Journal of Indigenous Issues*, Vol. XI, No. 2, Summer 1994, pp. 67–71; Margara Millán, "Mujeres indígenas y zapatismo: nuevos horizontes de visibilidad" in *Cuadernos Agrarios*, No. 13, January–June 1996, pp. 152–67; Giomar Rovira, *Mujeres de Maíz* (Mexico City: Editorial Era, 1997).

5. For an example of how academic work silences the voices of indigenous women in Chiapas, see Jesús Morales Bermúdez, "El Congreso Indígena de Chiapas: Un Testimonio," in Anuario 1991, Instituto Chiapaneco de Cultura, Tuxtla Gutíerrez, 1992, pp. 241–371.

6. For an analysis of these changes in the campesino economy, see George Collier, *Basta! Land and the Zapatista Rebellion in Chiapas* (Oakland: Food First, 1994), and Diana Rus, "La crisis económica y la mujer indígena: El caso de San Juan Chamula, Chiapas," INAREMAC, San Cristobal de las Casas, 1990.

7. See Collier and Merielle Flood, "Changing Gender Relations in Zinacantán, Mexico," in *Research in Economic Anthropology*, Vol. 15, 1994.

8. See June Nash (ed.), "Maya Household Production in the Modern World," in *The Impact of Global Exchange on Middle American Artisans* (Albany: State University of New York Press, 1993).

9. This organization plays a very important role in the formation of the National Network of Rural Consultants, which brought together organizations working on gender issues from various parts of Mexico.

10. This brief survey of feminist organizations' work in rural zones is by no means exhaustive. Many other organizations have followed the work of the pioneer organizations that established dialog with indigenous women. An important example of these is K'inal Antzetik, whose work with women from the National Coordinating Committee of Indigenous Women (CNMI) and other feminist organizations that are part of the National Network of Rural Consultants.

11. "Mujeres Indígenas protestan contra el Ejército," *La Jornada*, April 9, 1996, p. 12.

12. See R. Aída Hernandez Castillo, "Fratricidal War or Ethnocidal Strategy? Women's Experience with Political Violence in Chiapas," in Victoria Sanford (ed.), *Engaged Observer: Anthropology, Advocacy, and Activism* (Rutgers University Press, 2002).

13. Mission Statement from 1997 of the National Indigenous Coordinating Committee of Indigenous Women (CNMI).

14. See Sylvia Marcos, "Mujeres indígenas: Notas sobre un feminismo naciente," in *Cuadernos Feministas*, Año 1, No. 2, 1997; Sara Lovera and Nelly Palom, *Las Alzadas* (Mexico City: ed. CIMAC, 1999).

15. R. Aída Hernández Castillo, *The Other Word: Women and Violence in Chiapas* (Santa Cruz, Bolivia: ed. IWGIA, 2001).

16. In the Mexican context I use the term *hegemonic feminism* to refer to the

academic feminism from the center of the nation, for which the struggle for reproductive rights and abortion has been central. I analyze the tension between hegemonic and emerging indigenous feminism in my article in the collective book *Dissident Women: Gender and Cultural Politics in Chiapas* (University of Texas Press 2006).

Shane Greene

Incas, Indios *and Indigenism in Peru*

Peruvian President Alejandro Toledo entered office in July 2001 raising ethnic banners to mobilize the masses against the corrupt and authoritarian regime of his predecessor, Alberto Fujimori. Labeled as a modern-day Pachacútec—the Incan emperor widely credited with expanding and renovating the ancient empire— and waving the rainbow-colored flag of the Inca, Toledo configured his place within a centuries-old mythology still lodged in the popular Peruvian consciousness: the return of the Inca.[1] But he mixed these strategically deployed images of his Incaic ancestry with the adoption of a coastal and urban *cholo* status, thanks to the clear signs of upward mobility afforded to him by a prestigious education at Stanford University. In the Peruvian imagination his popular nickname, "*El Cholo*," connotes someone who has emerged from humble Andean roots to achieve a less provincial, and thus—according to Peruvian racial logic—an implicitly less "Indian" status.

During his electoral campaign and the battle against Fujimori's attempts to steal the election, Toledo continued to rely on these contradictory symbols related to Peru's racial hierarchies. He was at once an ascending Andean prophet, a capable coastal politician, the new Inca messiah and only the latest in a long line of "indigenous mestizos."[2]

Toledo's gestures to the Inca past are not new to mainstream Peruvian politics. Paying rhetorical homage to Peru's Incaic roots has long been prominent in the political discourses of even the most aristocratic and evidently non-indigenous Peruvian ideologues, nation-makers and *indigenista* intellectuals. Historian Cecilia Méndez aptly describes how the political elite has historically constructed Peruvian nationalism with constant rhetorical praise for the purity of the Inca past. Implicit in this, she perceptively adds, is the disparagement of assimilated present-day indigenous people. Peru's nationalist ideology, she says, is best captured in the phrase *"Incas sí, indios no"* ("Incas yes, Indians no").[3]

Since assuming office, however, the Toledo administration has lessened its use of neo-Incaic symbolism. It has been forced to move beyond this conventional posturing in the face of overtly political demands from social movements that have tired of facile rhetorical flirtations with Peru's pre-Columbian past. Movement leaders from both Andean and Amazonian regions now seek to unite their causes, putting an end to decades of organizing separately under different banners: the Andeans as "campesinos" and the Amazonians as "natives." They are clearly motivated in their move toward ideological unification and political invigoration by more than just the particularities of Peru's national historical context. Indeed, they are participants in an emerging ethnic movement—patently global in size and scope—that seeks legitimation from a regime of rights, responsibilities and opportunities afforded by a transnational indigenous citizenship.

At the 2004 Independence Day celebrations, Toledo made a clear concessionary gesture to the country's growing indigenous movement. Faced with single-digit approval ratings and continual threats of removal from office, he was undoubtedly anxious to heal at least one of the many political wounds from which his administration had suffered. He delivered a speech to Congress proposing the creation of a Development Institute for

Andean, Indigenous, Amazonian and Afro-Peruvian Peoples (INDEPA).

The forthright announcement of a new multicultural institute conceals much of the political complexity and dispute that brought the proposal into being in the first place. It followed a year of controversy over first lady Eliane Karp's initiative to establish a state agency that represents the interests of Peru's ethnic minorities. Notably, the year-long dispute served as a catalyst that provoked a strengthening of what was previously a weak, virtually non-existent alliance between Andean and Amazonian community leaders who now seek to explore the political potential of global indigeneity.

The first lady's initiative, the National Commission on Andean, Amazonian and Afro-Peruvian Peoples (CONAPA), had come under frequent attack by indigenous leaders and members of Congress. CONAPA's detractors claimed the effort masked some potentially nefarious private interests and moved forward despite growing discontent among indigenous organizations. Toledo's legislative proposal to create INDEPA signified the possibility of a new start by recognizing the troubled relationship between the first lady's ethnic rights agency and those whose interests it was meant to address.

Indigenous leaders responded to Toledo's announcement by setting out to work on a proposal for constitutional reforms that would address the collective rights of Peru's constitutionally recognized "campesino" (Andean) and "native" (Amazonian) communities. Peru's major Andean and Amazonian organizations submitted the proposal to Congress in October 2004 and held a press conference in Lima in which the leaders of "peasant" unions and "native" organizations publicly reaffirmed a shared identity as *"pueblos indígenas"* ("indigenous people").[4]

Méndez's ideological formulation now faces the possibility of a significant inversion: *"¡Indios sí, Incas no!"* No more romantic rhetoric. Peru's indigenous peoples are clearly focusing on indigenous rights legislation as the ultimate source from which an effective politics of recognition will emerge. The epigraph of an earlier proposal prepared by indigenous organizations expressly for Toledo's administration is similarly resolute: "For a Constitution for everyone . . . indigenous peoples and communities stand and be counted."[5]

The government has responded to these demands with new and contradictory indigenist rhetoric similarly influenced by tendencies originating from outside Peru's national context. Worldwide trends toward an inclusive multicultural politics shaped the state's revised indigenous agenda from the beginning. These trends consist of complex attempts to reconcile the rights and responsibilities of the individual citizen with those of collective citizens, which are often defined by a combination of racial and ethnic status, cultural criteria and a history of past wrongs for which the group seeks restitution.[6]

The Toledo Administration's embrace of this deceptively innocent global rhetoric illustrates how contested "multiculturalism" is as an ideological program, particularly when utilized in the top-down fashion characteristic of Peru's political culture. CONAPA represented the Toledo Administration's attempt to institutionalize this multicultural rhetoric. Although the agency got off to an apparently good start, it experienced a series of difficult growing pains as it sought to establish a participatory multicultural framework explicitly modeled on similar efforts in the region—particularly, Colombia's 1991 constitutional reforms. To CONAPA's credit, however, it called together national-level organizations representing Amazonian and Andean communities to propose reforms to the Constitution that would grant greater autonomy to Peru's ethnic minorities and promise greater inclusion in national and local governments.

Karp resigned from CONAPA midway through 2003, stating

it was time for the entity to be under the direction of a person representing one of Peru's ethnic minorities. Following her departure the commission spiraled deeper and deeper into a series of public scandals. Part of the conflict resulted from the poorly managed appointment of her successor. Initially, Toledo and Karp offered the job to Gil Inoach, a member of the Aguaruna peoples, in June of 2003. Inoach had recently completed his second term as president of the Interethnic Association of Development in the Peruvian Jungle (AIDESEP), an indigenous Amazonian organization, and had actively participated in CONAPA's initial phases. But according to Inoach, they later retracted the job offer because he refused to accept a pre-packaged list of persons the President and first lady planned to invite as acting members of the commission.

"They presented me a list of persons that would make up CONAPA, which I looked over," says Inoach. "Then I presented another list as a counterproposal, arguing that if CONAPA was betting on a change toward an inclusive state, then it would be advisable that CONAPA be composed of indigenous representatives that were authorized and representative . . . because of that, they later told me I was not ready to take over its presidency." The position went temporarily to Miguel Hilario, a member of the Amazonian Shipibo-Conibo peoples. Because Toledo and Karp failed to consult indigenous organizations on either candidate's nomination, several indigenous leaders inter-preted their actions as a clear instance of secretive bureaucratic cronyism.

Other factors also added to the crisis that plagued CONAPA. First, Karp's decision to accept a privately funded research project on indigenous movements, following her pro-bono work to create CONAPA, raised questions among members of Congress regarding her motives. Secondly, allegations surfaced accusing CONAPA of grossly mismanaging a World Bank "indigenous" fund. And finally, it was revealed that ranking members of CONAPA had close associations with consultants to a plan that would extend gas-extraction activities in a natural reserve inhabited by an isolated native population.[7]

The conflict over CONAPA came to a head on August 14, 2003, when 36 signatories from Peru's major indigenous organizations publicly declared their refusal to recognize the institution as representative of their interests. Their declaration cited a series of tough criticisms about CONAPA's bureaucratic inefficiency, its lack of legal status and its increasing tendency to "act behind the backs of indigenous organizations."[8]

These debates about indigenous leadership and the events following Karp's resignation contributed to a dramatic yearlong standoff. As late as April 2004, Toledo was still restating his faith in CONAPA. However, the relatively young umbrella indigenous organization, the Permanent Conference on Peru's Indigenous Peoples (COPPIP), which coordinates with both Andean and Amazonian community organizations, continued to push for a completely new institutional framework. Leaders from COPPIP, the Amazonian-based AIDESEP and three other national level indigenous organizations called community delegates to Lima to discuss CONAPA's government-backed constitutional reform process. Among the other organizers was the increasingly important National Coordinator of Communities Affected by Mining (CONACAMI), an environmental organization born in the late 1990s. CONACAMI's main base of support is found in various Andean "campesino communities" that are now being encouraged to reconsider their status as "indigenous" through their association with Peru's ethnically defined organizations. All the controversy led to Toledo's July 2004 proposal for the creation of INDEPA.

The existence of a burgeoning national movement moving toward the consolidation of Andean and Amazonian interests under an ethnic banner may take some by surprise. Many observers continue to insist that there is no significant indigenous movement in the country.[9] In fact, Peru is often cited as a notable exception in the Latin American context, an aberration from general trends of the regionalizing and globalizing ethnic-based political claims now trumping class-based politics. Explanations for this vary but they inevitably assume that the Peruvian national context is somehow peculiarly insulated from today's global indigenism and Latin America's growing grassroots indigenous mobilization.

Some prominent Peruvian thinkers have provided an impressively deep historical and cultural analysis to explain what they perceive as a lack of ethnic identity-based movements among Peru's Andean communities.[10] In this view, "indigenous" identity remains a highly devalued political currency for native Peruvian Andeans. Instead of appropriating their indigenousness as an appealing political tool, the argument continues, Andean peoples in Peru still articulate political projects for progress by utilizing other, non-indigenous ideologies. They adopt the symbols of ethnic hybridity and social mobility implied by mestizaje and "cholofication." Or when staking explicit political claims, they identify themselves as agrarian campesinos, utilizing a class-based rather than ethnic paradigm. Considering the explosion of ethnic politics during Toledo's presidency, it might be time to rethink these assumptions. It is important to note not only the emergence of new ethnic-based organizations that integrate Andean and Amazonian leadership, but also the realignment of older "campesino" organizations that now seek solidarity with ethnic organizations.

It is true that use of the term *"indígena"* remains uncommon in many Andean communities when compared to "campesino" or provincial forms of self-identification. But the increasing circulation of *"indígena"* in peasant and ethnic movement organizations suggests something about the impact of global ethnic politics in Peru and the possibility of a rediscovery of indigenousness in the Peruvian Andes.[11] Many commentators alleging the "insignificance" of Peruvian indigenous movements have failed to perceive how this broader global context is transforming Peru, as it has many other Latin American nations.

The emergence of joint Andean and Amazonian indigenous claims in Peru during the Toledo presidency is partly the outcome of processes that predate the administration and that extend beyond the country's internal regional dynamics. Peru's emerging ethnic movement draws significantly from several international arenas of rights claims and social advocacy that are decades in the making and central to indigenous projects everywhere. These include conventions recognizing indigenous peoples' rights—the International Labor Organization's Convention 169, for instance—and other ongoing indigenous agendas within diverse contexts like the UN or the Organization of American States. The dramatic worldwide impact of indigenous-environmental advocacy alliances is also of great importance.

Since the early 1980s, the UN has become the primary legal context in which indigenous leaders infuse local causes with a more universalistic notion of indigenous rights and cultural citizenship. Through the Working Group on Indigenous Peoples, the UN helped promote and release the "Draft Declaration on the Rights of Indigenous Peoples" in the early 1990s and declared a decade for indigenous peoples starting in 1995. The Draft is emblematic of global multiculturalist ideology at work. It proposes to recognize a series of collective rights that would redress the wrongs indigenous populations suffered under European colonialism and the assimilationist campaigns of postcolonial nation-states.

These international legal proposals, debated extensively by indigenous representatives, are careful to define collective rights in concert with the West's historically dominant notions of human and individual rights. Attempting to tie indigenous peoples to the rule of law within liberal state democracies avoids the thorny issue of ethnic separatism, which most indigenous groups do not advocate. But it still legitimates contemporary discourse about distinct indigenous "peoples" possessing a fundamental right to collective "self-determination." Ideologically, this guarantees them a sense of semi-autonomous existence within their respective nation-states and allows them to perceive themselves as part of an emerging indigenous citizenry on global and regional scales.

In international legal contexts, indigenous identities are most often defined by a combination of cultural, linguistic, historical and political criteria. But self-ascription as indigenous remains essential. This leaves the door open to those in the process of discovering or, in the case of Andeans in Peru, rediscovering their indigeneity. Furthermore, it raises hotly debated questions about who exactly can be considered indigenous as particular groups arise to claim the rights and responsibilities associated with this status.

Unquestionably central to this bundle of emerging rights and responsibilities are those directly associated with environmental justice and the privileged moral position indigenous peoples have come to occupy with respect to the environment. Although promoting indigenous peoples as inherently conservationist is a matter of great contention, one thing is clear: since the end of the 1980s, many indigenous groups have emerged as the most visible global representatives of environmental conservation.

Many indigenous movements now strategically display their cultural traditions, material practices and spiritual values as symbols of sustainable societies in opposition to the rampantly destructive tendencies of corporate capitalism. However, images of the indigenous as spokespersons for sustainability do not merely circulate as symbolic currency. They also serve as political capital convertible into real-world opportunities. Indigenous rights are now closely entwined with the recognition that global measures for environmental conservation are needed to address the ills of a resource-hungry world economy. The worldwide move toward promoting ecologically sustainable development by international aid institutions increasingly broadens the forms of support indigenous groups receive along with their chances for establishing a successful political platform.

In Peru, the international advocacy networks and conservationist alliances of Amazonian movements in the 1980s and 1990s helped create the ideological space necessary for Andeans to reevaluate their "peasant" status and consider exchanging it for, or combining it with, that of "indigenous."

The agrarian identity of Peru's Andean peoples was made official by the state's re-classification of Andean "indigenous communities" as "peasant communities" during General Juan Velasco's reformist military revolution of the late 1960s and early 1970s. Yet the revolution also gave birth to a distinct popular political consciousness that did define itself in ethnic and cultural terms. The Velasco state, for instance, recognized Amazonian peoples' titled settlements as "native communities." Influencing the military regime's recognition of Amazonian nativism were the pioneering efforts of the indigenous Amuesha Congress, which was founded in 1969 and incorporated the first ethnically federated Amuesha communities. Velasco enacted the Native Communities Law in 1974, resulting in the rapid growth of local organizations among all the major ethnic groups in the Amazon and the birth of the national organization AIDESEP, which has sought to represent Amazonian peoples nationally and internationally since 1980. Both local and national Amazonian organizations were engaged with international actors—

missionaries, researchers, activists and others—since their founding in the 1970s. This movement was decidedly "global" well before "globalization" became part of our everyday vocabulary. The Amazonian natives' organizational efforts initially sought to federate and protect their newly won communal land holdings. During the 1980s, the movement expanded and diversified with the emergence of dozens of new local federations and a rival national-level organization. AIDESEP and its founding president, Evaristo Nugkuag, played an absolutely critical role in expanding the global reach of the Amazonian cause. In 1984 he received help from the international nongovernmental organization Oxfam to host an international meeting in Lima.[12] AIDESEP invited national indigenous organizations from four other Amazonian countries, resulting in the creation of the now globally recognized Coordinator of Indigenous Organizations from the Amazon Basin (COICA). Nugkuag, who eventually served as president of both AIDESEP and COICA, became a key promoter of a strategic global alliance between Amazonian and environmentalist organizations. During his tenure, COICA and its participating indigenous organizations, invited every major international environmental NGO to Peru in 1990 to sign the Iquitos Declaration. The document formalized a strategic eco-indigenous alliance between Amazonian natives and global conservationists.

Only since the 1990s have the political projects of Andean and Amazonian Peruvians started to converge. Key sectors of the peasant leadership are exploring the potential of an alliance based on sharing a distinct form of ethnically and culturally defined citizenship. The indigenous umbrella organization COPPIP, which resulted from a 1997 human rights meeting in Cusco, seeks to realign the Andean "campesinos" with the Amazonian "natives" under an explicitly indigenous political program. Amazonian leaders initially played a strong role in the organization and promoted the expansion of an indigenous agenda to address the interests of Andeans. Leaders of Peru's "peasant communities" became increasingly involved in COPPIP when the organization forged a close alliance with CONACAMI's Andean-based anti-mining initiatives. Through advocacy and several massive protest marches, CONACAMI has sought to draw attention to the environmental impact of foreign mining activities in Andean communities. It has also tried to counter the threat posed by constitutional articles changed under Fujimori's neoliberal reforms that regulate community land titles and impede communal land management. Leaders from these organizations have come to recognize how well their environmental and community rights concerns fit within a broader indigenous rights framework.

It is not only through anti-neoliberal environmentalist rhetoric that Peru's Andean organization leaders follow the example of the Amazonians and assert a renewed interest in pragmatic community politics. Movement actors also explicitly justify their claims by looking to the international legal arena for political possibilities. They hope to intervene in Peruvian politics by engaging in that broader global sphere of post-cold war ideologies, which reward initiatives of the indigenous more readily than protests of the peasantry. Tellingly, COPPIP's declaration from its Second National Congress in 2001 denounced the ideological effect of the Velasco regime, which "erased from juridical and political language the denomination 'indigenous communities', substituting for it 'peasant communities', taking away the only name for our identity the colonizers allowed us." Of course, "indigenous" resonates with its own complex historical ambivalence, particularly in the Peruvian Andes. But in contemporary circumstances it takes on a certain appeal by virtue of its adoption into international legal settings and its successful and strategic use by other marginalized ethnic groups. Citing virtually every known UN legal proposal and international agreement that favors indigenous peoples, COPPIP leaders go on to declare, "It is our inalienable right to retake this [indigenous] identity, and to use it as an internationally recognized juridical status."[13] Indeed, they began retaking this indigenous platform in 1997 when the organization was founded, long before Toledo's ascent—and, as it turned out, his descent—as Peru's new Pachacútec.

In word and action, Peru's Andean leaders are joining with their Amazonian counterparts to explore the possibilities of a shared indigenous framework. The contentious trajectory of Karp's initiative and Toledo's resulting concessionary gesture to Peru's indigenous movement, hints at the political potential of the movements' increasing unification. This trend shows they are clearly drawing from a global movement and moment, and their emerging ethnic (and environmental) alliance is gaining momentum. Where exactly the steady globalization of Peru's indigenous movement will lead is to be determined as much by the force of global indigenism as by Peru's internal region-to-region and president-to-president dynamics. For now, it is probably a safe bet that Toledo, having arrived to office with the pomp and circumstance of an Incan emperor's second coming, will leave with a more pragmatic view of Peruvian politics.

ABOUT THE AUTHOR

Shane Greene is assistant professor of anthropology at Indiana University. He is currently working on a book titled *Customizing History: Indigenous Movements, Cultural Politics and the Neoliberal Order in Peru.*

NOTES

1. "Peruvians Elect an Inca Ancestor; President Wins Anti-Spanish Racial Vote," *Toronto Star*, June 5, 2001.
2. I borrow this phrase from anthropologist Marisol de la Cadena. See her

Indigenous Mestizos (Durham: Duke University Press, 2000).

3. Cecilia Méndez, "Incas sí, indios no: Notes on Peruvian Creole Nationalism and its Contemporary Crisis," *Journal of Latin American Studies*, Vol. 28, 1996, pp. 197–225.

4. "Indígenas y campesinos demandan cambios legislativos," *Servindi Actualidad Indígena*, Vol. 1, No. 6, October 29, 2004.

5. "Consulta indígena sobre la reforma constitucional," a document prepared by the indigenous organizations COPPIP, AIDESEP, CONACAMI, COICAP and CONAP from a meeting held on April 12–14, 2003.

6. On multicultural reforms in Latin America see Donna Lee Van Cott, *The Friendly Liquidation of the Past* (Pittsburgh: University of Pittsburgh Press, 2000). On multiculturalism more generally see Will Kymlicka, *Multicultural Citizenship* (Oxford: Clarendon Press, 1995). On guilt and historical restitution see Elazar Barkan, *The Guilt of Nations* (New York: Norton, 2000).

7. "Comisión de fiscalización encuentra irregularidades en la Conapa," El Comercio, June 24, 2004. Zachary Martin, "Peruvian Indigenous Organizations Declare CONAPA Defunct," *Cultural Survival Weekly Indigenous News*, 2003.

8. "Declaración pública de los pueblos indígenas del Perú ante la crisis institucional de CONAPA," document signed August 14, 2003, by representatives of COPPIP, AIDESEP, CONACAMI, COICAP, CONAP and others.

9. Xavier Albó, "Ethnic Identity and Politics in the Central Andes," in J. Burt and P. Mauceri (eds.), *Politics in the Andes* (Pittsburgh: University of Pittsburgh Press, 2004). Kay Warren and Jean Jackson (eds.), *Indigenous Movements, Self-Representation, and the State in Latin America* (Austin: University of Texas Press, 2002). Deborah Yashar, "Contesting Citizenship: Indigenous Movements and Democracy in Latin America," *Comparative Politics*, Vol. 31, No. 1, 1998.

10. Carlos Degregori, "Movimientos étnicos, democracia, y nación en Perú y Bolivia," in C. Dary (ed.), *La construcción de la nación y la representación ciudadana en México, Guatemala, Perú, Ecuador, y Bolivia* (Guatemala: FLACSO, 1998). See also Marisol de la Cadena, *Indigenous Mestizos*.

11. Here, I owe thanks to Cecilia Méndez for her helpful comments on an earlier version of this article. She pointed out that thus far "indígena" status seems to circulate mostly at the organizational level and has not really been revived at the community level where other forms of identification are much more common.

12. See Richard Chase Smith, "Las Políticas de la diversidad: COICA y las federaciones étnicas de la Amazonia," in Stefano Varese (ed.), *Pueblos indios, soberanía y globalismo* (Quito: Abya-Yala, 1996).

13. COPPIP, II Congreso Nacional de Pueblos Indígenas del Peru, 2001.

Mario A. Murillo

Beset by Violence, Colombia's Indigenous Resist

Colombian president Álvaro Uribe and his many supporters in and out of government often point out that under his "Democratic Security" strategy implemented since 2002—with the unwavering support of the White House—the government has been able to regain control of over 500 municipalities, bringing a level of security to the Colombian people not felt in generations. Indeed, this was one of the clarion calls of Uribe's successful campaign to get legal approval of a re-election bid for an unprecedented second term in office.

But as is the case with most things in Colombia these days, the optimistic assertions about security resonate primarily with the urban middle and upper classes, which remain largely isolated from the daily reality of the internal conflict. For peasant and indigenous communities in the countryside, the security promised by Uribe is at best a mixed blessing, if not a step back for their communities. Such is the case in the southwestern department of Cauca.

Northern Cauca was recently dubbed "Caguán II" by the Army in reference to the demilitarized safe haven of five municipalities former President Andrés Pastrana granted the Revolutionary Armed Forces of Colombia (FARC) during the 1999 peace talks. In a highly publicized special Security Council session of the Army in early July 2005, officials described in great detail how, over the last 20 years, the FARC had converted this region in the heart of indigenous territory into one of its most important strategic outposts. According to the military, the FARC has built a 350-kilometer network of clandestine roadways throughout the mountainous region to facilitate passage between rebel camps, as well as a training camp for new guerrilla recruits.

Last April, in one of the most dramatic manifestations of the current security situation, the FARC and state security forces clashed in an intense battle in the town of Toribío that lasted 11 days, resulting in the deaths of a 9-year-old boy and several police and soldiers. When it was over, local Army commanders proclaimed that the guerrillas had been "neutralized," and that security had arrived for the people of the region. Currently in Toribío, as is the case in other small towns of northern Cauca, the National Police maintains a massive presence. Highly fortified bunkers are scattered at different strategic points, and M16-bearing soldiers are stationed at just about every corner of the town. Although the guerrillas still maneuver relatively freely through the unpaved roads between the region's many small towns, the large police presence in places like Toribío presents at least a temporary deterrent to another attack from the FARC. Nevertheless, the mostly indigenous residents of the region uniformly express a greater sense of tension and insecurity.

"For us, both the guerrillas and the military are unwanted, because they directly interfere with the community process we have been working on here for more than 30 years," said one community leader who asked not to be identified, a Nasa Indian who works in the mayor's office in Toribío.

The indigenous leadership has been on edge since early July, when at the aforementioned Security Council session the Commander of the Army's Third Brigade, Gen. Hernando Pérez Molina, stationed in Cali, stated unequivocally that "in that area of northern Cauca, there existed a co-government where the

FARC used resources from the European Union that were directed to the Nasa Project for the guerrillas' own benefit." Pérez Molina was referring to the Nasa Project, a multifaceted community development plan started by the Nasa people in 1980 in the municipality of Toribío that encompasses three indigenous reserves—San Francisco, Tacueyo and Toribío. The Nasa Project incorporates political consciousness-raising, community organizing, and economic development based on sustainable agriculture and conservation. It also includes traditional education, health and family assistance programs—all under the rubric of an unwavering demand for indigenous autonomy and respect for their collective rights.

The Nasa Project is recognized internationally as an important community development program that has had outstanding success in reducing poverty through the conservation and sustainable use of biodiversity. In 2004, it was awarded special recognition from the Equator Initiative of the United Nations Development Program.

According to representatives of the Nasa Project, by linking their organization with the FARC, Gen. Pérez Molina was unilaterally trying to discredit its autonomy, thus exposing its leaders to reprisals from the state, and eventually, as in other parts of Colombia, even paramilitary operations.

"First of all, we have never received any money from the European Union," said the mayor of Toribío, Arquímedes Vitonás. "But more importantly, we are completely independent of any of the actors in this conflict, and we have been extremely diligent about accounting for all the resources that come to the community. For the General to say there is a co-government with the FARC is very irresponsible."

The tone of the general's comments is consistent with President Uribe's position regarding the alternative social programs of indigenous communities throughout the country, which on more than one occasion the President has described as illegal in their claims of autonomy from the state. Since taking office over three years ago, Uribe has been irked by the indigenous movements' claims of autonomy—particularly as they relate to his national security programs.

Early on in his term, Uribe proposed a series of constitutional reforms that would have chipped away at some of the hard-fought guarantees that indigenous people won in the 1991 Constituent Assembly that rewrote the Constitution. The President charges that some of the guarantees threaten the authority of the central government. Among these constitutional provisions is the recognition of indigenous territorial entities as autonomous zones where indigenous councils, or *cabildos*, have ultimate jurisdiction. Uribe's counter-reforms would have limited the scope of what are currently recognized as indigenous territories.

Another source of friction between the government and the indigenous communities has been the ongoing negotiations of a Free Trade Agreement (its Spanish acronym being TLC, for *Tratado de Libre Comercio*) with the United States. These trade negotiations are seen as the main reason Uribe and his supporters in Congress have been pushing new forest management laws that would hand over control of resources on indigenous lands to major corporate interests that stand to benefit most from the trade accord. Indigenous, peasant and Afro-Colombian organizations, along with the trade union movement, have been actively mobilizing against the trade agreement. These groups argue the agreement will devastate local economies, while "handing over sovereignty to multinational corporations who do not recognize the authority of indigenous communities," as Héctor Mondragón, an activist who has worked for years with Colombia's peasant and indigenous communities, told me recently.

Last August, the second of a series of nonbinding public referenda, sponsored by indigenous and peasant organizations, was held in northern Cauca on the TLC. A similar *consulta* was held in March as a symbolic gesture to allow the communities to express their feelings about the trade accord. On both occasions, over 95% of voters rejected the agreement. Nevertheless, the government gave it little weight. One minister described the outcome as the result of "dark forces" influencing the indigenous and peasant communities—a not-so-veiled reference to the guerrillas.

As this organizing against "free trade" agreements continues, the government finds itself struggling to implement its Democratic Security strategy in indigenous territory. Two controversial components of this strategy have been the creation of part-time "peasant armies" in rural areas and the establishment of a network of civilian informers who ostensibly collaborate directly with state forces in helping weed out guerrillas. The approach of involving civilians in local security has heightened tensions between the government and a growing number of "peace communities," which have declared their "active neutrality" in the conflict.

This confrontation has been especially acute in Cauca, where the indigenous leadership has been adamant about refusing to cooperate with any of the armed actors in their territories, citing the constitutional provision protecting indigenous autonomy. The FARC's attempt to consolidate its control in the region has inevitably led to clashes with state forces, leaving the indigenous communities caught in the middle. The vicious attack in Toribío was seen as the most extreme example of this type of violent escalation.

"The attack of last April was no surprise for us. We saw it coming as the National Police began stepping up its presence in the municipality in the weeks prior to April 14th," said Toribío native Mauricio Casso, who is the administrative coordinator of the Association of Indigenous Councils of Northern Cauca (ACIN). "The FARC really messed things up with the attack on the town, alienating everybody in the community with their brutality. But the state forces were just as much part of the problem. Their presence now opens the community up to even more reprisals from the guerrillas."

This is precisely why the indigenous leadership resented what they described as President Uribe's grandstanding in the immediate wake of the Toribío attacks: when he arrived to the town, Uribe openly challenged the FARC "cowards" to confront the state forces. The President and several members of his cabinet also used the incident to condemn the FARC for violating indigenous autonomy and threatening their rights.

"Those same people in the government who said the indigenous community's rejection of the free trade agreement was the manipulation of 'dark forces' suddenly became indigenous protectors," said José Domingo Caldon, a Kokonuco Indian and representative of the National Indigenous Organization of Colombia (ONIC). "The same people who have opposed indigenous self-government denounced the FARC's violation of our autonomy and said we should bring in the Army to protect us, to bring us democratic security."

Indigenous leaders fear this may be the beginning of a much more intensified process of violence in the months to come. "In Urabá [in the 1990s] we saw something similar, where the military accused banana workers of collaborating with the guerrillas, leading to the introduction of paramilitaries who waged an all-out war against the people," said Carlos Andrés Betancourt, the indigenous governor of Jambaló, a town about an hour further up the mountain from Toribío. "You began to see targeted assassinations against the leadership, with complete impunity, followed by massacres and the forced displacement of entire communities. I hope it doesn't come to this in northern Cauca."

Betancourt adds that the indigenous community's high level of organization has up to now prevented a similar level of displacement, but how long they will be able to walk the security tightrope remains to be seen. "Will the people be able to withstand another battle like that in the future? This is another question entirely," he said.

The indigenous leadership in northern Cauca, through the ACIN and other indigenous organizations in the area, has consistently made three demands in order to stabilize the situation in their territories: a complete withdrawal of all armed actors from the municipalities and indigenous territories; an immediate cease-fire and end to hostilities; and a negotiated end to the conflict between the government and the FARC rebels.

It is unlikely that any of these community demands will be met anytime soon. President Uribe has made it clear that state security forces will remain anywhere he deems necessary in order to confront "illegal activity." In September, state security forces actually clashed directly with the indigenous communities in the town of Caloto, where Nasa leaders occupied a piece of land that was supposed to have been given over to the indigenous communities years ago as part of a settlement reached after the state was found complicit in a 1991 massacre of 20 Nasa Indians. A number of indigenous activists were wounded in the week-long assault, and despite a negotiated outcome to the land takeover acceptable to the indigenous communities, doubts remained about the government's intentions. (For example, one government official again hinted of "nefarious forces" behind the indigenous community's action.) Just a few weeks after the assault, President Uribe invited some indigenous activists to participate in one of his famous "community councils," or *consejos comunitarios*, in Bogotá. Most of the major regional organizations boycotted the session, accusing the President of trying to divide the community by not inviting representatives of the ONIC.

"The social organizations of the Nasa people in northern Cauca are the most important popular social movements in the entire country right now. They're the only social sector that to a certain extent has been able to defend its rights and maintain a certain level of recognition on the part of the state," said Mondragón. "And this will continue so long as there is an organization and a movement that makes sure these rights are recognized and respected. How will these rights be taken away? As in other recent examples in Colombia, through violence and attacks on the leadership."

These attacks have already begun. In late October, after receiving a series of threats on their lives, a number of community activists from the ACIN were forced to take extra security precautions, including Alcibiades Ulcué, a Nasa leader who in 2004 was kidnapped by the FARC, Ezequiel Vitonás, the chief counsel of the ACIN, and Manuel Rozental, the co-coordinator of the ACIN's Communication Project, who actually left the country and is now in exile in Canada. The threats have come from pro-government paramilitaries, left-wing guerillas, and state security forces. Clearly, democratic security for the indigenous communities in northern Cauca has been far from what the government promised. "It's the calm of *la Chicha*," one community resident said, referring to the traditional corn-fermented drink popular in the region. "On the surface everything seems normal, but below it, things are bubbling over, ready to explode."

ABOUT THE AUTHOR

Mario A. Murillo is associate professor in the School of Communication at Hofstra University in Hempstead, New York, and host of Wake-Up Call on WBAI Pacifica Radio in New York City. A member of NACLA's editorial board, he is author of *Colombia and the United States: War, Unrest and Destabilization* (Seven Stories Press, 2004).

Charles R. Hale

Rethinking Indigenous Politics in the Era of the "Indio Permitido"

> Ethnicity can be a powerful tool in the creation of human and social capital, but, if politicized, ethnicity can destroy capital. . . . Ethnic diversity is dysfunctional when it generates conflict. . . .
> World Bank Web site on "Social Capital and Ethnicity" [1]

During the 1990s, Dr. Demetrio Cojtí Cuxil gained a well-earned reputation as "Dean" of Maya studies in Guatemala.[2] A prolific scholar and public intellectual, Cojtí deeply influenced the debate on Maya cultural and political rights. Many dominant culture ladinos associated him with the most assertive of Maya demands that directly challenge their long-standing racial privilege. To express their anxieties about these challenges, they often distinguished between principles they endorsed, like the idea of cultural equality, and "extreme" Maya demands that they associated with violence and conflict. When asked to elaborate, they would often turn personal: "Ah, Demetrio Cojtí, for example—he is 100% radical."[3]

In 1998, I talked with Cojtí about the contradictory mix of opportunity and refusal in the policies of the Arzú administration (1996–2000) toward Maya, which he summarized succinctly: "Before, they just told us 'no.' Now, their response is '*si, pero*' ['yes, but . . .']." When Cojtí later accepted the post of Vice Minister of Education in the newly elected Portillo government, speculation reigned. Had he "sold out"? Was he out to test the limits of *"si, pero"*? Gaining experience for a time when Mayas would control the state? Three years into the Portillo adminis-tration (2000–2004), I lunched with some ladino school-teachers—participants in the teachers' strike of 2003 against neoliberal downsizing. They scoffed when I remarked that, a few years earlier, they had described Cojtí as a radical: "He's part of the government now, even worse than the others."

Like Guatemala, nearly every other country in Latin America has recently been transformed by the rise of collective indigenous voices in national politics and by shifts in state ideology toward "multiculturalism."[4] The latter, combined with aggressive neoliberal policies, forms part of an emergent mode of governance in the region. Far from opening spaces for generalized empowerment of indigenous peoples, these reforms tend to empower some while marginalizing the majority. Far from eliminating racial inequity, as the rhetoric of multi-culturalism seems to promise, these reforms reconstitute racial hierarchies in more entrenched forms. While indigenous move-ments have made great strides over the past two decades, it is now time to pause and take stock of the limits and the political menace inherent in these very achievements.

In its mid- to late-twentieth century heyday, the state ideology of *mestizaje* had the same dual quality of today's multi-culturalism: in some respects egalitarian and in others regressive. There were variations, but the overall pattern remains clear.[5] Latin American states developed a mode of governance based on a unitary package of citizenship rights and a tendentious premise that people could enjoy these rights only by conforming to a homogeneous *mestizo* cultural ideal. This ideal appropriated important aspects of Indian culture—and of black culture in Brazil and the Caribbean—to give it "authenticity" and roots, but European stock provided the guarantee that it would be modern and forward-looking. This ideology was "progressive" in that it contested the nineteenth century thesis of racial degeneration and extended the promise of equality to all; its progressive glimmer, in turn, gave the political project—to assimilate Indians and marginalize those who refused—its hegemonic appeal.

Although seeking assimilation, state ideologies of mestizaje also drew strength from the continued existence of the Indian Other. Sometimes temporal distance separated this Other from the ideal *mestizo* citizen, as with the celebrated Aztec past in Mexico.[6] Elsewhere, this distance was spatial, as with the people of the Amazonian jungle lowlands, portrayed as inhabiting a world apart. Most often, these two dimensions merged, creating a powerful composite image of the racialized Other against which the *mestizo* ideal was defined. This image deeply influenced *mestizo* political imaginaries. Darker-skinned *mestizos* were lower on the hierarchy, a disadvantage invariably attributed to proximity to "*lo indio*" ("Indianness"). The more "*indio*" you looked, the more this proximity explained your failings. Or, in colloquial terms: "*te salió el indio*" (you let the Indian in you come out).

While this *mestizo* project remains strong, its power as an ideology of governance is slipping. For good reason, it has been the first object of indigenous resistance across the region. Policies of assimilation threaten ethnocide. Unitary citizenship precludes culturally specific collective rights. And the racism embedded in *mestizo* societies delivers a double blow, denigrating the unassimilated while inciting the assimilated to wage an endless struggle against the "Indian within."

Yet the decline of the *mestizo* ideology of governance results from other forces as well. Neoliberal democratization contradicts key precepts of the *mestizo* ideal. Downsizing the state devolves limited agency to civil society, the font of indigenous organization. The return to democracy—even the "guardian" or "low intensity" variants predominant in the region—provides these organizations space for maneuver. Even aggressive economic reforms, which favor the interests of capital and sanctify the market, are compatible with some facets of indigenous cultural rights. The core of neoliberalism's cultural project is not radical individualism, but the creation of subjects who govern themselves in accordance with the logic of globalized capitalism.[7] The pluralism implicit in this principle—subjects can be individuals, communities or ethnic groups—cuts against the grain of *mestizo* nationalism, and defuses the once-powerful distinction between the forward-looking *mestizo* and the backward Indian. Governance now takes place instead through the distinction—to echo a World Bank dictum—between good ethnicity, which builds social capital, and "dysfunctional" ethnicity, which incites conflict.

Explanations for the shift toward a "multicultural" public sphere in Latin America take two principal tacks. The first highlights the creative and audacious political agency of indigenous peoples. The second, exemplified by the work of political scientist Deborah Yashar, emphasizes structural or institutional dimensions. She explains the upsurge of indigenous politics as an unintended consequence of two broader developments: the wave of democratization, which opened new spaces of participation, and neoliberal reform, which eliminated corporatist constraints on indigenous autonomy and accentuated economic woes.[8] Although both explanatory tacks are valid, they miss the way neoliberalism also entails a cultural project, which contributes both to the rising prominence of indigenous voices and to the frustrating limits on their transformative aspirations. The essence of this cultural project, the desired outcome of the government's "*si pero*," is captured in the figure of what Rosamel Millamán and I have called the "*indio permitido*" ("permitted Indian").[9]

The phrase "indio permitido" names a sociopolitical category, not the characteristics of anyone in particular. We borrow the phrase from Bolivian sociologist Silvia Rivera Cusicanqui, who uttered it spontaneously, in exasperation, during a workshop on cultural rights and democratization in Latin America. We need a way, Rivera noted, to talk about how governments are using cultural rights to divide and domesticate indigenous movements. Our use of the word "*indio*" is meant to suggest that the aggregate effect of these measures—quite apart from the sensibilities of individual reformers—has been to perpetuate the subordination the term traditionally connotes. Multicultural reforms present novel spaces for conquering rights, and demand new skills that often give indigenous struggles a sophisticated allure. The menace resides in the accompanying, unspoken parameters: reforms have pre-determined limits; benefits to a few indigenous actors are predicated on the exclusion of the rest; certain rights are to be enjoyed on the implicit condition that others will not be raised. Actual indigenous activist-intellectuals who occupy the space of the *indio permitido* rarely submit fully to these constraints. Still, it would be a mistake to equate the increasing indigenous presence in the corridors of power with indigenous empowerment.

A reasonable starting point for exploring this new form of governance is the distinction between cultural rights and political-economic empowerment. Throughout Latin America, first round concessions of newly christened "multicultural" states cluster in the area of cultural rights, the further removed from the core concerns of neoliberal capitalism the better. In Guatemala, government endorsement of the Academy of Maya Languages signaled the beginning of the multicultural era. Soon thereafter, the Minister of Culture and Sports has become known as the "Indian" cabinet post, filled by a Maya in the last two administrations. The Ministry of Education also showcases the multicultural ethic with its programs in bilingual education and *interculturalidad* (intercultural dialogue). The preposterous idea that an Indian would become Minister of Finance is another matter altogether. At times, the contrast between cultural and political-economic opportunity turns blatant and brutal. Newly inaugurated Guatemalan President Oscar Berger held a ceremony upon naming Rigoberta Menchú "Goodwill Ambassador," and turning over the Casa Crema (a building formerly assigned to the Ministry of Defense) to the Academy of Maya Languages. He announced that the Casa Crema would also house a new television show, ". . . to carry programs on Maya culture, *interculturalidad*, and spirituality." Simultaneously, Berger stood by as the Armed Forces began the violent eviction of landless indigenous campesinos that had occupied over 100 farms in the prior three years.[10]

It would be wrong, however, to let this stark dichotomy between "cultural" and "political-economic" rights stand. The crude Marxist distinction between superstructure and base does injustice to the holistic political visions of indigenous movements. Cultural resistance forges political unity and builds the trenches from which effective political challenge can later occur. Moreover, even if the dichotomy had residual validity on its own terms, it would not withstand close scrutiny. The most important current indigenous demand—rights to territory and resources—cannot be construed as a "cultural" right. Yet instead of the belligerent "no" that one might expect, neoliberal institutions have responded to the indigenous clamor for land with a resounding "*sí, pero.*" Throughout Central America, for example, the World Bank is funding land demarcation projects, intended to assure black and indigenous communities rights to lands of traditional occupation.

Neoliberal multiculturalism is more inclined to draw

conflicting parties into dialogue and negotiation than to preemptively slam the door. Civil society organizations have gained a seat at the table, and if well-connected and well-behaved, they are invited to an endless flow of workshops, spaces of political participation, and training sessions on conflict resolution. In Guatemala, the great wave of such government initiatives came just after the signing of the Peace Accords in December 1996. The country was soon awash in international aid, with Maya civil society as the privileged recipient. This example helps explain why the pattern is so widespread: indigenous rights are, in bureaucratic jargon, a "donor driven" priority. Web sites of the World Bank and Inter-American Development Bank are awash with glowing articles about indigenous and Afro-descendent empowerment. At issue, then, is not the struggle between individual and collective rights, nor the dichotomy between the cultural and the material, but rather the built-in limits to these spaces of indigenous empowerment.

Once the cultural project of neoliberalism is specified, these limits become more evident. As a first principle, indigenous rights cannot violate the integrity of the productive regime, especially those sectors most closely linked to the globalized economy. If an indigenous community gains land rights and pulls these lands out of production, this poses no such threat, especially given the likelihood of the community's return to the fold through a newly negotiated relationship with the market. All the contrary if, for example, indigenous movements were to challenge the free trade zones that shelter maquila-type production, declare a moratorium on international tourism or create their own banks to serve as the "first stop" for remittances from indigenous peoples working abroad. These latter demands would be sure to evoke the wrath of the neoliberal state. More generally, this principle dictates a sharp distinction between policies focused on "poverty reduction," which are ubiquitous and heavily supported, and those intended to reduce socioeconomic inequality, conspicuous for their absence. This first principle has an increasingly globalized character, driven less by the interests of national economic elites than by the constraints and opportunities of a global economic system.

A second principle, also limiting the scope for possible change, has to do with the accumulation of political power. Neoliberal multiculturalism permits indigenous organization, as long as it does not amass enough power to call basic state prerogatives into question. These prerogatives are not about the state as the primary locus of social and economic policies, which now generally derive from the global arena. Nor do they revolve around the state's role as legitimate representative of the people, a dubious proposition for many. Rather, at issue is the inviolability of the state as the last stop guarantor of political order. The Central American countries offer an especially dramatic case in point. If the current massive flow of international aid, loans and development funding were cut off, these tiny dependent states would collapse. Without the state, however, neoliberal economic development would lack the coercive means and minimal legitimacy to proceed. Cultural rights, up to and including many forms of local autonomy, do not threaten to contravene this principle, especially as neoliberal elites gain the wisdom to respond to their indigenous critics not by suppressing dissent, but by offering them a job.

Although these two principles have a repressive side, it is striking how infrequently it appears. Land rights, again, are illustrative. Indigenous demands for territorial sovereignty could present a radical challenge to neoliberal regimes, if they were extensive enough to support an alternative system of productive relations or sufficiently potent politically to undermine state authority. Yet such a challenge blurs fairly easily into less expansive positions with which the state can readily negotiate.

Crucially, this negotiation is no longer about the all-or-nothing ideal of mono-cultural citizenship, which any expression of collective rights would contradict. Instead, it is about the more reasonable proposition of nudging "radical" demands back inside the line dividing the authorized from the prohibited. The critique that accompanies this account does not focus primarily on the limited character of the spaces opened by neoliberal multiculturalism, but rather on the prospect that these limits would define what is politically possible. As long as neoliberal principles are critically scrutinized as opportunities to be exploited, the spaces they open could be productively occupied, fighting the good fight to circumvent their pre-inscribed limits. I have engaged in precisely such an effort, with results that were mixed but positive enough to keep on trying.[11] Although sometimes viable and necessary, this strategy is risky, especially when the full ideological repercussions of neoliberal multiculturalism are taken into account.

With the *indio permitido* comes, inevitably, the construction of its undeserving, dysfunctional, Other—two very different ways to be Indian. The *indio permitido* has passed the test of modernity, substituted "protest" with "proposal," and learned to be both authentic and fully conversant with the dominant milieu. Its Other is unruly, vindictive and conflict prone. These latter traits trouble elites who have pledged allegiance to cultural equality, seeding fears about what empowerment of these Other Indians would portend. Governance proactively creates and rewards the *indio permitido*, while condemning its Other to the racialized spaces of poverty and social exclusion. Those who occupy the category of the *indio permitido* must prove they have risen above the racialized traits of their brethren by endorsing and reinforcing the divide.

One potentially deceptive image that flows from this analysis depicts a small indigenous elite benefiting as representatives of a majority from whom they are structurally alienated. To portray the divide strictly in class terms misses the point, and could reinforce the assertion that "real" Indians are poor, rural and backward, while middle class Indians are "inauthentic."[12] Rather, the dichotomy is cultural-political: moderate versus radical, proper versus unruly. Indians on the "radical" side of this divide are said to act in self-marginalizing ways; their resentment feeds "reverse racism"; and in the post-9/11 climate, criticism of these negative traits gives way to the ultimate term of opprobrium, the indigenous "terrorist."[13] Even those who occupy the category of the *indio permitido* are contaminated by proximity to the radicals, and must constantly prove they belong in the sanctioned space.

The point is not to lionize radicals or to place them beyond critique, but to challenge the dichotomy altogether, and thereby redefine the terms of indigenous struggle. A crucial facet of resistance, then, is rearticulation, which creates bridges between authorized and condemned ways of being Indian. Political initiatives that link indigenous peoples who occupy varying spaces in relation to the centers of political-economic power are especially promising. The same goes for efforts to connect diverse experiences of neoliberal racial formation, especially among indigenous and Afro-descendant peoples. Blacks are more apt to be skeptical of the "good ethnics" trope, cutting through to its underlying racist premises. Indigenous people are better positioned to work the newly opened spaces of cultural rights, putting assumptions about Indians as inherently pre-modern to good use. By placing both experiences under the same analytic lens, we see more clearly how neoliberal multiculturalism constructs bounded, discontinuous cultural groups, each with distinct rights that are discouraged from mutual interaction.[14]

As globalized economic change continues, strategies of

rearticulation can only become more difficult to achieve. Growing numbers of indigenous peoples are leaving rural communities for urban areas, where education, jobs and some hope of upward mobility can be found. Many continue northward to the United States. With few exceptions, the locus of economic dynamism has shifted from agriculture to activities such as maquila production, remittance-driven financial services, tourism and commerce. Rural Indian households are most likely to remain stuck in a cycle of critical poverty. Despite these rapidly changing demographic and economic conditions, indigenous leaders— increasingly urban and urbane—still draw heavily on the utopian discourse of indigenous autonomy, exercised in quintessentially rural, culturally bounded spaces. This discourse can reinforce the ideology of the *indio permitido*, creating authorized spokespeople, increasingly out of touch with those whose interests they evoke. Rearticulation, in contrast, would build bridges among indigenous peoples in diverse structural locations: from rural dwellers, to workers in the new economies, to those who struggle from within the neoliberal establishment. To be effective, rearticulation will also need to draw on reconfigured political imaginaries, and on utopian discourses of a different hue.

Rearticulation may also require shifting strategy from a focus on keeping the state out, to exerting control over the terms under which the state, and the neoliberal establishment more generally, stay in. Indeed, this shift has already begun. The short and unfortunate experience of the Confederation of Indigenous Nationalities of Ecuador (CONAIE) with "co-govern-ment" in Ecuador demonstrated how unprepared it was to take advantage of the fantastic success of ousting one government and being elected to help run its successor. The Bolivian indigenous uprising of October 2003 has given rise to a similar predicament. This dramatic political achievement revealed the profound vulnerability of the *indio permitido* and the explosive potential of rearticulation as resistance. Ahead lies the task of imagining the kind of reconstituted state and alternative productive regime that would stay true to that momentarily unified, but now highly fragmentary, indigenous majority.

The decade-old Zapatista uprising in Chiapas raises the same basic question, from the opposite point of departure. To survive a decade of state-orchestrated hostility while staying the course of defiant political innovation is an impressive feat. As the experiment enters its second decade, however, the prospects for rearticulation grow increasingly remote. Radical refusal of any engagement with the neoliberal state gains transformative traction to the extent that it simultaneously articulates, symbolically and in daily political practice, with those who struggle from other sociopolitical locations. As the potential for forging such articulation diminishes, this space of refusal starts to look like the *indio permitido*'s Other—unruly and conflict prone, but otherwise readily isolated and dismissed.

Perhaps, then, Dr. Cojtí's strategy requires a second look and a more subtle reading. During the same visit to Guatemala in which I spoke with my teacher friends about their strike, I asked Cojtí about the inner workings of the Ministry of Education. He divided the overwhelmingly ladino bureaucracy into three groups: hard-core racists and race progressives, both minorities; and an ambivalent majority that implemented the new "multicultural" mandate without conviction, as the path of least resistance. With ironic humor and characteristic cogency, he offered his own explanation for having taken the job: "to carry out a critical ethnography of the 'ladino' state!"

There is no point in trying to neatly classify this experience as either cooptation or everyday resistance; both are blunt conceptual tools, too focused on the practices themselves rather than on the consequences that follow. These consequences will remain unclear, in turn, until the process of Maya rearticulation begins. Given the genocidal brutality of Guatemala's ruling elite, amply demonstrated in recent history, this process is sure to turn ugly. It would be fatalistic to abandon hopes for rearticulation in anticipation of this ugliness, but irresponsible to advocate Maya ascendancy without imagining some means to assuage the fears and lessen the polarization. To occupy the space of the *indio permitido* may well be the most reasonable means at hand. If so, it will be especially crucial to name that space, to highlight the menace it entails, and to subject its occupants to stringent demands for accountability to an indigenous constituency with an alternative political vision. Otherwise, it will be safe to assume that those who occupy this space have acquiesced, if only by default, to the regressive neoliberal project that the *indio permitido* is meant to serve.

ABOUT THE AUTHOR

Charles R. Hale is associate professor of anthropology at the University of Texas, Austin; author of *Resistance and Contradiction: Miskitu Indians and the Nicaraguan State, 1894–1987* (1994), and *Más que un indio: Racial Ambivalence and the Paradox of Neoliberal Multiculturalism in Guatemala* (forthcoming).

NOTES

1. The basic analysis put forth in this essay was developed collaboratively with my friend and colleague Rosamel Millamán. The epigraph text is from the World Bank website on "Social Capital and Ethnicity": http://www.worldbank.org/poverty/scapital/sources/ethnic2.htm#neg.
2. A brief selection of Cojtí's key publications include his "Problemas de la 'Identidad Nacional' Guatemalteca," in *Cultura Maya y Políticas de Desarrollo*, COCADI, ed., pp. 139–62 (Chimaltenango: Ediciones COCADI, 1989); *Políticas para la reinvindicacíon de los Mayas de Hoy* (Guatemala: CHOLSAMAJ, 1994); *Ri Maya' Moloj pa Iximulew. El Movimiento Maya* (Guatemala City: Editorial Cholsamaj, 1997); and "Heterofobia y Racismo Guatemalteco," in *¿Racismo en Guatemala? Abriendo Debate sobre un*

Tema Tabú. C. Arenas, C. R. Hale, and G. Palma (eds.) (Guatemala: Ediciones Don Quijote, 1999).

3. This assessment tended to be based less on a systematic content analysis of Cojtí's position, than on the mere fact that a highly educated Maya dared to name the racial ills of Guatemalan society in a public, cogent and forthright manner. I address ladino responses to Maya ascendancy at length in my book, to be published with the School of American Research Press, titled: Más que un indio . . . Racial Ambivalence and the Paradox of Neoliberal Multiculturalism in Guatemala.

4. Ample documentation of this transformation can be found in Donna Lee Van Cott, *The Friendly Liquidation of the Past: the Politics of Diversity in Latin America* (Pittsburgh: University of Pittsburgh Press, 2000).

5. For example, the Guatemalan state, loath to give up the practice of separate and unequal, never fully embraced the mestizaje idea, except briefly during the 1944–54 period of social democratic reform. Peru and Paraguay constitute exceptions of a different sort, and each country had its particularities.

6. A good analysis of Mexico's Museum of Anthropology in this vein can be found in Nestor Garcia Canclini, *Culturas Híbridas: Estrategias para entrar y salir de la modernidad* (Mexico: Grijalbo, 1989).

7. For an analysis of "neoliberal" or "late" liberalism, see Nikolas Rose, *Powers of Freedom. Reframing Political Thought* (Cambridge: Cambridge University Press, 1999); Jean Comaroff and John L. Comaroff, "Millennial Capitalism: First Thoughts on a Second Coming," in *Millennial Capitalism and the Culture of Neoliberalism*, J. Comaroff and J. L. Comaroff (eds.), pp. 1–56 (Durham: Duke University Press, 2001); and Elizabeth A. Povinelli, *The Cunning of Recognition: Indigenous Alterities and the Making of Australian Multiculturalism* (Durham: Duke University Press, 2002). I develop a version of this argument more fully in my "Does Multiculturalism Menace? Governance, Cultural Rights and the Politics of Identity in Guatemala," *Journal of Latin American Studies*, 34: 485–524, 2002.

8. This summary is based on Yashar's presentation at the University of Texas, in May 2004. Her book is still forthcoming. See also her "Contesting Citizenship: Indigenous Movements and Democracy in Latin America," in *Comparative Politics*, 23–42, 1998; and "Democracy, Indigenous Movements, and the Post-Liberal Challenge in Latin America," in *World Politics*, 52 (October): 76–104, 1999.

9. This is the central concept in an essay that Millamán and I co-authored, focusing comparatively on my analysis of Guatemala and his of Chile. See our forthcoming "Cultural agency and political struggle in the era of the 'indio permitido'," in *Cultural Agency in the Americas*, D. Sommer (ed.) (Durham: Duke University Press).

10. See, for example, "Campesinos invaden 665 caballerías," *Siglo XXI*, 7/ 24/02. This article reports that CNOC, a coordinator of agrarian organizations, had occupied a total of 53 fincas in nine departments. A

top leader of CONIC, another indigenous agrarian organization, recently told me that the number of occupied fincas was much higher than 100. For an example of news reports on the violent expulsions, see "Plataforma Agraria: Exigen a Oscar Berger fin de desalojos," *Prensa Libre*, 2/20/ 2004. It appears that Berger may not have actively supported the expulsions, which have been carried forward by powerful business interests; rather, he lacked the political resources and will to stop them.

11. For a preliminary report and reflection on one such effort, see C.R. Hale, Galio C. Gurdian, and Edmund T. Gordon: "Rights, Resources and the Social Memory of Struggle: Reflections on a Study of Indigenous and Black Community Land Rights on Nicaragua's Atlantic Coast," *Human Organization*, 62 (4), 2003.

12. There is a direct analogy here, with a prominent line of critique of affirmative action in the United States. A good example is the article "Diversity's False Solace" by Walter Benn Michaels in the *New York Times Magazine*, 4/11/04. In this setting, also, to reduce the matter to class divisions is a simplification that mischaracterizes the dichotomy.

13. CIA concerns about indigenous movements in Latin America as a future security threat are laid out in the CIA publication, found at this web address: http://www.cia.gov/cia/reports/globaltrends2015/index.html. An example of the warning, cited from this report, is as follows: "Indigenous protest movements. Such movements will increase, facilitated by transnational networks of indigenous rights activists and supported by well-funded international human rights and environmental groups. Tensions will intensify in the area from Mexico through the Amazon region. . . ."

14. Sustained analysis in this dual analytical lens is exceedingly and surprisingly rare. One exception is Peter Wade, *Race and Ethnicity in Latin America* (London: Pluto, 1997).

Grassing the Roots

Harry E. Vanden

Brazil's Landless Hold Their Ground

Over the past few decades, there have been various forms of popular protest in Latin America against the austerity measures and conservative economic policies that have come to be called "neoliberalism." These protests have taken diverse forms: the Zapatista rebellion in Mexico, the neo-populist Fifth Republic Movement led by Hugo Chávez in Venezuela, the national indigenous movement led by the National Indigenous Confederation of Ecuador (CONAIE), the regime-changing popular mobilizations in Argentina and Bolivia, and the Landless Rural Workers' Movement in Brazil (*Movimento dos Trabalhadores Rurais Sem Terra*, MST), which is the subject of this article.

Such movements are also a recent and vociferous manifestation of the specter of mass popular mobilization against the governing elite that has haunted Latin America since colonial times. At present, a great many people—especially the poor—seem to feel that the much-touted return to democracy, the celebration of civil society and the incorporation of Latin America into the globalization process has left them marginalized both economically and politically. The reactions in Mexico, Brazil, Ecuador, Venezuela, Argentina, Uruguay and Bolivia have been strong and significant and, in varying ways, make one wonder if the dominant political project is working for common people. It is also quite possible that it is the democratization and celebration of civil society that allow—some would say encourage—the political mobilization that is manifest in the widespread emergence of forceful mass-based social and political movements.

There is a growing consensus that the traditional politicians' new political enterprise is leaving behind the great majorities and, effectively, further marginalizing specific groups within those majorities. Indicators of the growing malaise are many: general alienation from the traditional political process, increased crime, surging abstention rates in select electoral contests as suggested by the low turnout in Argentina in 2001.[1] The 1998 national elections in Brazil saw a similar phenomenon, with 40% of the electorate either abstaining or casting blank or annulled ballots.[2] Changing attitudes have often led to the abandonment of traditional political parties for new, more amorphous, ad hoc parties or coalitions like Chávez's Fifth Republic Movement in Venezuela, and Tabaré Vásquez's Broad Front in Uruguay. They have also produced an upsurge of new sociopolitical movements and mass organizations along with a plethora of national strikes, demonstrations and protests such as those that washed across Argentina at the end of 2001 and the beginning of 2002.

Mass communication systems and easy, relatively affordable access to the Internet have combined with higher levels of literacy and much greater political freedom under the democratization process.[3] This has occurred just as ideas of grassroots democracy, popular participation and even elements of liberation theology and Christian-Base Community organizing have been widely disseminated. There is growing belief that economic equality should exist and that systems working against such equality need to be changed. Unlike the radical revolutionary movements of the last few decades, these new movements do not advocate the radical restructuring of the state through violent revolution. Rather, their primary focus is to work through the existing political system by pushing it to its limits to achieve necessary change and restructuring.[4]

The end of authoritarian rule and the expansive democratization of the late 1980s created new political dynamics in many Latin American nations. Political spaces began to open up in what came to be labeled "civil society," and new forms of political action followed. The projection of an elitist armed vanguard as the spearhead of necessary change began to fade in the face of unarmed political and social mobilizations. The assertion of popular power reminiscent of mobilizations by the pre-coup Peasant Leagues in northeastern Brazil began to bubble up in new and varied forms.

By the time neoliberal economic policy became more widespread in the 1990s, it was becoming evident that the extant political systems in much of Latin America were unable to meet the needs of the vast majorities. Indeed, in the eyes of most Latin American popular sectors, the structural adjustments and neoliberal reforms advocated by international financial institutions like the IMF threatened their security and well being. Their insecurity and dissatisfaction drove them to seek new forms of protest and different political structures that might better address their needs since traditional parties and governments seemed increasingly unable to respond.

As the 1990s progressed, dissatisfaction with traditional political leaders and parties became more widespread along with doubts about the legitimacy of the political system itself. Traditional personalism, clientelism, corruption and avarice became subjects of ridicule and anger, if not rage. The effects of neoliberalism and continued classism and racism amid everstronger calls for equality were inescapable. With growing questions about the system's relevance and legitimacy, these demands were not exclusively addressed to the political system per se but to society more generally. Nor did the populace in most nations look to armed struggles and revolutionary movements to remedy their problems (Colombia is the significant exception here). They sought something different. Groups were looking for new political structures that allowed for their participation. There was a search for new structures that would respond to the perceived—though not always clearly articulated—demands emerging from the popular sectors.

The MST itself was formed as a response to longstanding economic, social and political conditions in Brazil. Land, wealth and power have been allocated in extremely unequal ways since the conquest in the early 1500s. Land has remained highly concentrated, and as late as 1996, 1% of landowners owned 45% of the land.[5] Conversely, as of 2001, there were some 4.5 million landless rural workers in Brazil. Wealth has remained equally concentrated. The Brazilian Institute of Government Statistics reported in 2001 that the upper 10% of the population received an average income that was 19 times greater than that of the lowest 40%.[6]

The plantation agriculture that dominated the colonial period and the early republican era became the standard for Brazilian society. The wealthy few owned the land, reaped the profits and decided the political destiny of the many. The institution of slavery provided most of the labor for the early plantation system and thus further entrenched polarized social relations between the wealthy landowning elite and the disenfranchised toiling masses laboring in the fields. Land remained in relatively few hands, and agricultural laborers continued to be poorly paid and poorly treated.

The commercialization and mechanization of agriculture beginning in the 1970s made much of the existing rural labor force superfluous. As this process continued and became more tightly linked to the increasing globalization of production, large commercial or family estates fired rural laborers, expelled sharecroppers from the land they farmed and acquired the land of farmers who owned small plots. This resulted in growing rural unemployment and the growth of rural landless families, many of whom had to migrate to cities, swelling the numbers of the urban poor. Others opted for the government-sponsored Amazon colonization program, whereby the government transplanted entire families to the Amazon region where they cut down the rainforest for planting. Few found decent jobs in the city, and the easily eroded rainforest subsoil allowed for little sustained agriculture, worsening their collective plight.

The immediate origins of the MST go back to the bitter struggle to survive under the agricultural policies implemented by the military government that ruled Brazil from 1964 to 1985. The landless rural workers in the southern Brazilian state of Rio Grande do Sul began to organize to demand land in the early 1980s. Other landless people soon picked up their cry in the neighboring states of Paraná and Santa Catarina.[7] They built on a long tradition of rural resistance and rebellion that extends back to the establishments of *quilombolos* (large inland settlements of runaway slaves) and to the famous rebellion of the poor peasants of Canudos in the 1890s. In more recent times it included the well-known Peasant Leagues of Brazil's impoverished northeast in the 1950s and early 1960s and the Grass Wars in Rio Grande do Sul and other southern states in the 1970s.[8]

When the MST was founded in southern Brazil in 1984 as a response to rural poverty and the lack of access to land, similar conditions existed in many Brazilian states. Indeed, there were landless workers and peasants throughout the nation, and the MST soon spread from Rio Grande do Sul and Paraná in the south to states like Pernambuco in the northeast and Pará in the Amazon region. It rapidly became a national organization with coordinated policies and strong local participatory structures characterized by frequent state and national meetings based on direct representation. By 2001 there were active MST organizations in 23 of the 26 states.[9]

Today the MST is arguably the largest and most powerful social movement in Latin America. The ranks of those associated with it exceed 200,000 and perhaps even double that number. It has a high mobilization capacity at the local, state and even national level. In 1997, for instance, the organization was able to mobilize 100,000 people for a march on Brasília.

Their views are well articulated. They have a clear understanding of the increased commercialization of agriculture and its consequences for the way production is organized, if not rural life more generally. Similarly, they are fully conscious of how globalization is strengthening these trends and threatening their livelihoods. In small classes, meetings and assemblies, and through their newspaper, *Jornal Dos Trabalhadores Sem Terra*, their magazine, *Revista Sem Terra*, and numerous pamphlets, they inform their base through a well-planned program of political education. They even establish schools in their encampments, settlements and cooperatives to make sure the next generation has a clear idea of the politics in play.[10] The next generation of leaders attends their national school ITERRA, where they get a strong political and popular orientation, well-grounded instruction in political and organizational theory and practical skills such as accounting and administration.

The MST also facilitates the organic development of highly participatory grassroots organizing rooted in groups of about ten families, which constitute a "Base Nucleus" in each neighborhood. Local general assemblies convene frequently and all members of the family units are encouraged to participate. Frequently held regional, state and even national assemblies in turn incorporate representatives of these local-level units.[11] Leadership is collective at all levels, including nationally, where some 102 militants make up the National Coordinating Council.[12]

Their political culture and decision-making processes clearly break from the authoritarian tradition. The movement has been heavily influenced by liberation theology and the participatory democratic culture generated by the use and study of Paulo Freire's approach to self-taught, critical education. Indeed, the strongly participatory nature of the organization and the collective nature of leadership and decision-making have made for a political culture that challenges traditional authoritarian notions and vertical decision-making structures.[13]

One of the characteristics of recent social movements like the MST is a broad national vision. The *Sem Terra* envision a thoroughgoing land reform and complete restructuring of agrarian production in all of Brazil, as suggested by their pamphlet prepared for their fourth national congress in 2000, "Agrarian Reform for a Brazil Without Latifundios."[14] The MST believes that it is impossible to develop the nation, construct a democratic society, or alleviate poverty and social inequality in the countryside without eliminating the *latifundio*. But they go on to say that agrarian reform is only viable if it is part of a popular project that would transform Brazil's economic and social structures.[15]

Like many of Latin America's recent social and political movements, the *Sem Terra* are well aware of how their struggle is linked to international conditions. Thus, they begin by challenging the positive vision of neoliberalism presented by global media.[16] In a draft document on the "Fundamental Principles for the Social and Economic Transformation of Rural Brazil," they note that "the political unity of the Brazilian dominant classes under Fernando Henrique Cardoso's administration (1994–2000) has consolidated the implementation of neoliberalism [in Brazil]," and that these neoliberal policies have led to the increased concentration of land and wealth in the hands of the few and the further impoverishment of Brazilian society. "Popular movements," the document goes on to say, "must challenge this neoliberal conceptualization of our economy and society."[17]

Mass political mobilization is another fundamental organizational principle as seen in their massive mobilizations for land takeovers and street demonstrations.[18] This strategy is widely communicated to those affiliated with the organization. A pamphlet disseminated by the organization, "Brazil Needs a Popular Project," calls for popular mobilizations, noting that "all the changes in the history of humanity only happened when the people were mobilized," and that in Brazil, "all the social and political changes that happened were won when the people mobilized and struggled."[19]

As has been the case in other Latin American countries, traditional politics and political parties have proven unable and/or unwilling to address the deteriorating economic conditions of marginalized groups who suffer the negative effects of economic globalization. In turn, the social movements have responded with grassroots organization and the development of a new repertoire of action that breaks with old forms of political activity. Developing organization and group actions, sometimes with the outside assistance of progressive organizations concerned with social justice, have tied individual members together in a strongly forged group identity.

In the case of Brazil and the *Sem Terra*, this outside role was played by the Lutheran Church and even more so by the Pastoral Land Commission of the Catholic Church. Although these organizations assisted the MST along with some segments of the Workers' Party (PT), the organization never lost its autonomy. It was decided from the onset that this was to be an organization for the Landless Workers, to be run by the Landless Workers and for their benefit as they defined it.

They have taken over and occupied large estates and public lands; constructed black plastic-covered encampments along the side of the road to call attention to their demands for land; and have marched and staged confrontations when necessary. They even occupied the family farm of President Fernando Henrique Cardoso shortly before the 2002 election to draw attention to his land-owning interests and the consequent bias they attributed to him. At times they are brutally repressed, assassinated and imprisoned, yet still, they persevere, forcing the distribution of land to their people and others without land. Their ability to mobilize as many as 12,000 people for a single land takeover or 100,000 for a national march suggests the strength of their organizational abilities and how well they communicate and coordinate at the national level. They also garner a great deal of national support, having created a consensus throughout the country that land distribution is a problem and that substantial reforms are necessary.[20]

The Landless remain keenly attuned to, and consider themselves part of, the international struggle over globalization. They helped organize and participated in the World Social Fora of Porto Alegre, and have sent representatives to demonstrations and protests throughout the world. Struggles that were once local and isolated are now international and linked.[21] International communications networks, including cellular phones and, especially, e-mail, have greatly facilitated the globalization of awareness about local struggles and the support and solidarity they receive. Combined with dramatic actions like massive land takeovers, the MST has generated considerable support at both the national and international level and has helped transform local struggles into national events, redefining local problems as national problems that require national attention and resources.

The interaction between the MST and the PT is also

instructive. Relations between the two organizations are generally excellent at the local level with overlapping membership, but the national leaderships have remained separate and not always as cordial. The MST has maintained a militant line in regard to the need to take over unused land and assert their agenda, whereas much of the PT leadership has wanted to be more conciliatory. Thus, the *Sem Terra* generally support the PT in most local campaigns and backed Luiz Inácio Lula da Silva in his successful campaign for the presidency. They helped achieve significant regime change in Brazil: Lula was elected with an unprecedented 61% of the vote in the 2002 runoff.

Indeed, realizing the PT's historic challenge to neoliberal policies and elitist rule, the landless turned out heavily in the election to join some 80% of registered voters who participated in both rounds of voting. Once the election was over, the MST did not demand to be part of the government. Rather, they continued to press the government for a comprehensive land reform program and a redistribution of both land and wealth. There would be no return to "politics as usual." The PT would pursue its "Zero Hunger" program and other social and economic initiatives and the MST would press the PT government for the structural reforms—like comprehensive agrarian reform—that it considered necessary.

By 2004, the MST displayed considerable dissatisfaction with what it considered the relative inaction of the government in regard to land reform, and it was threatening to once again engage in massive land takeovers. At the same time, the Lula government was facing increasing pressure from international financial institutions and national economic interests for moderate policies. MST believed the government was promoting agribusiness over distributing land to small family farms. And in early 2005 the MST pressured the Lula government to make good on its promises of land distribution by staging a national march on Brasília. By functioning in civil society and not *being* part of the government, the MST was free to pursue its original demands for land reform and socio-economic transformation, and maintain a critical stance toward Lula's accommodation with national and transnational elites.

Like the MST, many of the region's social movements have grown and have become increasingly politicized. They have come to represent a clear response to the neoliberal economic policies that have been forced on Latin American nations by international financial institutions, the U.S. government and national economic elites. In the 20 years since Brazil's military left government, the MST has embedded itself in civil society, taking advantage of the considerable political space that has opened up with the institutionalization of nominal democracy. Currently, the leftist Workers' Party is in control of the national and many state and municipal governments and has promised reform and structural change. Though they may lack the political will to implement many of their promised policies like land reform, they are not totally opposed to the policies being advocated by the MST and the landless continue to pressure them to carry out necessary structural changes. They do so in a changed political situation that makes repression unlikely and allows for considerable political space in which social movements like the MST can maneuver.

As they engage in grassroots organization and massive local and national mobilizations, the MST and social movements elsewhere have challenged the patterns of policymaking in Brazil and many other Latin American countries. Their growth and militancy have generated a whole new repertoire of actions that include national mobilizations so massive that they can topple governments—as in Bolivia—or force them to change their policies. They have left the traditional parties far behind as they forge new political horizons and create a non-authoritarian, participatory political culture. Such movements are using existing political space to maximum effect. In the process they are substantially strengthening participatory democratic practice.

They have vigorously resisted the corporate-led economic globalization process that has been heralded as the panacea to underdevelopment and poverty. Indeed, the economic realities that the masses of people all over Latin America are living, provide a potent empirical antidote to the universal prescription to globalize. The formulation of highly political social movements and the participatory democracy they practice provide a new and promising response to global neoliberalism. Further, these responses represent a substantial change from previous forms of political action, and they are transforming the conduct of politics in Brazil and Latin America.

ABOUT THE AUTHOR

Harry E. Vanden is a professor of political science and international studies at the University of South Florida, Tampa. He has published some thirty scholarly articles and six books, including *Politics of Latin America: The Power Game* (Oxford University Press, 2nd edition, 2006).

NOTES

1. Susan Kaufman Purcell, "Electoral Lessons," *América Economica*, December 6, 2001, p. 40.
2. Banco de Datos Políticos das Américas, "Brazil: Eleções Presidencias de 1998," , accessed April 19, 2002.
3. See United Nations Development Program, *Human Development Report, 1999* (New York: Oxford University Press, 1999), pp. 3–9.
4. CONAIE's very brief participation in a would-be junta that held the Ecuadoran Congress building overnight in January of 2000 is the exception. See Jennifer N. Collins, "A Sense of Possibility, Ecuador's Indigenous Movement Takes Center Stage," in "!Adelante! The New Rural Activism in the Americas," *NACLA Report on the Americas*, Vol. 35, No. 5, March/April 2002, pp. 40–46.
5. James Petras, "The Rural Landless Workers' Movement," *Z Magazine*, March 2000, p. 35.
6. Brazilian Institute of Statistics, *Statistical Report 2001*, as cited in "Pais

Termina Anos 90 Tão Desigual como Comencou," Folha de São Paulo (April 5, 2001).

7. See João Pedro Stedile, "Memories of Struggle in the MST," *NACLA Report on the Americas*, Social Movements: Building From the Ground Up, Vol. 38, No. 5, March/April 2005, and João Pedro Stedile and Bernardo Mançano Fernandes, *Brava Gente: a Ttrajectorai do MST e a Luta Pela Terra no Brasil* (São Paulo: Fundacão Perseo Abramo, 1999). See also Angus Wright and Wendy Wolford, *To Inherit the Earth, the Landless Movement and the Struggle for a New Brazil* (Oakland, CA: Food First Books, 2003), and Sue Branford and Jan Rocha, *Cutting the Wire, the Story of Landless Movement in Brazil* (London: Latin American Bureau, 2002).

8. See Elide Rugai Bastos, *As Ligas Camponesas* (Petópolis: Vozes,1984).

9. See Bradford and Rocha, *Cutting The Wire*, and interview with Geraldo Fontes, member of the National Coordinating Council, São Paulo, September 17, 2003.

10. In field research in Rio Grande do Sul State in 2001, the author observed a mixed grade class in one of the campamentos learning about "trasgenicos"—genetically engineered crops, their hazards and the corporations that control them. The MST produces educational material and guides—as well as training and orientation—on how to develop schools and popular education. See "O que queremos com as escolas dos asentamientos," *Caderno de Formacão*, No. 18, March 1999; and "Como fazemos a escola de educacão fundamental," *Cuaderno de Educacão*, No. 9 (MST, Education Sector, 1999).

11. The neighborhood organization of ten families could be the base unit (nucleo de base) in a larger cooperative or settlement, or even a temporary encampment. Each group then sends two representatives to a ruling council in each settlement, cooperative or encampment. General meetings in which all can participate are also held. These organizations in turn send representatives to the regional and state congresses. Special meetings are held to pick the representatives to the National Encounters (every two years) and National Congresses (every five years). As per Geraldo Fontes, member of the National Coordinating Council, in an interview in São Paulo, September 17, 2003.

12. Geraldo Flores, interview, September 17, 2003.

13. See "O MST e a cultura," *Caderno de Formacão*, No. 34 (São Paulo: Ademar Bogo, 2000), and Carlos Rodrigues Brandão, "História do menino que lia o mundo," *Fazendo História*, No. 7 (Veranópolis: ITERRA, 2001).

14. "Reforma Agraria, por um Brasil sem latifundio" (São Paulo: Movimiento dos Trabalhadores Rurais Sem Terra-MST, [2000]).

15. "Reforma Agraria," p. 4.

16. See, for instance, the political education pamphlet that the MST uses to explain neoliberalism to its affiliates: "O Neoliberalism, ou o mecanismo para fabricar mais pobres entre os pobres," Notebook No. 5 (São Paulo:

Consulta Popular, 1993).

17. The Landless Rural Workers Movement (MST), "Fundamental Principles for the Social and Economic Transformation of Rural Brazil," translated by Wilder Robles, *Journal of Peasant Studies*, Vol. 28, No. 2, January 2001, p. 153–54.

18. See João Pedro Stedile, "Memories of Struggle in the MST," *NACLA Report on the Americas*, Social Movements: Building From the Ground Up, Vol. 38, No. 5, March/April 2005.

19. MST, "O Brasil precisa de um projeto popular," Cuartilla No. 11 (Sào Paulo: Secrtaria Operative de Consulta Popular, 2000) pp. 1–29.

20. It should, however, be noted that much of the press was not always sympathetic and condemned their land takeovers as illegal actions. The rural landowners also did all in their power to stop their actions and discredit them in the public eye.

21. See Donatella de la Porta and Sidney Tarrow (eds.), *Transnational Protest and Global Activism* (Lanham, MD: Roman and Littlefield, 2005).

Sue Branford and Jan Rocha

Testimony of an MST Settler: Romilda da Silva Vargas

"I was born in Redentor near Tenente Portela in the north of Rio Grande do Sul state. My father farmed a small plot of land. I was only two and a half when my mother died in childbirth. My father married again after a year. When one of my elder sisters was 21 years old, she married and I went to live with her in a nearby town. I looked after the house, washed the clothes, made bread and looked after my nephew. And soon there was another child too. I went on studying for a while, but it wasn't easy. My sister and her husband didn't have their own land so they had to rent. They had to give half of their produce to the landowner. Money got so short that we had to buy food on credit in the local shop. After harvest, we had to pay our debts. I remember one year we wanted to buy a chair for the house, but there wasn't enough money left for that. The next year it was even worse. My brother-in-law had to sell some of his dairy cows to cover the debts.

"It was 1986, right at the beginning, that the MST arrived in the region. I was only 14 or 15 at the time. We were living close by an MST settlement. We saw the way the families progressed. They lived in black plastic tents when they arrived, but soon they had built proper houses, bought furniture, got electricity. We'd been there all those years and we hadn't even got electricity! At first, my brother-in-law got angry. He said, 'Here we are, killing ourselves with work and paying all that rent. And these vagabonds come in and get all this help from the government.'

"But after a while, we started making friends with them. They joined our church. They were active in the trade union. We were still very poor. We never had any money for clothes, for anything. So my brother-in-law decided to join the MST. Three months later I joined them. I was 16 or 17 years old at the time and I loved the camp. It was a wonderful communal experience. We all shared everything. I was in the liturgy commission and I traveled all over the state. I lost my shyness.

"But the owner of the estate got an eviction order from the courts and we all had to leave. Eventually, on March 9, 1989, we occupied the Santa Elmira ranch in the northwest of the state. The landowner was very angry. He got his gunmen together and launched an attack. First of all, his planes sprayed tear gas on the camp. And then the gunmen tried to take all the children away from their mothers. They'd brought a bus to take them to a home. The mothers screamed and wouldn't let go of their children. The men grabbed people by the hair, the clothes, anything. By chance, I wasn't there that day. My sister had gone to town to have another baby and I was with her. But I heard all about it.

"Then they took all the men away. They made them lie down, they beat them, they trampled on them. A lot of them had ribs broken. They accused the men with beards of being priests, the bigger men of being leaders. They put revolvers in their mouths and knives under their nails. They stripped off their clothes and put them on anthills. There was a priest there—Frei Sérgio Gorgen. They broke his teeth with a blow to his mouth. And then they arrested 30 men, including Frei Sérgio. On the way to prison in the town of Sobradinho, they pulled them all out of the police van and threatened to throw them into a gully. They treated the men like criminals in the jail, shaving their heads and beating them. There was huge uproar; lots of mobilizations and marches. The state governor, Pedro Simon, had to back down. He had to free the men and give land to all the families that had been in Santa Elmira. It all happened quickly, in just two weeks. That's how we got the land for our settlement, Conquista da Fronteira."

ABOUT THE AUTHORS

Sue Branford and Jan Rocha, from *Cutting the Wire: The Story of the Landless Movement in Brazil* (Kumarian Books, 2002).

Nicholas Watson

Homeless Movement Builds Momentum

Brazil's Landless Rural Workers' Movement (MST) is widely regarded as one of the world's most dynamic mass movements. In the 20 years since its inception, the MST has mobilized hundreds of thousands of rural workers in the struggle for land reform. Despite frequently violent responses to their occupations of idle land, the movement has managed to settle an estimated 350,000 families in small rural holdings throughout the country. But in recent months, attention has focused on one of the MST's younger and less well-known urban cousins: the Roofless Movement of Salvador (MSTS). The organization boasted 12,000 members only six months after its founding in Salvador da Bahia, Brazil's third most populous city after São Paulo and Rio de Janeiro. As a homeless peoples' movement, the MSTS tries to correct the jarring inequalities of the city by focusing attention on the plight of the excluded and urban poor.

Utilizing strategies similar to those of its rural cousin, the MSTS occupies abandoned or empty buildings and lots across the city to house homeless families and pressure the government to redress Salvador's enormous housing deficit. A local government spokesman claims that homes need to be built for 90,000 people, a number MSTS coordinator Pedro Cardoso laughs at: "Get real, it's more like 150,000."

An accurate count of the homeless population is difficult to come by because Salvador, like other large Brazilian cities, has a vast number of poor inhabitants camping out on a near-permanent basis in the homes of friends and relatives. A name even exists for the practice: to live *de favor*. According to the 2000 census, 16.5 million people live *de favor* in Brazil—more than 10% of the total population. But these living arrangements are often inhumane and are rarely sustainable. Twenty-four-year-old Juciara Pereira lived with her husband Raimundo and their six children in her mother's two-room house in Salvador until it became untenable. Raimundo, who collects used cans and cardboard on the streets to sell to a local recycling company, simply doesn't earn enough for them to even consider renting a place of their own. Thanks to the MSTS they are now on the city government's subsidized housing list.

In the past, families like Juciara's would squat on a neglected city hillside, where they might build a shack and make their home. With the explosion of rural migration to the cities in the 1950s and 1960s came the growth of the notorious *favelas* (shantytowns) that still clutter the urban landscape. But now much of the available space is already inhabited. Space shortages in the *favelas* became more acute in the 1990s with the introduction of limited services in a concerted government effort to urbanize *favelas* in much of the country. Many, though certainly not most, of the *favelas* enjoy electricity, sewage, paved roads and transportation networks, linking them to the larger city. Although these services are welcome improvements, the already limited space in a *favela* now comes at an unattainable premium for people like Juciara and Raimundo, forcing them to settle on land ever further from Salvador's city center.

As settlements move further to the periphery, services become limited or non-existent and violence is a constant threat. The MSTS seeks to prevent this literal and figurative peripheral existence by using what already exists within the city. "It's a perverse logic," says Cardoso. "People go homeless while space and empty buildings in the city center abound. We want to see the right to housing respected as a basic element of citizenship, and we think that's best done by direct action. We occupy buildings that aren't being put to a socially beneficial use in order to house needy homeless people."

One such building is the Portuguese Club of Salvador. Once a chic private club with spacious reception halls, a restaurant and swimming pools in a prime seafront location, it underwent foreclosure in the mid-1990s, leaving it empty and boarded up. In February 2004, however, some 200 MSTS members tore down the barricades and took over the abandoned club. They organized work teams to clear debris and clean the buildings, allowing families to move in with their few possessions. The largest reception hall is now divided by sheets of plastic and pieces of wood and cardboard to afford some privacy to the 20 families living in the space. At last count, the entire club was home to 154 families.

Living conditions are basic and the clubhouse is in disrepair. Rainwater gushes through the moldy roof and the empty swimming pools are a worrisome hazard considering the many children in the camp. One MSTS member, Renato Moura, died in 2005 after falling from one of the clubhouse balconies. Water for cooking and washing is only available from a single tap behind what used to be the club's pool bar and has to be carried in buckets past the decrepit diving board and broken sun loungers. "It's still worth it," says Anderson Santos, a rangy 29-year-old standing under the crumbling balconies and broken windows. "Before joining the movement I lived in my parent's two-room house with my three brothers and sisters, my wife and my two kids. I've been unemployed for four years, unable to provide for my family, feeling alone." The future of the Portuguese Club occupation remains uncertain, and the building is barely able to house so many people, but Anderson is optimistic: "The occupation has raised awareness among the local population of the housing issue. That's what's important." The work of the MSTS does not end with the occupations. "We're here to try to build a sense of community," explains Cardoso. Every occupation elects coordinators who organize cleaning committees, childcare, night watch duties, and construction and repair teams. Camp meetings take place every Saturday to discuss issues that inevitably arise from living in such close proximity. Members must attend at least one in three meetings or risk expulsion. Alcohol and drugs are banned. Organizing in this way has helped overcome hostility from local neighborhoods. "They can see for themselves that we're not criminals, that all we want is to be listened to," says Cardoso. In fact, some occupations have even received donations of food and clothing from neighborhood groups.

"There's a real feeling of solidarity in this camp," says Luciana Moura, one of five coordinators at the largest MSTS occupation, a piece of unused land near Salvador's airport that is home to more than 350 families. "We had a fire at the beginning of January in one of the shacks and had to pull down some of the surrounding shacks to stop the fire from spreading. But we all helped to rebuild them afterwards, using whatever we could find." Luciana's fellow coordinators are all women, reflecting the movement's gender make-up. Around 70% of MSTS members are women, often single mothers, and in most cases unemployed. Luciana is undaunted by the challenges she faces: "We're taking responsibility for our lives, showing this macho society that we're capable, that we can organize and that we know our rights."

So what has the MSTS achieved so far? The violent evictions by police experienced in the early stages of the movement have been replaced with a more conciliatory policy on the part of the local government, which is promising to accelerate its affordable

304/ *Dispatches From Latin America*

housing program. In early 2005 construction began on 100 government-subsidized homes. But, says Cardoso, it is "too little, too slow—we will continue our policy of occupations to put pressure on the government." The MSTS is far from isolated. Similar movements exist in cities across the country. In São Paulo, the Movement of Homeless Peoples from the Center (MSTC) is pressing the government to deal with the anomalies of South America's wealthiest and most populous city. According to Manoel Del Rio, a lawyer representing the MSTC, 15,000 people live on the streets of São Paulo, while 400 buildings and lots lie empty and unused in the city center.

Cardoso hopes the government of former lathe worker and trade unionist Luiz Inácio Lula da Silva will move to address these problems. "The existence of the Lula government opens up a space for us to operate, since we know he's sympathetic to our demands," explains Cardoso. "With the government in the financial straitjacket of the IMF and international lenders, it's our job to mobilize in order to remind the government that we are here, that we are the government's true support base," warns Cardoso with a cautionary tone. "We're not opposing the government, but trying to keep it on the path that led us to vote for it. We haven't been around for long, but we're an army of citizens, no longer prepared to accept exclusion and poverty."

ABOUT THE AUTHOR

Nicholas Watson is a freelance writer specializing on Brazilian political and social issues.

Hilary Wainwright

Making a People's Budget in Porto Alegre

From the time it was founded in the early 1980s, the Brazilian Workers' Party (PT) has maintained that electoral success is not an end in itself but a springboard for developing radical, participatory forms of democracy that will enable the country to start redressing the enormous inequalities in Brazilian society. The city where the PT has made most advances in this sense is the city of Porto Alegre, capital city of the relatively wealthy state of Rio Grande do Sul, a busy industrial, financial and service center with a population of 1.2 million people. Porto Alegre has been continuously governed by the PT ever since a charismatic bank clerk, Olívio Dutra, was first elected mayor in 1989, though it lost the mayoralty in 2004 to a coalition of parties.

In some ways, Porto Alegre is not a typical Brazilian city, for it has always had an unusually high literacy rate; in 1991 the rate was 96%, well above the Brazilian average of 81%. But the city has not bucked the Brazilian trend of extreme social inequality: in 1981, one third of the city lived in slum areas. At the same time, 15 families own almost all the urban land available for development.

In Porto Alegre, as throughout Brazil, city departments and their leading officials had vested interests in this inequality. Corruption was endemic. The local PT believed that the only chance of achieving change was to open up secretive municipal institutions, particularly their finances, to a process of popular participation. So when the PT gained control of the municipal government, it instituted the *orçamento participativo*, or "participatory budget" (PB). PB is a form of co-decision making, or shared power, in which local citizens take part in deciding the priorities for the municipal investment budget.

The process includes a series of public meetings or plenaries in which participants critique the results of past budgets and voice their views about what the city's future investment priorities should be: should, for instance, building sewers be made a priority, or would citizens rather see new schools or clinics? Plenary participants also elect delegates to regional forums, where budget priorities are further refined, and to the citywide budget council, a powerful body that negotiates the final investment priorities for the city. The budget council draws up the overall budget and puts it to the mayor and municipal council for final approval. The municipal council has never rejected an investment plan drawn up by the budget council or made any damaging amendments.

The participatory budget process is limited by the fact that it only applies to that portion of the municipal budget that is spent on new investment, or about 15%. (The largest chunk of the rest of the budget is spent on salaries.) And the overall budget was squeezed as the previous national government instituted neoliberal policies and cut back funding to municipalities. Over its 15 years of existence, however, the PB has opened up a state bureaucracy that is normally hidden. Such openness repels corruption and forces municipal officials and employees to be more accountable to local residents. The PB process also provides an opportunity to pursue broader social goals.

I was able to see the participatory budget process in action at a plenary in one of the city's 16 regions in 2002. While people waited to register, a troupe of actors put on a kind of street theatre focused on local problems. To an outsider, the people streaming in seemed to be a cross-section of the community: white-haired matrons; eager schoolgirls; young Rasta men; the anxious poor, many of them black; glamorous tanned student types; confident-looking middle aged men of various shades of brown. But the coordinators said that some neighborhoods were much better represented than others and the registration enabled them to identify areas, or groups of people, that were not well represented and find out why. Around 600 people had come, out of a community of 3,000. The majority attending that night were women.

A survey by CIDADE, an independent research organization, shows that a large majority of the participants at PB plenaries are unskilled workers with only a primary level of education. Over the last four years more women than men have attended the plenaries, and more women than men have been elected delegates. This is impressive for a region that is renowned throughout Brazil for its machismo. And in a city that up until recently excluded black people from the main supermarkets and from factory jobs, it is particularly noteworthy that at least one quarter of the budget council delegates are black or indigenous people.

Once the long queue of people registering had snaked its way into the hall and we were settling down in our seats, the chair asked for an indication of how many were attending their first PB meeting. Over 300 hands went up. This is quite common; new people are constantly engaging with the process. Despite a hostile local media, recent surveys show that over 85% of Porto Alegrans know about and support the PB. They find out about it through their neighbors and friends, through leaflets and through delegates, like the ones they were to elect at this meeting. PB itself has become a form of media.

The people crowding into the vast school hall saw the meeting as an opportunity to vent their feelings to government representatives, as well as to win over their neighbors in support of their chosen causes. A local tradition of public story telling made for a hall full of people able to narrate vivid tales of municipal failings, and two groups were particularly vociferous. The first group complained that in the previous year's budget, sanitation had been a high priority and a lot of money had been spent on it but, fumed speaker after speaker, the problems of dirty water and open sewage remained. People from one neighborhood complained that a stream had become the local sewer; they wanted it covered so it could not be used in this way. Government officials at the meeting said that, for environmental reasons, the stream should remain a stream but they promised to clean it. Another vocal group came from a local school. This was the first budget plenary they had attended and they used it to simply shout out their complaints. Then-Mayor Raoul Pont responded, urging them to elect a delegate, turn their complaints into proposals and negotiate for funds through the participatory budget process.

Regional delegates elected at such plenaries meet together throughout the year to iron out problems, monitor progress and encourage ideas for next year's budget. And they keep in regular touch with the region's two representatives to the budget council. These representatives are accountable to the regional delegates and could in theory be recalled by a specially convened plenary, though this has yet to happen.

The municipal government holds other plenaries based around themes, bringing together people from across the city with a common interest in such areas as education, health, culture or economics. These important thematic plenaries also elect delegates to the budget council.

Delegates at both the regional and the city level are regularly under pressure from their electors. Jussara Bechstein-Silva, a charismatic leader in the poor Vila Planetário neighborhood who represents the central region on the budget council, explained: "You have to answer to local residents who are asking. 'Why is [a project] so delayed? Why is it failing?' And you have to answer to the council too. You are pressured on both sides." But city officials as well as employees who work specifically with the PB process provide some support for the delegates: "Mayor Olívio Dutra came [to a meeting] one night in the pouring rain and told us to be hopeful because our construction [project] would be completed. And we had a lot of support from our lawyer," said a woman who worked in the planning department, part of whose job was to provide the delegates with technical advice.

PB has clearly been successful in driving Porto Alegre's municipal administration to spend the bulk of its investment budget on making the city's poor neighborhoods fit to live in. Most social statistics indicate progress significantly ahead of other cities: 9,000 Porto Alegran families, who 12 years ago lived in shacks, now have brick housing and the legal status of these buildings has been regularized. Nearly the whole population (99%) has treated water; and the sewage system covers 86% of the city, compared with 46% in 1989. Over 50 schools have been built in the past ten years and truancy has fallen from 9% to less than 1%. The number of students going on to university doubled from 1989 to 1995. And a detailed analysis of the municipal budget after 1989 shows that the lower the average income of the PB region, the higher the volume of public investment per head. The report concludes that the participatory budget has functioned as "a powerful instrument of the redistribution of wealth."

Still, there are limits to what the PB, in its current form, can do: Argues Betânia Alfonsín, a young urban planner who used to be in the local leadership of the PT and now works with movements in the *favelas* (slums), "You cannot plan a city just on the basis of individual investments. We have to complement that by democratizing and strengthening urban planning. If not, you can get a gulf between city planning and specific investments. An example of this lack of coordination was the expansion of the sewage network. This work was not accompanied by an investment in water treatment, which has resulted in a considerable increase of untreated sewage flowing into the city's main water source, Lake Guaíba."

In response, municipal leaders have encouraged the urban planning department to embark on a major new initiative in participation. How exactly will the new participatory structure for urban planning link to the PB? "I'm not sure. I don't think the government knows either," says Alfonsín. There are some signs, however, that participatory planning is beginning to feed directly into the budget process, even becoming the basis on which delegates choose priorities.

The participatory budget can also strengthen the hand of the municipality when it wants to gain social benefits for the city from private investors. In the early 1990s, for example, the giant French supermarket chain Carrefour wanted to build a store in the North Central Region of Porto Alegre. This region has many small shopkeepers who felt the supermarket would threaten their businesses and these small entrepreneurs decided to take their concerns to the thematic PB plenary on economic policy. "We wanted to set up a committee to negotiate compensation for the small businesses in the area, as a condition [for building] the new supermarket," said one of the activists.

The outcome was unprecedented: while normally Carrefour supermarkets rent inside spaces for around 20 local shops, the Porto Alegre committee won agreement for 40. The company also agreed to employ young people and help fund training schemes. Carrefour had never before had to make real concessions to gain entry into a new market.

But, however good and successful its municipal policies, Porto Alegre cannot wall itself off from political reality in the rest of the world. Over the last two decades, many governments have willingly reduced their capacity to meet the needs of their poor by, for example, cutting public spending and lowering taxes on the rich. Under President Lula's predecessor, Fernando Henrique Cardoso, Brazil's federal government opened the national economy to the full, unrestrained impact of global deregulation, with concomitant pressures to privatize and run down the state's social capacities. As a result, the federal government strengthened central control over public spending and cut the funds going back to the cities. Funds going to local authorities were reduced from 17% of the revenue received in 1990 to 14% in 1999. Further cuts occurred in the interim between then and Lula's election. Under such circumstances, a single progressive administration like that in Porto Alegre can become unintentionally complicit in imposing on local communities the burden of clearing up the unregulated market's social mess.

Essentially, the logic goes like this: as neoliberal policies are imposed nationally and internationally, the poor communities that make up Porto Alegre face greater and greater social problems. Their needs intensify. In the meantime, the municipal council's budget to help meet these needs is cut. Its capacity for providing high-quality free services, such as childcare, health, education and housing, is reduced. The individual communities and neighborhoods put forward projects for solving these problems themselves. The participatory budget approves these grassroots solutions, for they fit the basic budget criteria. But what is not discussed is the quality of the service and the level of pay provided by the community project. Sérgio Baerlie, a long-time observer of the PB process, illustrates this problem with the example of community day-care centers: "The money that the municipal government needs to run by itself just one day-care center is enough to fund several, perhaps more than ten, day-care centers run by community associations, where labor costs are much lower. The result is that today Porto Alegre has 118 day-care centers run by community associations with funds from city hall." Baerlie suggests there is a danger here of unintentionally accepting a neoliberal transference of social policy from the state to the community and in the process undermining the principle of the provision of free public services as a universal social right.

In the face of such realities, however, Porto Alegre has not only tried to use PB to spend limited funds fairly, it has also worked to increase revenue through municipal enterprises. André Passos, chief of the municipal budget planning department, points to an information technology company, originally created to administer public departments, that now sells its services to the public. The increased revenue will enable the company to invest in optical fiber technology, which will be a future source of revenue. The city's water company is also municipally owned, and a highly successful company owned by the city council builds most of Porto Alegre's buses. There is also a growing network of municipally owned but cooperatively run recycling projects— all this at time when elsewhere in the world governments and corporations try to persuade us that "modernization" means privatization.

It is not an easy nor a quick process to construct the kind of participatory democracy practiced in Porto Alegre. In 1998 the PT won the elections for the government of Rio Grande do Sul, the state that has Porto Alegre as its capital. The new government began to extend PB across the state but faced resistance in many rural areas still dominated by reactionary landowners. It was unable to get the system running as effectively as it had hoped. Although other factors were involved—

including bickering between different PT factions—the PT lost the state government elections in Rio Grande do Sul in October 2002. It was a bitter disappointment for the local PT members, tempering their delight at Lula's triumph.

But in Porto Alegre, the transparency and publicly negotiated character of the rules for PB ensure that it is widely respected and supported. It is perceived to have a legitimacy distinct from the electoral institutions of the mayor and the municipal assembly. The government cannot change PB rules by its own authority—everything has to be negotiated in a process that, until the last moment before the budget is approved, is heavily weighted towards the popular participants. To close the process down now would provoke an eruption. And not just in the poor parts of town. PB is an extension of democracy, not a competing structure. It effectively makes the mayor's electoral mandate a daily living pressure on the state apparatus.

Celso Daniel—the PT mayor of the São Paulo town of Santo André who was murdered, probably by a drug mafia in 2001—believed that PB principles, so far applied only at the local level, could also be applied to the federal government, something that has gained a new relevance with Lula's victory: "If the president of Brazil becomes committed to the participatory budget process at the central level, this could be very important for the construction of a new kind of federalism in Brazil," he had told me. He explained how the present federal system in Brazil is "very tied to the old oligarchies, the old elites in Brazil." Daniel, who was a close Lula adviser, would undoubtedly have held a key position in the PT government.

Meanwhile, the local success of the participatory budget process has moved the Brazilian Workers' Party on to brand new political ground. In contrast to the conventional model in which a winning political party controls, or perceives itself to control, a state apparatus, PB has unleashed a more potent, more broadly based means of controlling a key part of the state. Traditionally a party that had won a local election, in this case the PT, would play the leadership role in the formation of municipal policy and strategy. The party would choose a direction, stay a step or two ahead, collectively develop a clear vision, and be, in effect, the brains behind the process. Under PB, instead of monopolizing the role of conscious political brain, the PT has encouraged many political "brains," many self-conscious agents of social change. This implicitly challenges the nature—though as yet not the fact—of the PT's leadership, in so far as the PT continues to act like a conventional political party.

Some of the potential tensions are apparent in Porto Alegre. When the PT came to office and turned to its own supporters to join the government, about 10% of the local membership moved into government jobs. This process led to what experienced PT member Luciano Brunet described as "a rupture between party and government, which weakened the party. At times it seemed as if people in government didn't care what the party thought."

This rift is still felt. There is a growing gulf between party members inside and outside the government. The weakness of the links between party and government except at election time has been reinforced, Luciano feels, by changes in party governance which made the PT more like other traditional social democratic parties, with elections for delegates to the party conference and other leadership positions held only once every three years. Luciano and others believe the PT should be moving in another direction, to become more pluralistic, more closely connected with the NGOs and campaigns that many party members are a part of anyway. "If you want to have a participatory democracy, you need a party which reflects it," concludes Luciano. In his view, if the PT is a conscious brain, it needs to adapt to the fact that in creating a source of democratic power beyond the state, it has dismantled its monopoly of radical brainpower.

Olívio Dutra, the Porto Alegre mayor who began the PB process there, is now serving as minister for urban policy in Lula's cabinet. If it is still unclear whether or how the new government could apply PB principles on a national level, PB's appeal to those who have already taken part in it is evident. Says Porto Alegre urban planner Betânia Alfonsín, "Participation is addictive."

ABOUT THE AUTHOR

Hilary Wainwright is the editor of *Red Pepper*, the London-based independent magazine of the green and radical left. This article is adapted from her book *Reclaim the State: Adventures in Popular Democracy* (Verso 2003).

Benjamin Witte

Multinational Gold Rush in Guatemala

Somewhere amid the chaos that erupted January 11, 2005, along a stretch of the Pan-American Highway in Guatemala, a protestor lost his life. The victim was later identified as Raúl Castro. He was 37.

With the exception of the man's name and age, information about what transpired that day in the northern province of Sololá is murky at best. Reports about how many police and soldiers the government dispatched vary from a couple of hundred to as many as 2,000. Nor is it clear who threw the first stone, fired the first shot or tossed the first Molotov cocktail. Simply put, the scene was pure chaos. Fires and exploded tear-gas canisters choked the air. The piercing sounds of gunfire, sirens and manic shouting replaced what would have normally been the hum of highway traffic. Hundreds of police, soldiers and campesino protestors scuffled half-blinded in the haze.

It's sad to say, but the death of a single person under violent circumstances doesn't usually constitute news in Guatemala, where murder and assassinations are rampant, even now, almost a decade after the official end of the country's 36-year civil war. Yet the story of Castro's death—presumably at the hands of government security forces—continues to arouse steady, albeit modest, public attention. There's something about that death, or more specifically, about the circumstances leading up to the conflict, that has set off persistent alarm—not only in Guatemala but also abroad.

Protests in Sololá actually began more than a month before Castro's murder. Starting in late November 2004, demonstrators—campesinos (mostly of Mayan descent), local leaders, environmentalists and Catholic Church-affiliated representatives—took up positions along the Pan-American Highway. Their goal was to impede the transport of materials and equipment for a soon-to-be-operating gold and silver mine in neighboring San Marcos province, some 93 miles away. For 42 days they were successful, and then the government called in its troops.

The mine, known as the Marlin Project, is located near the towns of Sipacapa and San Miguel Ixtahuacán. It is owned and operated by a company called Montana Exploradora de Guatemala. The company is not, as its name would suggest, Guatemalan. Instead, Montana Exploradora is a subsidy of Glamis Gold, a company that is registered in Canada (it has a post office box in Vancouver) but maintains its headquarters in the United States.

Glamis Gold stands to make a fortune on the Marlin Project. The mine, which is spread over some 250,000 acres, is expected to yield about 250,000 ounces of gold and 3.6 million ounces of silver per year, output that will quickly make it the company's most profitable venture. Furthermore, of the company's various operations, the Marlin Project will be its least expensive to run, with an estimated cash cost of just $90 dollars per ounce of gold, significantly lower than Glamis' overall cash-cost average of approximately $150 dollars per ounce. Best of all, boasts the company on its Web site, "The project is fully permitted and enjoys strong local support, as well as backing by the Guatemalan Government and the World Bank." Well, at least some of that is true.

The World Bank threw its weight behind the project with its private-sector arm, the International Finance Corporation (IFC), which granted Glamis Gold a $45 million loan for the development of the Marlin Project. The project enjoys full support from the Guatemalan government, as its willingness to send soldiers to aid the company suggests. Supporters of the project say Guatemala, one of the hemisphere's most impoverished countries, desperately needs this type of foreign direct investment. Foreign companies, they say, create jobs and boost government coffers by supplying tax revenue.

In fact, the government is so supportive of foreign mining ventures that in the last decade (since the signing of the 1996 peace accords), Guatemalan leaders have granted foreign companies more than 300 exploration requests and mining concessions. Many of those companies are Canadian.

Not surprisingly, Canada's Ambassador to Guatemala, James Lambert, threw his active support behind the country's budding mining industry. In an article published in late 2004 the Guatemalan daily *Prensa Libre*, Lambert penned a defiant defense of Canada and its mining companies as the Glamis controversy heated up.

"Is it possible," asked the Ambassador, "for a country to be recognized as one of the most socially and environmentally responsible countries in the world, near the top of the list in the Environment Sustainability Index and, at the same time, be a major mining country, with a mining industry that contributes $41.1 billion to its economy?" And he answered his own question. "Yes," said Lambert, Canada is that responsible country, and its companies mine responsibly at home. There's no reason, therefore, why they wouldn't do the same in Guatemala.

But there is a reason, said opponents to the project. The Ambassador's assurances aside, Glamis Gold and the other companies waiting in the wings cause tremendous social and environmental damage. Why? Because in Guatemala, with its weak, pro-investment government, tightly controlled media and general atmosphere of repression and impunity, foreign companies can simply get away with it.

Despite Glamis Gold's insistence that its operations "enjoy strong local support," the list of people and organizations opposed to the Marlin Project continued to grow. A poll conducted by the survey company Vox Latina suggested that in Sipacapa and San Miguel Ixtahuacán more than 95% of local residents disapprove of the mining activity. Almost as many residents think metal mining will have a destructive influence on their towns, while only just under 9% are buying the line that the Marlin Project will bring wealth to the area. The poll, conducted in October 2004, involved 400 interviews with adults and has a 5% margin of error.

Local Church leaders, labor unions, mayors from across the country and several environmental groups joined the townspeople in opposing the mine. Alvaro Ramazzini, the Archbishop of the Diocese of San Marcos, was a particularly outspoken critic of the project. In an open letter to Guatemalan President Óscar Berger, the Archbishop wrote that the country's current laws provide an open invitation for potentially harmful mining practices. "A mining company will invest in countries where the laws governing mining constitute an open door. This is the case for Guatemala," he explained. Ramazzini's public stance against the project earned him death threats.

Nevertheless, the opposition was not silenced. Three weeks after the January confrontation, thousands of protestors in Sololá once again took to the streets, this time with the backing of 19 of the province's town mayors. Also, Archbishop Rodolfo Cardinal Quezada Toruño, the country's highest-ranked Church leader, sided with the opposition, as did the San Marcos-based union, the Movement of Catholic Workers (MTC).

It was through the MTC that Father Ernie Schibli of the Montreal NGO Social Justice Committee first learned about the mining controversy in Guatemala. This is not simply a Guatemalan problem, say Schibli and other concerned Canadians. Glamis Gold, at least in name, is a Canadian company, as are several other mining companies with plans to operate in Guatemala. "The whole country's been mapped out," he says. And since the Canadian Ambassador is actively backing these exploitative projects, says Schibli, people in Canada must direct opposition to their own government. "That's where Canadians have the most leverage," he explains.

Schibli went to Guatemala to investigate the situation in San Marcos firsthand. What he encountered confirmed the findings of the Vox Latina poll. The local, mostly Maya, residents simply don't support the project. "Despite what the mining company has to say, the broader community and the indigenous people of Guatemala as a whole have rejected their claims. They're firmly opposed to the mine," says the priest.

Meanwhile, says Schibli, in Canada, opposition "has snow-balled." Canadian NGOs siding with Schibli's Social Justice Committee include the Canadian chapter of Friends of the Earth, the Toronto-based Rights Action and the Atlantic Regional Solidarity Network (ARSN) of Nova Scotia.

In March, ARSN sponsored a tour in Eastern Canada called "Mining the Connections." One of the principal participants was José "Filóchofo" Chacón, a well-known political cartoonist who also works closely with Madre Selva, one of several local environmental groups trying to bring attention to mining issues in Guatemala.

According to the cartoonist, the risks posed by Glamis Gold and other foreign mining companies are not only environmental but also economic and social. Problem number one, says Chacón, is the measly 1% in royalty fees companies like Glamis are required to pay under Guatemala's flexible mining laws.

"One percent," he emphasizes, "for every $100 that the

mining company takes in earnings, they leave 1% for the country. In other words, we're talking about a law that's shameful, a law that's defeatist, a law that belongs to governments that are willing to hand everything over. What's more, that 1% is divided in half. They leave 0.5% for the communities being affected. The other 0.5% goes to the state."

Undoubtedly, argues Chacón, communities such as Sipacapa and San Miguel Ixtahuacán are going to need every penny, because the Marlin Project will almost certainly result in environmental and health problems. One of the biggest effects of the mine will be increased competition for water. The average Guatemalan campesino, according to Madre Selva, uses roughly 30 liters of water per day. The Marlin Project, by its own estimates, will use 250,000 liters per hour, massive consumption that threatens to deprive local subsistence farmers of water they need to survive.

Pollution from the constant flow of trucks winding in and out of the mountainous region as well as from the oils and gases used to operate the mine's heavy machinery is a likely problem. Most alarming, however, is the vast amount of cyanide used by the mining process to extract gold and silver. Inevitably, say environmentalists, at least some of that cyanide will be absorbed by the environment and poison ground water, posing a long-term health risk to nearby residents.

Glamis Gold insists these concerns are blown way out of proportion. For one thing, it says, water competition need not be a concern, as the Marlin mine will only be using water pumped from its own 1,000-foot well. Nor should residents worry about cyanide poisoning. "The cyanide process," Glamis explains on its Web site, "is entirely contained in the process plant with redundant liners and safety systems." After all, boasts the company, in preparing the Marlin Project for operation, Glamis Gold dutifully conducted the requisite environmental impact study (EIS), and was subsequently granted approval by all the necessary parties. The EIS alone, says the company, should convince residents they have nothing to worry about. Or should it?

Colorado-based geologist Dr. Robert E. Moran, who's reviewed EIS's from all around the world, has carefully reviewed Glamis' impact study and isn't so sure the document offers anything in the way of assurances. Simply put, "the general quality [of the report] is poor," he says.

"Let me start by saying it's not the kind of report that would be acceptable in Canada and the U.S. It's too poorly written, too poorly organized. It lacks the basic information you need. There's not much data there." Moran says he's heard the 1,000-foot well promise before. "It's a pattern you see over and over with projects in developing countries." As far as potential cyanide pollution, it's the same story. "They all have redundant protection systems, but they almost all have leakages," says Moran. "It's over simplified to say waste doesn't get released. If you leave out about 50% of the facts, then their statement is OK."

Guatemalans have seen gold prospectors before, starting with the first Spanish conquistadors who ventured into the country during the early part of the sixteenth century. They've also had a tumultuous past with North American companies that have set up shop and, like the United Fruit Company in the 1950s, haven't hesitated to use any means necessary in protecting their interests.

In the early 1950s, Guatemalans remember, then-president Jacobo Arbenz instituted a number of "radical" measures, including a land reform plan that involved exercising the government's powers of eminent domain over uncultivated land owned by United Fruit. The government, said the President, was prepared to pay for the land fair-and-square, basing purchase prices on the company's own grossly undervalued land assessments. The plight of the well-connected U.S. company soon caught the attention of authorities in Washington, and in 1954 the CIA successfully executed an operation that resulted in Arbenz being ousted in a coup. In 1960 war broke out. The conflict didn't officially come to an end until 1996. By then, more than 200,000 people had been killed, most of them indigenous, murdered by government troops who forced their way into villages in the same highland regions that are now being prepped for exploitation by North American mining companies.

Taking all of that into consideration, it's easy to see why the specter of government troops, dispatched in the hundreds to break up a protest against Canadian and U.S. mining interests, might arouse a sense of foreboding among villagers in highland Guatemala and among the people who empathize with their plight. Indeed, Raúl Castro's death—even in a country that continues to be as violent as Guatemala—is eerily disconcerting. "When we talk about the army," says José Chacón, "we're talking about an army that's been accused of massacres. We're saying that now, during this time of peace, the army is returning once again to the communities. This produces a psychological impact."

In signing the 1996 peace accords, authorities in Guatemala agreed to abide by a number of international laws, including Convention 169 of the International Labor Organization (ILO). Among other things, this law states that indigenous peoples must be consulted and allowed ultimate say over any development plan that could affect them or the land on which they live.

Despite what Glamis Gold says on the matter, that consultation never took place. This is not, of course, the first time Guatemala's highland Maya have been shut out of national dialogues. But this refusal by the government and by companies such as Glamis Gold to inform, consult and ultimately listen, breeds frustration. Without avenues to express their political voices, Guatemala's campesinos take to the streets—they protest, they block highways. And on January 11 and on countless other days in the country's tumultuous past, their mobilization has been met with heavy repression. "Our concern is that democratic spaces, through dialogue, don't exist in Guatemala," says a wary Chacón. "In this very moment, every type of demonstration has been repressed brutally."

Despite the tireless efforts and stiff opposition of the communities and their allies, Glamis and the Guatemalan government plowed ahead. Even a referendum in June 2005 that passed with 98% approval in 13 indigenous communities rejecting the mine, failed to make headway in halting the project. Two months later, the *Financial Times* published the leaked results of a report compiled by the Compliance Advisor Ombudsman (COA), one of the IFC's own watchdogs. The report concluded what opponents to the project had been saying all along, that the bank not only failed to properly consult local communities, but also ignored the environmental and social risks of the project.

Nonetheless, in November 2005 Glamis Gold announced to its stockholders that the Marlin mine was at long last up and running. The president and CEO of the company, Kevin McDonald said, "Nobody can lose. We are all going to win."

ABOUT THE AUTHOR

Benjamin Witte is a Santiago-based freelance writer. A former editor of the *Santiago Times*, he also worked as a reporter for the *Tico Times*.

David Bacon

Stories from the Borderland

I. INDUSTRIA FRONTERIZA

Tijuana's oldest *maquiladora* closed last year.

It didn't fall victim to the dreaded Chinese competition, confounding a wave of near-hysterical alarms in south-of-the-border newspapers, warning that the days of all Mexico's *maquiladoras* (factories that create duty-free exports) were numbered. Instead, Industria Fronteriza owed its demise to a more prosaic cause: women stopped wearing nylons.

For almost four decades, seamstresses in this sprawling sweatshop churned out what was once the height of haut couture. Starting in the mid-1960s, the sleek hosiery caressing the slim legs stalking down New York's fashion runways passed through the rough working hands of hundreds of Mexican women bent over machines on a sweaty, deafening factory floor within a stone's throw of the U.S.-Mexico border.

Given changing styles, perhaps the company's end could have been easily predicted. Plans might have been made for easing these veterans of needle and thread into jobs in some other border sweatshop. Or they might have been trained to fill one of the high-value-added positions that policy wonks insist should, and will, replace the old labor-intensive jobs that started the industrial gold rush here 40 years ago.

Traditional Mexican labor law would have helped the dislocation of these seamstresses. Since the 1930s, when radicals wrote the country's labor legislation (and made it a model throughout Latin America), the Federal Labor Law has called for something U.S. workers would love to have: severance pay. A week's pay for every year at the machine seemed only just to the reformers of that more egalitarian age. For today's seamstresses, a little money to pay for training programs, some severance pay to live on and a government interested in finding new jobs for older workers might have made quite a difference.

Not in the world of the border. This world turns labor law on its head—old post-revolutionary legal rights are just so much ink on paper, and even the decisions of federal judges to enforce the law are simply ignored.

What actually happened at Industria Fronteriza, however, is strange even by Tijuana standards. First, workers got no notice that the company was planning to close. In itself, that's not unusual in a city and an industry where shops are suddenly emptied of their machines in the dead of night, leaving people to show up for work at the doors of a vacant shell the following morning. Second, Industria Fronteriza employees belonged to a pro-company *charro* union, whose casual lack of concern for their welfare was the source of many prior industrial battles. That's not unusual either.

What distinguishes the Industria Fronteriza experience, however, is that in the spring of 2003, the company conspired with the *charro* union and staged a strike against itself. The sole purpose of the phantom strike was to provide a legal obstacle to the implementation of the severance pay requirement, and leave the workers with nothing. Mexican law says that in the event of a strike, the claims of the striking union must be satisfied before company can close. Since the official closure of Industria Fronteriza was a precondition to distributing severance pay, the declared strike stopped the compensation process in its tracks. That was pretty extreme, even considering the long-established practice along the border of allowing factory owners to get away with virtually anything.

Throughout Mexico, factory owners sign "protection contracts" with pro-government and pro-company unions, called *sindicatos charros*. The phrase originally referred to unions led by Luis Morones, a Mexican labor leader from the 1920s. Morones was famous for dressing up like a cowboy, or *charro*. A notorious conservative in the Mexican labor movement, he signed sweetheart agreements with employers; consequently, workers "celebrate" his memory by referring to company unions as "*charro* unions." Protection contracts and *charro* unions are the primary system of labor control for foreign corporations that have built factories on the border. This system allows them to pay extremely low wages, even by Mexican standards, and to maintain dangerous and even illegal working conditions, with little fear of organized worker resistance.

Jesús Campos Linas, the dean of Mexican labor lawyers, says that thousands of such contracts in Mexico are arrangements of mutual convenience among corrupt unions, the government and foreign investors who own the factories. "Companies," he explains, "make hefty regular payments to union leaders under these contracts and in return get labor peace."

Over the two years following the closing of Industria Fronteriza, a lawsuit by the workers ground through the courts. Finally, four workers, who had been illegally fired in June 2002, won a decision forcing the Tijuana Labor Board to tell the company to collectively pay the workers $50,000 in severance. Of course, the company didn't pay, so the workers had to get another order, this one requiring that the board confiscate the sewing machines, industrial steam irons and the other equipment left in the abandoned factory.

On December 7, 2004, the workers stood ready at the gate, having come with a truck, forklifts, a lawyer from Mexico City and supporters to carry the equipment out. They had even reserved a storeroom in the *maquiladora* workers' barrio of Maclovio Rojas to house the confiscated machines. But the *charro* union stood at the door of the plant prepared for a hostile confrontation with about 40 people, including former company supervisors, holding big sticks ready to start a fight with the workers.

They needn't have bothered. When a Labor Board official noticed a strike flag in the door of the factory, he refused to perform the confiscation because a "strike" was in progress. Workers pointed out that the *charro* union itself had ended its phantom strike, but the labor board just needed a pretext. In a shouting match back at its downtown offices, Labor Board president Raúl Zenil y Orona refused to discuss any further action against the company, and he announced to the workers that the confiscation would never happen.

In some ways, the workers were lucky they didn't end up in jail. Tijuana is in Baja California, the free-trade state, where the advanced guard of Mexican industry and commerce live by a set of rules that the rest of the country is only beginning to adopt. In Baja, challenging the cabal of managers, government officials and compliant unions that set these rules provokes a grim and dangerous hostility. The state's prisons have been home to many activists from the social movements of "*los de abajo*," the people from below.

During the two strikes of Han Young workers in 1998 and 1999, the first legal strike by an independent union in the *maquiladoras*, strike leaders Enrique Hernández and José Peñaflor spent months slipping through the shadows from office to hidden office, seeking to avoid arrest. Julio Sandoval, a leader of indigenous migrant farm workers, spent three years in an Enseñada prison for leading land invasions to secure farm workers a place to live. Hortensia Hernández has been held in Tijuana's prison almost as long for fighting for land and housing for the city's maquiladora workers in the Maclovio Rojas barrio.

Laboring in the border's vital factory heart, Margarita Avalos describes the grinding economic pressure driving these social movements. Avalos worked at Industria Fronteriza for two-and-a-half years, and remembers her time ironing the sleek garments sewn by her friends: "In the factory, the administration was really authoritarian. They screamed orders. They threw on the floor the things we needed to use. They forced us to work extra time, and if we couldn't do it, they said they wouldn't pay us for any of the time we worked at all. Sometimes I had to work 24 hours straight, even going without eating, in order to get out the orders they demanded. The chemicals and the heat were hard on my body, and for those of us who were pregnant, it was even worse."

For that, Avalos was paid $65 a week. If she really churned out the nylons and bras the way the managers wanted, she could make another $30, but that meant ironing a lot more than the standard 2,000 pieces in an eight-hour shift, or one every 15 seconds.

Raúl Ramírez, Baja California's Human Rights prosecutor, faults the government's desire to protect investment above all else. "The authorities don't care about the poverty of these communities, or their social problems like lack of housing or drug addiction. But they are very concerned with the question of the land titles of the large landholders. They want to take care of their investments. So the government uses the law, the police, even the army. They say this provides safety and stability for investors. And they abandon the poor."

The social cost of this policy, Ramírez says, can be found in Baja California fields on any given day during the harvest season, when workers pick tomatoes and strawberries for U.S. supermarkets. Whole families work together in these agricultural *maquiladoras*—children alongside adults. Félix, a 12-year-old boy picking cilantro in Maneadero in June 2003, said his parents were making about 70 pesos a day (a little over $6), while he was bringing home half that. "We can't live if we all don't work," he said, in the tone of someone explaining the obvious.

At wages a tenth of those paid for the same job in Los Angeles on the U.S. side of the border, it might seem fair if *maquila* workers only had to pay a tenth of L.A. prices for food, rent or any of the basic necessities of life. But that's not the world of the border either. In 2003, a group of nuns, who organized the Center for Reflection, Education and Action (CREA), did an exhaustive survey of border prices. They found that for a kilo of rice, a Tijuana *maquiladora* worker had to labor for an hour and a half. Even an undocumented worker bussing dishes in Beverly Hills at minimum wage can take the same rice home with only 10 minutes' pay.

As usual, what appears to be a legal problem—in this case the enforcement of labor laws—is really about money. It's a recipe for confrontation, and all along the border economic pressure is fueling a wave of industrial unrest.

The National Labor Policy of Mexican President Vicente Fox caters to investors, not minimum-wage maquila workers. In 2001, the World Bank recommended rewriting Mexico's Constitution and Federal Labor Law, eliminating protections for workers in place since the 1920s. The new law would drop mandatory severance pay and stipulations that require companies to negotiate over factory closures. No longer would employers have to grant permanent worker status after 90 days, limit part-time work or abide by the 40-hour week. And the law would also eliminate the historical ban on strikebreaking. Mexico's guarantees of employer-paid job training, health care and housing, would be scrapped as well. Essentially, these recommended changes would institutionalize in the rest of Mexico the kind of labor relations that already exist, on the ground, in the *maquiladoras*.

Fox embraced the Bank's report, calling it "very much in line with what we have contemplated." The recommendations were so extreme that even the head of a leading employers' association, Claudio X. Gonzalez, called them "over the top," noting the Bank didn't dare to make such proposals in developed countries. "Why are they then being recommended for the emerging countries?" he asked.

In Mexico City, Jesús Campos Linas, the labor lawyers' dean, was appointed to head the local labor board. Campos Linas rejects Fox's argument that gutting worker protections will make the economy more competitive, attract greater investment and create more jobs. "Mexico already has one of the lowest wage levels in the world," he charges, "yet there's still this cry for more flexibility. The minimum wage in Mexico City is [less than $4] a day—no one can live on this. And [in 2002] we lost 400,000 jobs. Changing the labor law will not solve this problem."

Tiburcio Pérez Castro, professor of education at the National Pedagogical University, accuses the Baja California government of only enforcing those provisions of the law that protect private property. "There's a law guaranteeing people the right to health care, but no one has any," he notes bitterly. "There's a law which protects the right to food, but thousands of people go hungry every day."

So in the end, according to Pérez Castro, the rule of law itself is in question in Baja California, "at least insofar as it protects people, especially the poor, in the enforcement of their rights. They pass laws to protect the *maquiladoras*, so the rule of law exists in that sense," he admits. "But there is a danger to social stability, because it's so one-sided."

Whose priorities will prevail in Mexico, those of workers or those of free-trade investors? "The changes proposed by the Bank would be a gigantic step backwards for workers," Campos Linas emphasized. "The bankers don't understand that it took a revolution—a million people died—to get our constitution and labor law. Our problem isn't that we need a new law; it's to enforce the one we have."

In Baja California, the free-trade state, that's not so easy.

II. CUSTOMTRIM/AUTOTRIM

In early September 2002, the coalition for Justice in the Maquiladoras (CJM), a group that brings together unions, churches and community groups in the three countries of the North American Free Trade Agreement (Canada, Mexico and the United States), put out a call to border activists, urging them to act quickly to salvage one of the few remaining complaints filed under the North American Agreement on Labor Cooperation (NAALC): the case of mistreated workers at the Customtrim and Autotrim plants.

What followed that call, and the ultimate fate of the Customtrim/Autotrim complaint, is not only a stark illustration of the failure of the NAALC, but also a grim warning. As the Bush Administration pushes hard for the Free Trade Area of the Americas (FTAA), free trade's defenders argue that the rights of workers in Central and South America under these agreements can be protected in much the same way that the NAALC protected the rights of workers in Mexico. The bitter experience of the workers at Customtrim/Autotrim and their supporters, however, indicates that exactly the opposite is true. Labor protections embodied in the NAALC not only failed in this one case, but in every other effort made by workers to use the same mechanism to protect their health, their safety and their rights at work. Basing protection for workers in future agreements on this experience condemns them to the same fate.

The labor cooperation agreement is usually referred to as the "labor side-agreement" to the North American Free Trade Agreement (NAFTA). It set up a process that free-trade supporters argued would protect the health, safety and labor rights of workers in the three NAFTA countries. Under the side-agreement, workers, unions and community organizations could file complaints if worker protection or health and safety laws were not being enforced. NAFTA also had a second side-agreement, the North American Agreement on Environmental Cooperation. Its process, similar to that of the labor side-agreement, supposedly allowed communities to file complaints over cases of environmental contamination.

Both agreements were crucial to residents of the U.S.-Mexico border, since violations of labor rights, dangers to worker health and safety, and extreme cases of environmental contamination have been commonplace in this region since long before the agreements were proposed. These problems are a result of a longstanding development policy in which both the Mexican and U.S. governments encouraged corporations to relocate production to border factories, or *maquiladoras*, by creating a border zone within which labor protection, health and safety, and environmental laws were essentially not enforced. By 2001, more than 2,000 such factories were employing more than 1.3 million people, and Mexican border cities like Tijuana and Juárez had mushroomed into industrial urban centers with over a million residents each.

The CJM's urgent call of September 2002 was motivated by its learning of a secret discussion between U.S. and Mexican government officials, held in the San Diego Convention Center, supposedly to find ways of protecting the safety and health of *maquiladora* workers. From the perspective of the activist group, the secret meeting highlighted just how empty the promises of the side-agreements have been. The first problem was that the workers themselves, the very victims of the conditions that the side-agreements were intended to remedy, were excluded from the process.

Workers at the Customtrim and Autotrim plants, owned by the U.S. auto-parts giant Breed Technologies, had filed a complaint that they had been systematically exposed to toxic chemicals at work in violation of Mexican health and safety laws. The sickest ones were referred to by management as "junked workers" and were forced to labor in a special area. When workers began organizing an independent union to protest, the most active participants were fired, another violation of Mexican labor law. Complaints to the authorities went nowhere, and workers filed a case under the labor side-agreement, assisted by the CJM along with U.S.-based health and safety activists.

The body responsible for resolving the workers' complaint—the Binational Working Group on Occupational Safety and Health—organized the San Diego meeting, but the discussion inside the convention center was really about dumping the workers' case, not resolving it. A year before, a report issued by the National Administrative Office of the U.S. Department of Labor concluded that extensive violations of Mexican health and safety laws had taken place in the two Breed Technologies plants in the cities of Matamoros and Valle Hermosa.

Workers testified at the hearing that prompted the report, risking their jobs and ensuring that they would be blacklisted for years. Independent health and safety experts from both countries had also submitted massive documentation. Workers and their supporters thought there was yet a chance that, for the first time, monetary penalties might be imposed on Mexico for not enforcing its own laws, since the side-agreement allows for heavy fines in cases of health and safety violations.

In the end, however, the secret and exclusive San Diego meeting proved to be the only actual outcome of the NAFTA process. The meeting was "a charade and a disgrace," fumed CJM director Martha Ojeda. "Instead of specific, effective action to improve conditions at Autotrim/Customtrim, and throughout the *maquiladora* industry along the border, the injured workers are promised 'chats' between government officials whose refusal to listen and to act was the exact basis of the complaint in the first place," she railed.

By 2002, the number of new complaints filed under the labor side-agreement had slowed to a trickle and finally to none at all. Under U.S. President Bill Clinton, appointees to the National Administrative Office of the Department of Labor, which is responsible for hearing evidence on complaints, often tried to maintain at least the appearance of a commitment to workers' rights. For some judges, like Irasema Garza, who took testimony from Customtrim/Autotrim workers, that commitment was more than just window dressing. With the Bush Administration, however, the United States has ceased to even bother with pretense. Bush's unmistakable message was that any effort to restrain trade and investment was politically wrong-headed. And for his part, Mexican President Vicente Fox did nothing to change the basic hostility to the appeal process evidenced by his predecessors.

The problem with the side-agreement process, however, isn't the attitude of the public officials responsible for administering it, although they often make it clear that even an appearance of fairness depends on the political will of the administration in power. Whether liberals or conservatives hold office, in Washington D.C., Mexico City or Ottawa, they are all committed to corporate-defined free trade. Enforcing labor rights and environmental protections runs contrary to the purpose for which NAFTA was negotiated—creating conditions favorable to investment.

The Bush Administration is simply more open in its embrace of this goal and sees nothing wrong with making money from low wages and relaxed controls over pollution. This attitude will also be the hallmark of agreements designed to extend NAFTA southward like the FTAA. Mindful of the Customtrim/Autotrim case, those considering their positions relative to the FTAA should heed the warning by Connie Garcia of the San Diego-based Environmental Health Coalition as she stood outside the closed San Diego meeting: "NAFTA fails to protect workers or the environment. Its terms should not be reproduced in new agreements."

The move to hold a secret hearing on the Customtrim/ Autotrim situation surprised no one, and most border activists saw it for what it was—a last gasp of the NAFTA side-agreement process sputtering to a halt.

III. METALES Y DERIVADOS

Metales y Derivados is an abandoned battery recycling plant sitting on the lip of Otay Mesa adjoining Tijuana. Standing outside the plant walls on the chemical-encrusted ground, it's possible to look over the mesa's edge and see people moving about in the working-class barrio of Chilpancingo below. There, six years earlier, the Border Region Workers' Support Committee (CAFOR) and the Citizens' Committee for the Restoration of Cañon del Padre had documented the growing number of children born with anencephaly (that is, without brains). Two of CAFOR's Mexican organizers, Eduardo Badillo and Aurora Pelayo, along with their U.S. supporters were stopped from making annual counts of the growing number of cases after the issue began to appear in the press. But enough data had been accumulated, they believed, to cite Metales y Derivados as a likely source of the pollution causing the horrific birth defect.

In 1998 the San Diego-based Environmental Health Coalition (EHC) and the Citizens' Committee in Tijuana filed a case under the environmental side-agreement. They alleged that Mexican authorities hadn't enforced environmental laws against the plant's owners, the New Frontier Trading Corporation, based in San Diego. Staff working for the North American Commission for Environmental Cooperation (NACEC) investigated the complaint and reported their findings in February 2002.

Their study documented the illegal storage of 7,000 tons of toxic waste and the presence of lead, arsenic and heavy metals in the soil surrounding the defunct plant. It also mentioned an inconclusive survey of lead contamination among Chilpancingo residents conducted by a team from the University of California at Irvine. Cesar Luna, the lawyer who headed the EHC's border project at the time the case was filed, documented one case of anencephaly himself and heard reports from residents of at least half a dozen others.

But NACEC staff had no power to investigate the actual health conditions in Chilpancingo, and no official record of contamination existed because Mexican authorities never conducted a health survey in the barrio. They had good reason not to do so. Reports of anencephaly had been increasingly frequent in industrial communities all along the border, but the lax enforcement of environmental laws is an important, albeit unspoken, means for attracting new factories. A scandal about children without brains might discourage any future flow of investment.

So just as in the labor case, that was it. "All we got was a report, and an incomplete one at that," grumbled EHC policy advocate Connie Garcia. "Nothing changed on the ground. NAFTA provides for no cleanup plan or enforcement mechanism, and the community continues to be poisoned."

ABOUT THE AUTHOR

David Bacon is a freelance writer and photographer; he writes regularly on labor and immigration issues. His latest book is *The Children of NAFTA: Labor Wars on the U.S./Mexico Border* (University of California Press, 2004).

Raúl Zibechi

Worker-Run Factories: From Survival to Economic Solidarity

Factories "recovered" by their workers are a response to two decades of neoliberalism and deindustrialization. In a movement unprecedented in Latin America, workers have taken direct control of production and operation without bosses—and sometimes even without foremen, technicians, or specialists—in about 200 factories and workplaces in Argentina, some 100 in Brazil and more than 20 in Uruguay.

The workers acted not as a result of ideological debates but out of urgent need. The massive closure of factories and companies supplying the domestic market prompted a handful of workers to prevent at least some of these plants from becoming abandoned warehouses.

Though this new workers' movement is heterogeneous, many of the problems it faces are common to a broad range of factories in different productive sectors. These include legal issues to gain recognition of the factory's ownership, assuring supplies of raw materials, the lack of working capital, product marketing, and technical difficulties stemming from obsolete machinery or the exodus of technicians and managers. Such problems have been addressed and have often been resolved by the workers themselves.

The demise of military dictatorships (1983 in Argentina, 1985 in Uruguay and Brazil) gave birth to democratic regimes, but these governments were tightly constrained from the outset by the economic, political and social structures inherited from the authoritarian period. That legacy—characterized by huge foreign debts—led these governments to accede to the recommendations promoted by the "Washington Consensus." These changes included rolling back economic regulations and dismantling the feeble welfare states that had been built in most of the countries of the region.

Beginning in 1990, financial and economic deregulation, privatization and the shedding of protective tariffs and subsidies, caused many factories to close. These policies led to unemployment for many workers and more precarious working conditions for those who still had their jobs. When import restrictions were lifted, it opened the floodgates to imported products, and local industries often could not compete. Hardest hit were small and medium-sized enterprises that supplied the domestic market.

The massive closure of these companies was but one aspect of the deep restructuring of production undertaken in the 1990s. Meanwhile, leading industrial sectors became highly concentrated. This aggravated unemployment and it soon became a permanent structural feature of the economy.

The process of deindustrialization in Argentina, Uruguay and Brazil was followed by renewed growth based on the simplification of production strategies and transforming the technical and social organization of labor. Restructuring not only raised unemployment rates—to above 10% of the economically active population in nearly every Latin America country and above 20% toward the end of the decade in Argentina. It also prevented most former workers from being rehired at the modernized automated or robotized plants, since they lacked the training necessary for the new positions created in these plants. Moreover, this type of modernization exacerbated the trends toward social exclusion and the isolation of the poor.

For many workers, the closure of the companies where they worked condemned them to a lifetime of exclusion. This was especially true for workers over 40, who had very little chance of re-entering the formal labor market. Unemployment meant not only a loss of income but also the forfeiture of benefits such as health insurance, retirement pensions and housing. This explains why some workers chose to fight to recover their source of employment; that is, to keep their factories operating even without the owners.

In Brazil, the movement to recover factories preceded similar efforts in Argentina and Uruguay. In 1991, *Calzados Makerly* in São Paulo closed its doors, eliminating 482 direct jobs. With the support of the Footwear Workers Union, the Inter-Union Department of Studies and Statistics, and grassroots activists, *Calzados* workers spearheaded a process toward worker-managed production.

In 1994, the *Asociação Nacional dos Trabalhadores em Empresas de Autogestão* (National Association of Worker-Managed Enterprises, ANTEAG) was formed to coordinate the creative responses that emerged in the wake of the industrial crisis. ANTEAG currently has offices in six states and seeks to support worker-management projects by linking them to initiatives by nongovernmental organizations and state as well as municipal governments.

Solving the movement's serious funding problem is one of the association's most important tasks. ANTEAG now works with 307 worker-managed cooperative projects that employ some 15,000 workers; of those, 52 are companies that were recovered by their workers. The worker-managed companies are found in all branches of industry from mineral extraction (*Cooperminas*, for example, has 381 workers) to textiles (scores of small companies, nearly all operated by women) and tourism services.

ANTEAG sees worker management as an organizational

model that combines collective ownership of the means of production with democratic participation in management. The model also implies autonomy, which is why workers are responsible for decision-making and control of the companies. The autonomy model discourages the hiring of professional managers, and if professionals are hired, they must always be under the control of the collective.[1]

Argentina has traveled a different road to worker-run factories. There, the movement emerged at the peak of the country's economic crisis and progressed very rapidly. The creation of these enterprises in Argentina was linked to grass-roots experiences within the resistance movement spawned by the crisis. The worker-run factory movement grew out of a combination of workers' efforts to keep their jobs, organization among middle-class groups (professionals, employees, technicians) in neighborhood assemblies, and meetings of organized unemployed workers called *piqueteros*. All of these groups continue to promote their own demands and proposals, while building links with worker-run enterprises.

The vast majority of recovered factories in Argentina are small or medium-sized, and most of them were hurt by the economic liberalization imposed by Carlos Menem's government in the 1990s. They cover a wide range of sectors: over 26% are in the metallurgical industry, 8% cold storage plants and 8% electrical appliance manufacturers. Printing presses, transportation, food processing, textiles, glass and health companies each represent under 5%. Half of the workplaces have operated for more than 40 years and, when reclaimed by their workers, had an average of 60 employees. Only 13% had more than 100 workers.

Some 71% of worker-run factories distribute income in an egalitarian manner (janitors earn the same as more highly skilled workers), and only 15% have maintained the wage policies that were in effect before they were occupied. Though the factory-recovery process began in the mid-1990s, two-thirds of the enterprises were taken over during the socially cataclysmic years of 2001 and 2002. This underscores the close ties between the grassroots resistance movements of the economic crisis and factory takeovers.

Seven of every 10 factories were recovered only after fierce struggles—physical takeovers in nearly half the cases and *"acampadas en la puerta"* (prolonged sit-ins at factory gates) in 24% of the cases. In these cases, forced occupation lasted for an average of five months, which reveals the intensity of the conflict waged by workers before gaining control of the plants.

Surveys indicate that the factories in which long, intense conflicts were waged are the most likely to employ an egalitarian distribution of earnings and to take part in neighborhood assemblies in middle-class neighborhoods. Only 21% of the recovered companies have maintained their former foremen, and only 44% have kept their administrative personnel. Thus, more than half of the reclaimed plants began to produce with only manual labor. Despite the intense and often exhausting battles fought to gain control of the factory, workplaces where highly combative struggles were waged have been the most successful—an average of 70% of the output capacity is being used in these factories compared with 36% in those with a low degree of conflict. Likewise, facilities abandoned by supervisors and managers use a higher degree of productive capacity than those where the supervisors and managers have remained (70% versus 40%).[2]

A quick overview of specific experiences reveals one of the most interesting aspects of the Argentine movement—the close ties being forged between the workers in recovered companies, residents organized in neighborhood assemblies and *piquetero* groups. Through many forms of close collaboration, workers have been able to extend their networks well beyond the factory floor.

Two recovered businesses—*Chilavert* (a graphics shop) and *El Aguante* (a bakery)—have survived thanks to the leading role played by neighborhood assemblies in taking over the facilities. In late May 2002, the management of *Chilavert*, located in the Pompeya neighborhood of Buenos Aires, called in the police to evict the workers who were occupying the plant. The Popular Assembly of Pompeya, as well as other assemblies and groups of residents, got involved by calling meetings to discuss the problem and then by communicating via phone or word of mouth to send in groups of neighbors to support the workers during the repeated eviction attempts.[3] Similar situations arose in other factories. In many cases the alliance between workers and neighborhood residents proved crucial, whether the neighbors were organized in assemblies or not formally organized at all.

Panificadora Cinco (as the *El Aguante* Cooperative was formerly known) shut down in October 2001, laying off 80 workers without severance pay. In April 2002, the Carapachay neighborhood assembly, seeking ways to obtain cheaper bread, linked up with a group of 20 workers who had been fired from the bakery. Following a joint meeting, neighbors and former workers took over the plant. For 45 days they resisted eviction attempts, as local residents camped out with workers in a tent outside the bakery in an *aguante* (loosely translated as "endurance").[4] They finally succeeded in gaining ownership of the plant.

Neighborhood solidarity was decisive: assembly members, *piqueteros* and leftist activists in charge of security patrols held three festivals, a march through the barrio, a public denouncement of the owner, a May Day ceremony, talks, debates and cultural activities. Although exceptional, this case reveals how a social struggle can redraw territories, establishing linkages where indifference was once the norm.

In the case of the metallurgical company IMPA, the workers' organization helped consolidate the local neighborhood group and cemented a stronger alliance between the two. The employee-run factory enjoyed the support of local residents even before its workers had organized assemblies in the zone. Then the workers decided to create a cultural center as a way of reaching out to the community and building solidarity with the neighborhood and social movements.[5] The center was a success and paved the way for efforts now being undertaken by other recovered factories whose workers realize the importance of not remaining isolated within their plants and warehouses.

Similarly, amid a conflict at a bread stick cooperative called New Hope, a group of neighborhood assembly members, psychologists linked to *Topía* magazine, and local artists brought a proposal before the workers' assembly to create an arts and cultural center to garner the support of neighborhood residents and raise the cooperative's social profile. Now the cultural center hosts daily workshops on music, theater, dance, puppetry, literature and gardening; offers recitals and plays; features movies for both adults and children; and organizes conferences by prominent intellectuals.

These examples demonstrate one of the worker movement's novel characteristics: an incipient but growing of spreading territorial roots. The link between worker-run enterprises and neighborhood assemblies points to society's growing interest in committing to the success of these companies and to workers' willingness to go beyond the factory gates and feel part of the broader social movement. In some cases, this is manifested by a factory's commitment to hire unemployed neighborhood residents to fill job openings. Thus, by maintaining community activism, rebuilding social ties, and moving toward "territorialization" of the struggle, the job-recovery movement seeks to address one of the main problems it faces: the relationship of employee-managed operations to the local market.

Solidarity begins when collaboration arises between neighbors (acting individually or through assemblies), worker-run factories, student groups and *piqueteros*. When a factory begins operating under worker-control, this solidarity usually takes one of two paths: it may become institutionalized through large, stable organizations such as ANTEAG in Brazil, or, as has occurred at many Argentine workplaces, horizontal linkages may be established with other initiatives, such as cultural centers in factories or initiatives to address the needs of the overall movement, particularly regarding its relationship with the market.

Brazil has developed a broad movement linked to economic solidarity, with an entire distribution network of products made by landless peasants and production cooperatives. In Argentina, these links had been bureaucratized but are now re-emerging at the grassroots level. At the peak of the economic crisis, barter networks grew exponentially, at one point involving two to five million people. Although the barter movement later declined, it contributed to the debate on how to trade outside of the monopolist market. New experiences being developed in Argentina seek to avoid the creation of large structures that exceed the control of the grassroots collectives and instead to favor "face-to-face" relationships.

Following the mass protests of December 19 and 20, 2001, that led to the fall of Argentine President Fernando de la Rúa, production links between recovered factories, *piqueteros*, peasants and neighborhood assemblies have multiplied. A common trait of these social sectors and movements is that they tend to produce for their own needs. Groups of *piqueteros* plant crops, bake bread and produce other articles, and some are setting up hog and rabbit farms or fish hatcheries. A few neighborhood assemblies bake bread, cook meals, concoct cleaning and cosmetics products, or collaborate with *cartoneros* (people that get by scavenging and recycling trash).[6]

Some neighborhood assemblies are doing interesting work that blurs the division between producers and consumers. There are 67 popular assemblies in Buenos Aires and well over half are autonomous and coordinated at the territorial level. This sector actively promotes fair trade and solidarity though conscientious consumption. Some commercial activity has also fostered efforts across sectors: rural producers, *piqueteros*, assembly members and recovered-factory workers are beginning to weave direct ties without the mediation of the market. In a sense, these experimental endeavors are recuperating the original nature of the market, described by Fernando Braudel and Immanuel Wallerstein as characterized by transparency, modest profits, controlled competition, freedom and, above all, the domain of "common people."[7]

Several experiences demonstrate these principles at work: Palermo, a suburb of Buenos Aires, holds a fair-trade fair two days a week with more than 100 stalls. The fair only sells products made by the neighborhood assemblies, *piquetero* groups and recovered factories.[8] Items for sale include bags made of waste material, cleaning articles, bread, diapers, recycled computers, recycled paper, homemade pastas, handcrafts and marmalades.

In another instance, workers and residents collaborate in the production and distribution of a brand of *yerba maté* (a tea popular in the region) known as Titrayjú (the acronym for *Tierra, Trabajo, y Justicia*, or Land, Work and Justice). The tea is produced by an organization of small rural producers in northern Argentina called the Agrarian Movement of Misiones. The operation has avoided exploitation by intermediaries for the last year by partnering with 30 neighborhood assemblies that sell and distribute the tea directly in Buenos Aires, assisted by *piqueteros* and other grassroots organizations.

Utilizing the creative space opened by the protests against Argentina's economic crisis, the Assembly Cooperative (*Cooperativa Asamblearia*) was founded in 2004 by assemblies in the middle- and upper-income neighborhoods of Nuñez and Saavedra. The assemblies first began with community purchasing, then organized a cooperative that distributes products from five recovered factories, an agrarian cooperative and several other neighborhood assemblies. Something similar is being done by the former employees of *El Tigre*, a worker-managed super-market in the city of Rosario that sells products from recovered factories throughout the country as well as from community gardens and small growers.

Although the Argentine movement is in its early stages, it has already invented new forms of marketing that go far beyond the early barter arrangements. The purpose of bartering was to create a currency that could facilitate a massive alternative economic system. The new efforts, on the other hand, prioritize ethical and political criteria related to how goods are produced and marketed, and they seek to close the gap between producers and consumers by promoting direct, face-to-face relationships. The Assembly Cooperative, for example, seeks to "promote the production, distribution, marketing, and consumption of goods and services from worker-managed factories, that is, products that are the fruit of the labor and the collective property of workers," according to a brochure introducing the Cooperative.[9] Three basic principles guide the group's actions: worker-managed production, responsible consumption and fair trade. These principles form part of the solidarity economy that worker-run enterprises and neighborhood organizations are trying to build to break their dependence on the dominant market.

NOTES

This article is translated for International Relations Center (IRC) by Laura Carlsen.

1. For more information, see http://www.anteag.org.br/.
2. All statistics were taken from a study coordinated by Gabriel Fajn, *Fábricas y empresas recuperadas* (Buenos Aires: Centro Cultural de la Cooperación, 2003).
3. Cafardo, Analía and Paula Domínguez, *Autogestión obrera en el siglo XXI*, Cuaderno de Trabajo No. 27 (Buenos Aires: Centro Cultural de la Cooperación, 2003).
4. *Aguante* literally means "endurance" or "resistance," but in recent years it has been used in the grassroots movement to refer to active solidarity in critical situations.
5. *IMPACTO* newspaper, published by IMPA workers.
6. *Cartoneros* are jobless residents of large cities who salvage cardboard and sell it to wholesalers.
7. Immanuel Wallerstein, "Braudel y el capitalismo o todo al revés," *Pensar las ciencias sociales* (Mexico: Siglo XXI, 1998), p. 231.
8. Muracciole, Jorge, "Economía asamblearia en acción," *Proyectos, Vol. 19/20*, No. 4, May/June 2003.
9. For more information, see http://www.asamblearia.com.ar/.

Raúl Zibechi

Another World is Possible: The Ceramics of Zanon

On some occasions, rare as they may be, the slogan "Another world is possible," becomes reality. The workers of the Zanon Ceramics factory, who took control of the company and have been functioning as a cooperative for four years now, demonstrate that even working for a large, high-tech business, it is possible to create another life.

"The poetry of life can be greater than the poetry of paper," said the Argentine poet Juan Gelman, upon contemplating "a square meter of poetry" impressed into ceramic tiles that the workers of Zanon take wherever they go as a gift. When he learned his poetry decorated the 25 squares of ceramics, he emotionally wrote: "Never in my life did I imagine that I would see my poems published on ceramics. Never in my life did I imagine that the workers of a reclaimed factory would interrupt their work in order to make it happen. It appears my imagination fell short."

The more-than-five-year struggle of the workers of Zanon Ceramics has much of the makings of a lyric poem. They had to confront a successful Italian businessman, labor unions from the southern Argentine province of Neuquén as well as governmental authorities and the police before they became the country's largest reclaimed factory—and the most successful of them, from a "business" standpoint.

Zanon is Argentina's most important ceramics factory,

covering almost 20 acres (80,000 square meters), or 9 hectares, and utilizes the latest technology: mobile production lines for transporting the tiles, mechanical Caterpillars and robotic cars that slide along rails, robots that impress different patterns into the clay, gigantic funnels for mixing and automatic kilns. The large machines are run, nevertheless, through cooperative rather than hierarchical structures.

At first glance, the experience of Zanon Ceramics is hardly different from other businesses taken over by their workers—a total of 200 in Argentina. But one of its major accomplishments was the recuperation of the labor union by the workers. In Argentina, labor unions do not defend the workers, but rather, the businessmen, and the Labor Union of Workers and Ceramics Employees of Neuquén (comprising four factories in the province) was no exception. The company paid an extra salary to the union leaders and made donations to the union to ensure that there would be no conflict.

Within the factory, fears ran high, recall workers Mario Balcazza and Jose Luis Urbina: "If the boss told a worker he had to stay 16 hours to work, he had to, because if not, the next day they would suspend him." When they began to put together a list of alternative candidates to run in the union elections in 1998, internal repression spiked drastically: "If you spoke with someone from the union, the company marked you and then fired you, and no one would defend you because that kind of behavior would also get you fired," says Balcazza.[1] But finally, more than 60% of the 300 workers opted to renovate the union and distance the bureaucrats.

And so began another chapter of Zanon's history: The new union would not allow itself to be bought or intimidated by the company. It made the appropriate denouncements when illegal actions were taken, and it gained the confidence of the workers. In order to overcome difficult operational and commercial situations, the company intensified the rhythm of work, which caused numerous work-related accidents. Starting in 2000, the chain of events came to a head: an employee died in the factory without medical attention because the factory, which runs 24 hours a day, did not even have an ambulance or doctor on hand. When Daniel Ferras, age 22, passed away, the workers stopped production for eights days demanding, and finally receiving, an ambulance and nurse. Afterwards, the company began to get behind on its wage payments (up to three months without pay) until September of 2001 when it decided to turn off the kilns.

The company's proposal was to downsize to just 60 employees, but the workers interpreted this as a way of "cleaning out" the labor union. By that time, Zanon had incurred substantial debts with the provincial government, which had lent money to the company so it could pay back wages. The workers rejected the layoffs, burnt the telegrams in front of the provincial government's headquarters, erected a tent in front of the company for five months and, thanks to a judicial seizure of 40% of the ceramic stock, they began to sell it off to compensate for their lost salaries. Nevertheless, despite having gone months without their salaries, a section of the ceramicists donated their pay to restore the provincial hospital, while members of the local Movement of Unemployed Workers (MTD, in its Spanish initials), known as *piqueteros*, provided the labor for the renovation.

In March of 2002, 220 of the 330 workers decided to occupy the factory and begin production "under worker control." Through an assembly, they all agreed to receive the same salary, and formed commissions on sales, administration, security, expenditures, production, planning, safety, health and public relations. The local indigenous Mapuche, who, up to that moment had been degraded and exploited by the ceramics industry, gave the workers access to their clay quarries. On April 5, 2002, the first production of 20,000 square meters of tiles left the factory. Three months later they produced 120,000 square meters, half of what the factory produced under the previous owners.

From the point of view of growth in production, the development of Zanon under the ownership of its workers has been a success: in January 2006, they were producing 300,000 square meters of tile, exceeding previous production levels, and they expect to reach 400,000 square meters in the near future. With help from the Universities of Comahue (Neuquén) and Buenos Aires, they have reclaimed and updated the production process, and in two years they invested $300,000 into the maintenance and improvement of machinery. From the 300 accidents per year that occurred under previous ownership, they have brought the number down to 33, and there has not been a single death, whereas before, approximately one worker died every month.

Under the management of the workers, various new tile designs have been introduced. In the former era, European and Italian medieval designs prevailed. However, when the workers took control of the designs, they began making changes, using Mapuche designs—created in conjunction with the indigenous communities themselves—to celebrate the culture and to pay homage to the community that offered its clay deposits to the ceramicists.

One notable difference between Zanon and other businesses recovered by their employees is its relationship with the community. The factory has legally changed its name to Fasinpat (short for *Fábrica Sin Patrón*, or Factory Without Owner), become a cooperative, and started making a countless number of donations: to hospitals, schools, nursing homes, soup kitchens, indigenous groups, firefighters and the Red Cross of Neuquén. The Zanon workers have awarded thousands of square feet of ceramics as a sign of recognition and thanks for the community's help and support. The workers believe the profits of a business should be returned to the community. The most important and emblematic donation was the construction of a health center for the neighborhood of Nueva España. Under the guidance of the community members—400 families who had for 40 years run a first aid center—the Fasinpat employees donated the materials and constructed a health center for the neighborhood. Moreover, when they need to hire more employees, they call on the organizations for the unemployed and neighborhood organizations to hear their proposals. Indeed, the 100 new positions created so far have been filled by young people, who face particularly hard times on the job market.

But the community also supports Fasinpat. The factory is open to all who wish to visit it. Each week students and people from all over Argentina (and a good number of foreigners) arrive at the Zanon plant to see and experience one of the few modern factories—totally automated and with some robotic processes— in the hands of the workers. In turn, when the police attempted to remove the workers on April 8, 2003, thousands of neighbors surrounded the factory to stop them. Soon after, 9,000 people gathered for a rock festival inside the factory to show the solidarity of community with the workers.

Currently, they maintain a Web site, host a radio show and distribute a monthly newspaper with national circulation.[2] They have also produced several videos relating various aspects of their experiences. They maintain a good relationship with other worker-recovered businesses and they frequently take trips to tell the story of their experience and to meet other workers in similar situations. They recently participated in the First Latin American Gathering of Worker-Recovered Factories, which took place in Caracas, Venezuela.

In the pamphlet "Zanon under worker control," Zanon workers explain their work methodology: "We are interested in letting you know that behind each ceramic tile there is a history and a reality that has made it possible for the wheel to keep on turning. All processes and decisions are in the hands of the workers. We are the ones who decide what to buy, how to sell, what and how to produce." Perhaps the major difference between Zanon-Fasinpat and other companies is the organization of the production process: "This factory is an intricate machine where each one contributes his part, where there are no hierarchies and where the commitment to and responsibilities of work determine the quality of the product and the future of our management."

The differences between the current and previous management are striking. A former employee recalls, "We were not allowed to leave or go to the bathroom. The pathways were marked out with different colors. Red indicated places where there were automatic machines and you had to move with caution, and blue was for places you could go. Back then, the kiln operators had to wear red clothes, electricians green and so forth. That way, they could tell if someone from another sector was somewhere they weren't supposed to be. It was like a jail."[3] The managers were on the upper floor, in offices with glass windows so they could keep watch, and close by were the union organizers, who followed on the heels of all the workers.

When the workers took over production, the assemblies of each sector began naming coordinators to take charge of the production process and dialogue with their peers when problems arise. Every few months, the coordinators rotate out so that after a certain amount of time, each person has had a shift as coordinator. According to those interviewed, the coordinator earns the same salary as the rest but has more responsibilities.

Carlos Saavedra, who was general coordinator of the whole factory, recognizes that the duties require more time than normal, but adds, "I do not control anyone and no one controls me. We simply all report the work that we do so it can be accounted for. The numbers are clear. Anyone can see them. Whether I am coordinator, or not, is a decision made by the assembly, and if I am not, then that is their decision. Everyone does what he or she is asked."[4] Now, instead of control, the workers of Zanon have created mutual confidence and responsibility.

The factory is divided into 36 sectors that work during three eight-hour shifts. Each sector has its own coordinator. "Each Monday there is a coordinating meeting and there they decide what each shift needs; problems of individual sectors are resolved and if they cannot be resolved, they are brought before an assembly of all the shifts. But the final product that goes to market is the responsibility of everyone, not just the person who makes it, because we all work on the same level, in conjunction with each other from the raw clay until the final ceramic piece is finished and put up for sale."[5]

Once a month, the factory calls a daylong meeting in which every member participates. It is the most important meeting, and it covers all topics—from the type of footgear necessary for each section, to the purchases they will make and external actions of solidarity in which they will participate. "The social, political and production aspects are all discussed. For each point, we have a specific order that we go in, and we will not adjourn the meeting until every last issue is agreed upon," recount the workers. Nevertheless, they recognize that this way of functioning—democratic, participatory and horizontal—requires a lot of energy: "It is exhausting, but it is productive because you find solutions to all of the problems debating them with everyone. It is worse to let time go by because everyone ends up with doubts. There are many things that probably are not understood immediately; there are sectors that manage money, expenditures, sales, administration. To do this, we assigned two individuals, whom we call auditors, to manage the expenses.

Each month, they produce a report of how much is being spent and bought. This report is given to demonstrate transparency to everyone. If there is money left over, we can use it to fix machinery or buy raw materials. And everything is resolved at the section assembly or general assembly."

The assembly established some rules for coexistence. Everyone must arrive at the factory 15 minutes before their shift begins and cannot leave until 15 minutes after it technically ends, so that they can find out or relay the news of the day to members of a different shift. Two examples demonstrate the achievements and difficulties of this system: on one occasion they were forced to make a painful decision and fire an employee who had been stealing, but on another "they paid for a worker with addiction problems to go into treatment and the employee was able to continue working."[6]

Strange as it may seem, the time dedicated to equal debate improves the level of production per hour, something that goes against the current of the hegemonic business model. Perhaps because, as Saavedra notes, "hours no longer mean what they used to. Back then, I worked 12 hours and returned home feeling exploited and destroyed. Now, if I return home tired, it is a different kind of tiredness. Because inside you is passing a caravan of satisfactions that is sometimes difficult to explain."[7] Before, when the horn sounded indicating the end of a shift, the workers left running to their houses so they could forget about work. "Now I stay longer even when I don't have to," says Saavedra, implying that work can exceed being just an obligation and become a satisfaction. For his part, the assembly-line worker Juan sums up many of the feelings of the workers: "Back then, I would pass a ceramicist on the line, and he was just a ceramicist. Period. Now, each ceramicist that I pass on the line is like something of ours in its rightful place, something that belongs to you."[8]

Today, the ex-Zanon workers hope that the Argentine government will decide to recognize their status and let them continue to operate under their own control. They hope that someday the state, which to this day has yet to make a purchase from them, can become a client that will contribute to the growth of a project that is demonstrating that another world really is possible.

NOTES

This article is translated for International Relations Center (IRC) by Nick Henry.

1. Author interviews, Mario Balcazza y José Luis Urbina.
2. The newspaper's name is *Nuestra Lucha* (Our Fight) and the Web site is http://www.obrerosdezanon.org.
3. Hernán López Echagüe, *La política está en otra parte* (Norma, Buenos Aires, 2002), p. 178.
4. Carlos Magnani, *El cambio silencioso* (Prometeo, Buenos Aires, 2003), pp. 143–44.
5. Author interviews, Mario Balcazza y José Luis Urbina.
6. Lavaca, *Sin Patrón: Fábricas y empresas recuperadas por sus trabajadores* (Buenos Aires, 2004), p. 40.
7. Carlos Magnani, *El cambio silencioso* (Prometeo, Buenos Aires, 2003), p. 144.
8. Analía Cafardo y Paula Domínguez, *Autogestión obrera en el siglo XXI* (Centro Cultural de la Cooperación, Buenos Aires, 2003), p. 36.

Acknowledgments

The editors would like to thank past and present NACLA staff and contributors. Without their dedication and hard work for social change, this book would not exist. Thanks also to Shehla Hashmi Grewal, who has drawn the maps of Central and South America on pages 8 and 9. Individual essays are reproduced with permission from the following sources:

Teo Ballvé, "Is Venezuela the New Cuba?," *NACLA Report on the Americas*, Mexican Workers Since NAFTA, Vol. 39, No. 1, July/August 2005.

Teo Ballvé, "*¡Bolivia de pie!*," *NACLA Report on the Americas*, Empire & Dissent, Vol. 39, No. 2, September/October 2005.

Maruja Barrig, "Latin American Feminism: Gains, Losses and Hard Times," *NACLA Report on the Americas*, The Body Politic: Gender in the New World Order, Vol. 34, No. 5, March/April 2001.

Sue Branford and Jan Rocha, "Portrait of an MST Settler, Romilda da Silva Vargas," *NACLA Report on the Americas*, Crisis and Change: Colombia and Brazil, Vol. 36, No. 5, March/April 2003.

Laura Carlsen, "Timely Demise for Free Trade Area of the Americas," (Silver City, NM: International Relations Center, November 23, 2005).

Jennifer N. Collins, "A Sense of Possibility: Ecuador's Indigenous Movement Takes Center Stage," *NACLA Report on the Americas*, ¡Adelante! The New Rural Activism in the Americas, Vol. 33, No. 5, March/April 2000.

Steve Ellner, "Venezuela: Defying Globalization's Logic," *NACLA Report on the Americas*, Empire & Dissent, Vol. 39, No. 2, September/October 2005.

Jonah Gindin, "Chavistas in the Halls of Power, Chavistas in the Streets," *NACLA Report on the Americas*, Social Movements: Building from the Ground Up, Vol. 38, No. 5, March/April 2005.

Shane Greene, "Incas, *Indios* and Indigenism in Peru," *NACLA Report on the Americas*, The Paradoxes of Racial Politics: The Politics of Race and Globalization, Part II, Vol. 38, No. 4, January/February 2005.

Andrés Gaudin, "The Krichner Factor," *NACLA Report on the Americas*, The Paradoxes of Racial Politics: The Politics of Race and Globalization, Part II, Vol. 38, No. 4, January/February 2005.

Luis A. Gómez, "Evo Morales asume la presidencia y pone fin al neoliberalismo en Bolivia," *La Jornada* (Mexico), January 23, 2006.

Guillermo Delgado-P., "The Making of a Transnational Movement," *NACLA Report on the Americas*, Racial Politics, Racial Identities: Race and Racism in the Americas, Part III, Vol. 35, No. 6, May/June 2002.

Charles R. Hale, "Rethinking Indigenous Politics in the Era of the '*Indio Permitido*'," *NACLA Report on the Americas*, Changing Identities: The Politics of Race and Globalization, Part I, Vol. 38, No. 2, September/October 2004.

R. Aída Hernández Castillo, "*Zapatismo* and the Emergence of Indigenous Feminism," *NACLA Report on the Americas*, Racial Politics, Racial Identities: Race and Racism in the Americas, Part III, Vol. 35, No. 6, May/June 2002.

Forrest Hylton and Sinclair Thomson, "The Roots of Rebellion I: Insurgent Bolivia," *NACLA Report on the Americas*, Bolivia Fights Back, Vol. 38, No. 3, November/December 2004.

Chris Jochnick and Paulina Garzón, "A Seat at the Table," *NACLA Report on the Americas*, Well of Contention: Oil in the Americas, Vol. 34, No. 4, January/February 2001.

Peter Lambert, "Paraguay's Enigmatic President," *NACLA Report on the Americas*, Social Movements: Building from the Ground Up, Vol. 38, No. 5, March/April 2005.

Gerardo Rénique, "Strategic Challenges for Latin America's Anti-Neoliberal Insurgency," a longer version of this article appeared as "Introduction. Latin America Today: The Revolt against Neoliberalism," in *Socialism and Democracy*, Issue 39, (2005) Vol. 19, No. 3, http://www.tandf.co.uk.

Silvia Rivera Cusicanqui, "The Roots of Rebellion II: Reclaiming the Nation," *NACLA Report on the Americas*, Bolivia Fights Back, Vol. 38, No. 3, November/December 2004.

Emir Sader, "Taking Lula's Measure," a longer version of this article appeared *New Left Review*, No. 33, May/June 2005.

Richard Stahler-Sholk, "Time of the Snails: Autonomy and Resistance in Chiapas," *NACLA Report on the Americas*, Social Movements: Building From the Ground Up, Vol. 38, No. 5, March/April 2005.

Harry E. Vanden, "Brazil's Landless Hold Their Ground," *NACLA Report on the Americas*, Social Movements: Building From the Ground Up, Vol. 38, No. 5, March/April 2005.

Hilary Wainwright, "Making a People's Budget in Porto Alegre," *NACLA Report on the Americas*, Crisis and Change: Colombia and Brazil, Vol. 36, No. 5, March/April 2003.

Nicholas Watson, "Homeless Movement Gains Ground," *NACLA Report on the Americas*, Beyond Revolution: Nicaragua and El Salvador in a New Era, Vol. 37, No. 6, May/June 2004.

Benjamin Witte, "Multinational Gold Rush in Guatemala," *NACLA Report on the Americas*, Mexican Workers Since NAFTA, Vol. 39, No. 1, July/August 2005.

Raúl Zibechi, "Worker-Run Factories: From Survival to Economic Solidarity," (Silver City, NM: International Relations Center, August 1, 2004).

Raúl Zibechi, "Izquierda uruguaya: La construcción de la hegemonía," IRC Americas (Silver City, NM: International Relations Center, Americas Program, October 25, 2004).

Raúl Zibechi, "Another World is Possible: The Ceramics of Zanon," (Silver City, NM: International Relations Center, January 20, 2006).

Index

ABOUT SOUTH END PRESS

South End Press is a collectively run, nonprofit book publisher with more than 250 titles in print. The majority person of color, majority women collective tries to meet the needs of readers who are exploring or already committed to the politics of radical social change. Since our founding in 1977, our goal has been to publish books that encourage critical thinking and constructive action on the key political, cultural, social, economic, and ecological issues shaping life in the United States and in the world. In this way, we hope to provide a forum for a wide variety of democratic social movements, and provide an alternative to the products of corporate publishing.

From its inception, the Press has organized itself as an egalitarian collective with decision-making arranged to share the rewards and stresses of running the business as equally as possible. Each collective member is responsible for core editorial and administrative tasks, and all collective members earn the same base salary. The Press also has made a practice of inverting the pervasive racial and gender hierarchies in traditional publishing houses; our staff has had a female majority since the mid-1980s, and has included at least 50% people of color since the mid-1990s. Our author list—which includes Arundhati Roy, Noam Chomsky, bell hooks, Winona LaDuke, Manning Marable, Ward Churchill, Cherríe Moraga, and Howard Zinn—reflects the Press's commitment to publish on diverse issues from diverse perspectives.

To expand access to information and critical analysis, South End Press has been instrumental in the starting of two on-going political media projects—Speak Out and Z Magazine. We have worked closely with a number of important media and research institutions including Alternative Radio; Political Research Associates; the Committee on Women, Population, and the Environment (CWPE); and INCITE! Women of Color Against Violence. Please consider making a donation to help support South End Press in its mission to continue expanding access and ensure our continued financial viability.

To make a donation or receive a current catalog of our books, please write to us at South End Press, 7 Brookline Street #1, Cambridge, MA 02139 or email us at southend@southendpress.org. To order books, obtain information about author events, or submit a review of a South End Press book, please visit our website: www.southendpress.org.